Contents

Introduction

When *Bittersweet* was published in 2003, chocolate in America was on the brink of a seismic shift that would forever change our understanding of and our experience with this beloved food.

New and more interesting chocolates—purer, more flavorful, less sweet, different, even exotic—had started to appear next to the familiar brands, and we were ready to, actually starting to, taste chocolate in a new way. But no one was explaining the difference between these chocolates and standard American chocolates, or providing guidance to cooks who would naturally want to make their favorite recipes successfully with the new chocolates.

In the decade since then, all of the changes presaged in the first edition have in fact occurred and have even sparked a new wave of chocolate innovation. This revised and updated paperback edition is (blessedly) simpler to use and understand, in part because terminology that had been new and unfamiliar is now common (it doesn't need repeated explanation anymore)

and most especially because these days bars of chocolate are almost universally labeled with percentages. This latter fact makes it easier to call for a specific chocolate in a recipe, easier to shop for the right ingredient, and easier to make a successful chocolate dessert with any chocolate you choose using the guidelines in the book. Meanwhile, because there are hundreds more foreign and domestic chocolates available than there were ten years ago, chocolate-loving home cooks and culinary school students will find this book even more useful and relevant.

In addition to being a primer on chocolate, *Seriously Bitter Sweet* is a collection of great recipes, sweet and savory, each with choices or commentary on the chocolate called for. And my story is woven throughout: growing up with chocolate in California in the 1950s; tasting my first handmade chocolate truffle in Paris in 1973; the role of my Berkeley shop, Cocolat, in the context of the larger food "revolution" of the 1970s and '80s; and, finally, the years leading to the era of what I call the New Chocolates, which were the primary motivation for the book.

In retrospect, my first hint that American cooks—even seasoned American cooks and pastry chefs—might need continuing education in chocolate came early. After I sold Cocolat in 1990, I had more time to write and publish cookbooks and experiment with new ingredients, including chocolates. When I started making desserts with a renowned European chocolate, one that I had tasted and loved but never worked with, I assumed that it would make my already superb desserts even better. I did not anticipate that a superior chocolate with 70% cacao—instead of the then standard American bittersweet with 54% to 59% cacao—would produce an inferior dessert, simply because of its higher cacao percentage.

By 1997 I was spending time with the late Robert Steinberg and John Scharffenberger as they launched their tiny company, Scharffen Berger Chocolate Maker. In short order, Scharffen Berger became the first new American bean-to-bar chocolate manufacturer in fifty years; the first to make an American 70% bittersweet chocolate; and the first American company to put cacao percentage on a chocolate bar, to market cocoa nibs, and to produce a premium-quality natural American cocoa powder for home cooks. I was a casual consultant at first, then a friend and regular advisor—often, in truth, a nag. I don't take credit for what they did, but I did know very early on (even before John and Robert knew) that Scharffen Berger would change chocolate in the United States forever. And that is exactly what happened. At the same time, my experience with the new American chocolate provided the true impetus for *Bittersweet.*

At first to help John and Robert, and then to satisfy my growing curiosity, I started adapting some of my recipes to make them work with a 70% chocolate, then a 62% chocolate, and then several in between. Soon I had a set of formulas, observations, and rules of thumb. Meanwhile, a colleague said it was not worth paying for special chocolate if you were just going to cook with it. But I was finding that although good chocolate made good desserts, better chocolate yielded even better desserts—as long as you knew how to use it. I was also discovering that the simplest recipes were best for showing off distinctive chocolates.

The relatively quick success of the new chocolate "upstart" had an impact. American manufacturers started to include the cacao percentage on their labels (as I knew they would); they also began making higher-percentage chocolates. The family-owned Guittard Chocolate Company in California responded by launching their own excellent artisan chocolate line, E. Guittard, for professionals and home cooks. Furthermore, more chocolates from Europe and Latin America were showing up. Suddenly choices were multiplying in the baking aisle (and, of course, in the candy aisle). Bittersweet chocolates—now with a spread from 54% to over 70% cacao—were no longer interchangeable with one another in a recipe.

Nor was the focus just on recipes for flourless chocolate cakes and chocolate mousse or even on new desserts. As the new century dawned, the focus was equally on the chocolate itself: the transformation of cocoa beans into chocolate, the source and quality of the beans, and the blending (or not blending) of them. There was talk of rare varietals and the possible existence of a fourth species, of fermentation and drying methods on cacao farms, and of chocolate production methods and choices. Now the focus was on the flavors inherent in the beans, new and diverse ideas about what chocolate really tasted like and how much sugar it should or should not have in it. Now there was even a chocolate flavor wheel modeled after the classic wine flavor wheel, custom-designed for discerning the flavors of chocolate. Chocolate had gained a new status—transcending candy—and a growing respect for the complexity of its flavor and the skill required to transform beans to bars.

Bittersweet came out at the beginning of this era. When it was published, most of the bars of American chocolates in the baking aisle were not yet labeled with percentages. They were simply called unsweetened chocolate, bittersweet chocolate, or semisweet chocolate; the last two were similar enough to be completely interchangeable in recipes. Home cooks (even culinary students and American chefs) had no idea of the cacao percentage of these unmarked bars or how they compared to the European, or new American, bars of bittersweet and semisweet chocolates that were marked with percentages. And of course they did not know what difference percentage would make in their desserts anyway. Excitement about tasting the new chocolates did not translate into knowledge about using them.

With so little consumer knowledge and such inadequate chocolate labeling at that time (established American manufacturers considered cacao percentage to be a trade secret), it was arguably ridiculous to think I could explain cacao percentage and its impact on flavor and texture in a dessert recipe and then guide readers in choosing chocolates. Just to be able to explain the difference between the old chocolates and the new, I estimated the cacao percentage of all of those unmarked American chocolates by extrapolating from information on nutrition labels and from my understanding of chocolate making. When percentage labeling became de rigueur, shortly after the publication of Bittersweet, it was an enormous relief to find that my calculations were very close to the mark, even taking into consideration that some manufacturers boosted cacao content just a tad before slapping percentages on their bars. Such was the new climate of competition in our world of chocolate that suddenly higher percentages were construed to mean better chocolate!

In the decade since Bittersweet's debut, chocolate has continued to evolve. Today, most American chocolate bars are labeled with cacao percentage, making it easier for consumers to choose what to nibble on or cook with, as well as easier for me and others to create a recipe that will be successful for any cook willing to follow it. Magazine editors and cookbook authors often—but not yet always—include cacao percentage when chocolate is called for in recipes. Nevertheless, Seriously Bitter Sweet is the only work available that explains how to use high-percentage chocolates in recipes, and I remain a missionary trying to persuade everyone who publishes recipes to call for chocolate by percentage. Although the former upstart Scharffen Berger was acquired in 2005 by the Hershey Company, there are scores of new American chocolate companies, including craft producers of artisan chocolate operating out of industrial garages and even storefronts or the backs of cafés, not unlike similarly dedicated coffee roasters, cheese makers, beer brewers, and jam makers. The new chocolate makers continue to redefine our expectations about the flavor and even the texture of chocolate: some eschew the traditional use of lecithin and vanilla, which are normally added to chocolate; some use goats' milk instead of cows' milk in milk chocolate; some use evaporated cane or raw sugars instead of refined white sugar; some grind the chocolate coarsely for a rustic effect; and so on. Some new producers are making raw chocolates; some even use unfermented cacao. There continues to be a strong focus on single-origin chocolates or blends that feature mostly beans of a single origin. Increasing interaction and relationships between chocolate makers and cacao farmers are improving the quality of the beans, pushing more revenues to farmers as well as encouraging better conditions and wages for cacao workers. There is more organic chocolate and more fair-trade chocolate. And botanists and cacao hunters have confirmed a fourth species of cacao, called Nacional. (A list of more than thirty of the newest American chocolate makers, mostly small-batch, bean-to-bar "craft" producers, starts on page 319.)

Two positive (although less dramatic) changes have occurred since *Bittersweet* was published. White chocolate, long known as "not real chocolate," now has an official definition and status as "real" chocolate; this designation distinguishes it from the white compound coatings (which are still not "real chocolate") that used to crowd it. Second, there are more premium cocoa powders available to home cooks, and several of them are natural cocoas. The latter are gaining deserved recognition and attention from cooks and chefs.

Chefs and confectioners are more open-minded and creative about what chocolate goes with, crossing the divide between sweet and savory often and with ease. The newest chocolate confections routinely involve savory herbs or spices, cheese, bacon, and, of course, salt. Meat and poultry, vegetables, salads, grains, and even fish are garnished, seasoned, or thickened with chocolate or cacao nibs. Chocolate today has most definitely transcended mere candy, and consumers, not just chefs and chocolate makers, are aware of this too.

BITTERSWEET

When I sold my first chocolate truffles in the early 1970s, take-out food was pizza or Americanized Chinese food or, in some cities, Jewish or Italian food from a delicatessen. Coffee had the strength of dishwater and cheese was always orange. We were not yet a nation addicted to fast food, but neither were we passionate about organic produce, the authentic tastes of foods from every corner of the globe, or handmade "artisan" foods. We loved chocolate, but we thought of it as candy: fudge or a candy bar—plain, nutty, or nougatty—or an assortment of boxed chocolates from Whitman's or See's. More than 70 percent of the chocolate purchased by Americans was milk chocolate. Home bakers melted gritty squares of one of two brands of bitter "baking chocolate" or spooned out cocoa to make cakes, brownies, and fudge.

A chocolate cake was a tall, fluffy affair made with shortening rather than butter and slathered with swirls of sugary fudge frosting. The prettiest desserts were usually disappointing. When I opened my first shop, American desserts were still more sweet than flavorful and more decorative than delicious. Even the darkest chocolate contained less pure chocolate (cacao) and more sugar than it does today. Ganache was an unknown foreign language, bittersweet rarely spoken. But in fewer than twenty-five years, everything changed.

Julia Child, and then a legion of baby boomers like me, brought home to America new tastes in food and new ideas about eating from life and travel in Europe or war in Asia. Wearing T-shirts and aprons rather than toques and starched jackets, would-have-been architects and teachers became chefs and bakers. We changed the way Americans ate and cooked. Some did it with small restaurants, wineries, cooking schools, and cookbooks; I opened my chocolate dessert shop. For me it had all begun in 1973, in Paris, with a single bite of a homemade chocolate truffle.

MME. LESTELLE'S FATEFUL TRUFFLE

The truffle was an unexpected jolt of pure bittersweet pleasure that left me momentarily speechless. I felt that I was tasting chocolate for the very first time. The truffle was intense: complex and earthy, dense and smooth. It was not candy, but a very tiny divine dessert. It was all about chocolate flavor rather than sweetness. Seriously sensual, it was a bittersweet poem. And it was fresh, as a true chocolate truffle should be, homemade by my elderly landlady on the rue Copernic, during my postgraduate year in Paris. Mme. Lestelle's truffle was the beginning of a year of tastes, little explosions that redefined my understanding of even the simplest foods. I tasted fragrant peaches and strawberries ripe beyond any previous experience of ripeness, chicken with so much flavor and a texture that, in retrospect, I compare with the first taste of pasta cooked "al dente" after a lifetime of mushy noodles. Cheeses (none of them orange) beguiled me. And wine. That truffle was only the beginning.

Back in California I seduced my friends with Madame's truffles. Hardly allowing graduate-school studies to get in the way, and with a business card proclaiming "Alice's Chocolates (truffles, cakes, pâtisserie diverse)," I made French cakes and truffles at home and sold them at the Pig by the Tail Charcuterie in Berkeley, across the street from a new little restaurant called Chez Panisse. By 1976, my miniature chocolaterie had overflowed my home kitchen and, instead of starting my master's thesis in marketing, I opened a small chocolate dessert shop I called Cocolat. I never did write the thesis.

The simplest French chocolate tortes and truffles were a revelation to my customers, as they had been to me. Dramatically bittersweet and far richer than anything Americans were accustomed to, Cocolat desserts transformed local standards. That influence rippled beyond the rarefied air of Berkeley and became part of the larger culinary revolution. Mme. Lestelle's bite-sized cocoa-dusted truffles created a local sensation, but my almost inadvertent invention of extravagantly large chocolate-dipped ganache truffles (see page 98) caused an explosion. When Zabar's in New York called to place an order, I first said, "No; truffles are too fragile and perishable to ship." But who could say no to Zabar's? Ultimately, I solved the shipping problem and Zabar's bought truffles. Then Gael Greene discovered them and wrote about them in *New York* magazine.

Cocolat became a destination for savvy chocolate lovers from all over the country. Europeans living in Berkeley shared the "secret" of Cocolat with visiting friends and relatives. One small shop eventually became seven, and then ten. *Gourmet* said, "Cocolat is to chocolate what Tiffany's is to diamonds." Meanwhile, "gourmet" food was becoming big business. Executives from food corporations came to see and taste what was going on at Cocolat. They came to sample desserts that tasted more of chocolate than of sugar, and cakes made with butter and topped with fresh whipped cream or bittersweet ganache rather than powdered-sugar frosting or sugary fudge. They came to see elegantly designed desserts, from tailored and simple to spectacular, without the old-fashioned bakery frills and fuss. And they came to try freshly made chocolate truffles, which didn't taste like ordinary candy. Cocolat-style desserts found their way onto menus across the country and into the pages of food magazines. Big chocolate truffles began to show up everywhere too, often to my chagrin, since they tasted nothing like a true truffle should. I didn't know whether to be proud or appalled when my dad reported seeing so-called chocolate truffles in a gas station mini-mart.

CHOCOLATE FOR ADULTS

Mini-marts notwithstanding, the idea and the image of chocolate shifted from sweet candy to suave dessert. I don't remember hearing the phrase "chocolate for adults" before I used it to explain the desserts and truffles at Cocolat. In the period between 1974, when I started making chocolate truffles for the Pig by the Tail, and the sale of Cocolat, in 1990, chocolate had become "gourmet." Meanwhile, chocolate truffles, flourless chocolate cakes, and chocolate mousse were becoming household terms and items, found everywhere from food magazines and cookbooks to television and restaurants. As a result, Americans were buying and using chocolate differently. Recipes called for good bittersweet or semisweet chocolate (and plenty of it) rather than the unsweetened "baking chocolate" typical of traditional American recipes.

With chocolate as a starring ingredient in desserts rather than just a flavoring, the quality and flavor and texture of the chocolate made more of a difference. Where there had been chocolate for baking (unsweetened and generic) and chocolate for eating (sweetened, smooth, and delicious), now your favorite bittersweet or semisweet chocolate bar was the perfect ingredient for making chocolate mousse or a chocolate torte or chocolate truffles. Americans were buying more dark chocolate than ever before, for eating and for baking.

Although 66 percent of Americans still preferred milk chocolate to dark, the shift toward dark chocolate was probably best reflected in the fact that even the big American candy manufacturers started offering dark chocolate versions of their most popular milk chocolate candy (such as Hershey's Kisses, Kit Kat bars, and Milky Ways).

By the late 1980s, there were many more recipes in books and magazines that called for bittersweet or semisweet chocolate, and more semisweet baking chocolate in the grocery store, next to the squares of unsweetened baking chocolate. This was dramatic evidence that even mainstream American baking habits had changed. However, unlike European chocolate for cooking, some of our American bittersweet and semisweet "baking chocolates" were grainy and the flavor too harsh for the chocolate to be eaten plain. The manufacturers got the message only half right: they understood that new-style recipes called for semisweet chocolate, but they clung to the notion that cooking chocolate and eating chocolate were two different things. I thought they missed the real trend: better quality and more variety.

THE NEW CHOCOLATES

By 2000, only a little over a decade later, there were many more chocolates to choose from, and the quality had never been better. Home cooks could buy all kinds of imported and domestic chocolates, in specialty stores and by mail and even in supermarkets, that were once accessible only to pastry chefs and candy makers. Here in Berkeley, where food things happen early (if not first), premium American, Swiss, French, German, and Dutch bittersweet, semisweet, white, and milk chocolates for eating and dessert making were stacked right beside those tedious baking squares in the supermarket. There were better-quality unsweetened baking chocolates and even tins of roasted cocoa beans. And no single chocolate tasted like any other. Any dessert maker who was still using only the old baking squares was missing the newest culinary adventure.

The very definition of chocolate was shifting again. Like winemakers blending grapes, chocolate makers differentiate their products according to the way they choose and blend cocoa beans of different varieties and from different sources. Now some chocolate makers were blending with a different vision and some were even making chocolates exclusively with beans from a single source. There is no one best chocolate, just as there is no one best wine. One man's divinely smooth chocolate with nutty flavors might not suit the person who wants chocolate with lots of fruity acidity.

In addition to better quality and greater variety, the composition of chocolate was changing too. The newest and most exciting chocolates were dark—bittersweet and semisweet—and made with more cocoa beans and less sugar than we Americans were accustomed to. Chocolates with a percentage on the label to indicate cacao (cocoa bean) content began to appear. The higher the percentage, the stronger and more intense the flavor. Bittersweet chocolate with "70%" cacao contained almost half again as much ground cocoa beans and more than a third less sugar than the bittersweet chocolate we were used to. Old-style American bittersweet chocolate (usually averaging 55%

cacao) tasted mild and sweet compared with a bar of 70% chocolate. But Americans were catching on fast to the pleasures of European-style flavors and stronger dark chocolates, and American manufacturers began to make their own new chocolates, blending cocoa beans differently and using more beans and less sugar as well.

Cooking and making desserts with the new chocolates was the obvious next step, and one of the primary reasons for this book. Stronger and more distinctive chocolates provide more variety and excitement in desserts—and sometimes more flexibility in creating desserts that are not as sweet as before—but they rarely substitute perfectly in recipes that were created for the older, sweeter chocolates. To make our favorite recipes with the new chocolates, we needed to crack the code for substituting one type of chocolate for another. But there was more to it than that. If our palates hadn't changed, we wouldn't have been enjoying stronger and more interesting chocolates in the first place. We needed a new approach to chocolate desserts— a new kind of recipe.

Desserts that seemed daringly bittersweet a decade before, including my own, now seemed too rich and sweet. Few did justice to the more interesting and better chocolates. Even at my favorite local restaurant, world renowned for exquisitely simple dishes that celebrate the perfection of each ingredient, the signature chocolate dessert was so rich in egg yolks and cream that it lacked the stunning clarity of flavor characteristic of every other dish on the menu. To taste more of the nuances in the chocolate, we didn't need to increase the chocolate in recipes—we had done that years ago. But we did need to adjust the proportions of fat, dairy products, and sugar, not for reasons of healthy eating or dieting but for pleasure, clarity, and flavor. Indeed, lessons I had learned from working on *Chocolate and the Art of Low-Fat Desserts* years earlier were suddenly even

more relevant: less fat and less sugar actually bring flavors into sharper focus and allow substitutes to be tasted. Cream can soften flavors too much, and egg yolks, sometimes so wonderful with dark chocolate, can blur flavors instead. I had been applying these lessons in all of my cooking, and teaching this gospel too. By the time I worked on the 1997 revision of *Joy of Cooking* a few years later, I already knew how to sharpen flavors in recipes that tasted too tame for the twenty-first-century palate.

MAKING DESSERTS WITH THE NEW CHOCOLATES

I could not have been better prepared for working with the new, more distinctive and complex chocolates. My friendship and consulting relationship with the founders of Scharffen Berger Chocolate Maker provided me with a stunning new chocolate to play with, which in turn led me to greater curiosity about all the newer interesting chocolates. I was immediately frustrated (but fascinated) at not being able to taste the specific characteristics, much less the nuances, of these chocolates in desserts. Even when restaurant chefs made special desserts to promote a particular chocolate, the desserts often didn't do justice to the distinctive flavors in the chocolate. As often as not, the special dessert simply tasted like another rich, sweet chocolate dessert.

I wanted recipes that let the complex flavors in these new chocolates speak. When I began to experiment, I realized that I already knew how to make the chocolate flavors pop: strategic reductions in sugar, butter, and cream, simplified recipes, and fewer ingredients. After one of my "minimalist" recipes appeared in *Food & Wine,* I bumped into a well-known local chef in the produce market. He greeted me with "So you make chocolate mousse with water instead of cream?" I urged him to try it if he wanted to taste more chocolate flavor.

I was also beginning to choose different chocolates to partner with different ingredients, for different recipes, for different occasions, or even just for fun—as a hostess chooses different wines to go with different food or company. This required that I taste chocolate with more attention, as though I had never tasted it before. But now I also needed information that I could not find in books or from classes. It was not enough to appreciate that the chocolates differed in flavor. I had to understand how chocolates with different cacao percentages behaved in all kinds of recipes. Why was it, for example, that I could substitute a 70% chocolate in my favorite chocolate torte recipe and produce something delicious, with minimal tweaking, while the same substitution wrecked my best ganache? I wanted to be able to work with all kinds of chocolates in all kinds of desserts and to help others do it as well. I approached the project in my usual trial-and-error mode, in the process learning how different types of recipes responded to the different percentages of cacao, sugar, and fat in different chocolates. Finally, I used what I knew about the composition of the chocolates to devise rough formulas that I could apply strictly or loosely, depending on the recipe, to substitute high-percentage chocolates in favorite recipes. Now I was playing with the chocolate in recipes like a musician playing variations; I was noticing flavors and textures that I had missed before. I was tasting chocolate for the first time—again, thirty years after I tasted my first chocolate truffle.

This book is about understanding the chocolate and rethinking recipes. It is filled primarily with simple recipes, sweet and savory, and new information for curious cooks who love chocolate and want to taste and use the different types. Here I share the tools I created for myself, to allow other enthusiasts to speak the language of chocolate more fluently: to experiment and convert recipes with ease and understanding. Readers will find a primer on working with chocolate, on making chocolate truffles, and on substituting one kind of chocolate for another. I've also included some low-fat recipes, savory dishes, and a great introduction to cocoa nibs (roasted cocoa beans), with recipes, for those who are not yet familiar with this exciting form of chocolate.

Along the way, I've shared memories and experiences, small tastes of my life with chocolate. Although my stories go back in time, the recipes themselves, even those for making childhood favorites, are infused with current knowledge and reflect a very contemporary taste for chocolate. In the years since the publication of *Bittersweet,* I have continued to use the tools and tricks that I developed in addition to the recipes. With so many more chocolates available with different flavor profiles and percentages, the ability to substitute and switch between them serves me well and often! Meanwhile, I continue to focus on simple recipes that honor the true flavors in the chocolate. At the same time, I am always looking for new ways to pair chocolate with unexpected ingredients in savory as well as sweet dishes.

I wish you all of the pleasures of chocolate, and I invite you to taste chocolate again, for the very first time. *Bon appétit.*

SERIOUSLY
BITTER
SWEET

1

BEFORE YOU START

Working with chocolate, dessert making, and baking are each different from cooking. Small, simple, but often nonintuitive details can significantly alter results. Unlike the cook, the baker can rarely taste and adjust or repair as he or she mixes a batter or creates a dessert. Knowing which details are important sets you free to be as creative and playful as you like, without any sad surprises.

Details That Make a Difference

MISE EN PLACE

Mise en place is a French phrase that means "put in place," or "set up." Professional chefs could not survive in a busy kitchen without relying on this practice. When you see TV chefs with all their ingredients measured in little dishes before any cooking begins, you are seeing mise en place!

The ritual of setting out and measuring ingredients focuses you. It clears your mind and promotes attention and connection to the task at hand. It allows you to determine before you start a recipe that you have all of the ingredients and equipment you need. You are less likely to measure incorrectly or forget to include an ingredient in a batter, regardless of any distractions.

Many desserts and chocolate confections turn out best when the recipe steps are performed without interruption. Mise en place ensures that once you begin a recipe, you will not have to run to the store, search the sandbox for your sifter, or rummage in the pantry for a particular pan while your melted chocolate hardens or your batter deflates. Mise en place makes both baking and dessert making more pleasurable and more successful.

MEASURING

Some inaccurate measurements will not always spoil a dessert. You can use a liberal hand with certain ingredients, such as raisins, nuts, chocolate chips, coconut, or even vanilla, and you can normally substitute dried fruits and nuts in equal measure one for another.

But for tender cakes with a perfect crumb, you must measure the baking soda, the baking powder, and, most important, the cocoa powder and flour *carefully*. Even, or especially, in the simplest recipes, baking is not as forgiving as cooking. If cakes are tough, dry, doughy, or leaden, chances are your flour measurement is at fault.

A cup of all-purpose flour can weigh anywhere from 4 to 6 ounces, depending on whether or not it is sifted before measuring or packed firmly or less so into the cup. That 2-ounce (50 percent!) discrepancy can make the difference between a moist, light poem of a cake and a highly effective doorstop.

How to Measure Flour

When a recipe says "1 cup all-purpose flour," this means 1 cup of all-purpose flour measured, without first sifting, as follows: If it is compacted, stir the flour briefly in the sack or canister with a spoon. Spoon the flour lightly into a 1-cup dry measure until it is heaped above the rim. *Do not* shake or tap the cup to settle the flour! Sweep a straight-edged knife or spatula across the rim of the cup to level the flour. A cup of unsifted all-purpose flour measured this way weighs 4½ ounces (130 grams); a cup of unsifted cake flour weighs 4 ounces (115 grams).

If a recipe calls for "1 cup sifted flour," the flour should be sifted before measuring: Set the measuring cup on a sheet of wax paper. Use a medium-mesh strainer (my preference) or a sifter to sift the flour over the cup until it is heaped above the rim. *Do not* shake or tap the cup to settle the flour! Sweep a straight-edged knife or spatula across the rim of the cup to level the flour. A cup of sifted all-purpose flour measured this way weighs 4 ounces (115 grams); a cup of sifted cake flour weighs 3½ ounces (100 grams).

Note: Ignore the "presifted" label on flour sacks. Presifting eliminates any foreign matter, but the flour gets compacted again en route to your grocer's shelf.

How to Measure Cocoa Powder

Normally my recipes call for unsifted cocoa. If your cocoa is very lumpy and compacted, press out most of the lumps with the back of a spoon, then stir it a little to loosen it before measuring it like unsifted flour (see opposite). If sifted cocoa is called for, use a medium-fine strainer to sift and measure it as for sifted flour.

Dry and Liquid Measures

Dry measures are measuring cups designed to measure dry ingredients. When using dry measures, you use a 1-cup measure to measure 1 cup, a ½-cup measure to measure ½ cup, and so forth. Unless the recipe calls for a "packed" or "lightly packed" cup, heap dry ingredients above the rim, as described for flour, without packing them down; do not tap or shake the cup to settle the ingredient. Sweep a straight-edged knife or spatula across the rim of the cup to level it.

Liquid measures are clear glass or plastic containers designed to measure liquids; they have pouring spouts and lines up the sides to indicate measurements. Set the measure on the counter before pouring in the liquid—you can't hold it completely level in the air. Lower your face so you can read the measurement at eye level as you pour in the liquid.

MIXING

For best results, use the specific type of mixing utensil suggested in each recipe. Mixing with a rubber spatula does not produce the same batter texture as mixing with a wire whisk. Folding, stirring, beating, and whisking all produce different results. When a recipe calls for mixing (or folding or stirring, etc.) "just until the ingredient is incorporated," this means that extra mixing may deflate the batter, result in a tough cake, or cause other problems.

Add and mix ingredients in the order called for. The order in which key ingredients are mixed can be critical. If a recipe calls for stirring A into B, it is safest to assume, especially when working with chocolatey batters, that stirring B into A will not produce the same result.

In order to blend flour and other dry ingredients into batters without excessive mixing, many recipes call for whisking the flour and the other dry ingredients (such as leavening, spices, and salt) together first. For very delicate cakes such as sponge or génoise, the dry ingredients are sifted two or three times as well. Whisking and/or sifting fluffs and aerates the dry ingredients so they blend easily and thoroughly into the batter or dough with very minimal mixing.

To prevent overmixing, recipes may call for turning the mixer off before adding the dry ingredients to a dough or batter. Then the mixer is turned back on to a low speed to prevent the ingredients from flying out.

Tough or Tender?

Tenderness in cakes, cookies, and pastry is often a matter of proper measuring, mixing, and timing. Toughness can result from measuring flour inaccurately, using too much flour or the wrong flour (bread flour or whole-grain flour rather than all-purpose or cake flour), or too much mixing after the flour has been moistened in the batter. Baking for too long or at a temperature that is too high or too low can also cause tough cakes, cookies, and pastry.

Hot and Cold

The texture of cakes and other desserts can be critically affected by the temperature of the individual ingredients called for in the recipe. Mixing cool or cold ingredients into tepid chocolate can cause a batter to harden precipitously. When a recipe calls for butter, milk, eggs, or any usually refrigerated ingredient to be at room temperature, that means at 65° to 70°F. The ingredient should still be cool, not warm. Remove such items from the fridge early, or bring them to room temperature more quickly as follows:

• Put eggs (still in the shell) in a bowl of warm water or crack them into a stainless steel bowl (which conducts heat better than glass) set in a larger bowl of warm water and whisk gently until blended, then let stand until no longer cold.

• Microwave milk or another liquid in a glass measure on Low (30%) power or Defrost for just a few seconds, or set the measure in a bowl of hot water, just until no longer cold.

• Cut butter into chunks and microwave on Low (30%) power or Defrost, a few seconds at a time, until pliable but *not* melted.

BAKING

Always preheat the oven for 15 to 20 minutes so that it reaches the correct temperature before you bake. Remember that heat rises, so baking something in the top of the oven will produce a different result from baking it in the bottom. Follow the instructions for rack placement in each recipe. I usually position a rack in the lower third of the oven so that a cake placed on the rack is just below the center of the oven. When baking a thin sheet cake or a single sheet of cookies, I position the oven rack in the center.

Unless the instructions say otherwise, baked items should be cooled on a rack. They should always be cooled completely before covering or wrapping. Wrapping baked goods before they are completely cool produces a damp, soggy texture and encourages the growth of mold and bacteria.

Equipment

Baking Sheets and Jelly-Roll Pans

Medium- to heavy-weight aluminum baking sheets and jelly-roll pans will not warp or bend and they heat evenly, without hot spots. I avoid dark or nonstick surfaces, which toughen and overbake tender cakes and cookies; nor do I like cushioned pans, because they yield uninterestingly uniform cookie textures. Professional aluminum "half sheet pans," which measure 12 by 17 by 1 inch, fit most home ovens and perform much better than lighter-weight 11-by-17-inch home-kitchen jelly-roll pans. You can buy them at specialty cookware stores, restaurant supply stores, and warehouse grocery discount stores.

Bowls

I use stainless steel and glass mixing bowls for different purposes. Stainless is best for melting chocolate in a water bath, for example; glass, for melting it in the microwave. Bowls that are nearly as deep as they are wide keep dry ingredients from flying out and are best for beating egg whites. One- and two-quart glass measures with handles also make wonderful mixing bowls and are perfect for melting large quantities of chocolate in the microwave.

Cake Decorating Turntable

A heavy, well-balanced lazy Susan or decorating turntable is the best tool for frosting and decorating cakes, but a lightweight plastic one will do in a pinch. Ateco turntables are available at restaurant supply and kitchenware stores or by mail (see Sources, page 317), and they last a lifetime (so far). A 12-inch metal banding wheel from a ceramics supply shop is just as good, at about half the cost.

Cake Pans

Experienced bakers normally avoid stainless steel pans because stainless steel does not conduct heat evenly. However, there are some heavy-gauge stainless pans with aluminum cores to ensure even heating; they are beautiful but quite expensive. For layer cakes and sponge cakes, I avoid glass pans and pans with dark finishes, even if they are non-stick. These tend to overbake the edges and bottoms of light and tender cakes, sometimes even before the inside is done. Richer or heavier pound cakes and loaf cakes are different—the deep golden brown crust produced by heavy (often decorative) dark tube and loaf pans is both delicious and beautiful to see. Always read the information that comes with these pans; you may be advised to lower the baking temperature by 25 degrees, which is also good advice if you must bake in a glass pan.

I use 8- and 9-inch round and square pans and 9-by-13-inch rectangular pans, all 2 inches deep. For springforms, I use pans with true 8- and 9-inch diameters (rather than European pans with metric sizes) and a depth of a full 3 inches. Even better than traditional springform pans are Parrish Magic Line "cheesecake pans" with removable push-up bottoms, in depths of 2 and 3 inches.

Cooling Racks

Racks for cooling cakes and cookies speed up the cooling process and keep baked goods from getting soggy. To save counter space, I have a multitiered rack that holds either four half-sheet pans or four cooling racks. The rack folds away when not needed.

Food Processor

The processor is invaluable for pulverizing nuts or chocolate, transforming ordinary granulated sugar into extra-fine sugar for making meringue, making fruit purees, and mixing some tart and cookie doughs. I keep a mini processor on hand too, for small quantities.

Immersion Blender

An immersion or stick blender is a handheld "wand" that enables you to blend or puree a sauce or soup in the pot or container it was made in, rather than have to transfer the mixture to the bowl of a food processor. It is very powerful and the best tool—even more effective than a food processor—for making perfect ganache for truffles.

Measuring Cups

For measuring liquids, I have 1-, 2-, 4-, and 8-cup glass measures. The two larger sizes double as mixing bowls. For measuring flour and dry ingredients, I keep at least one set of metal or sturdy plastic measuring cups including ⅛-, ¼-, ⅓-, ½-, and 1-cup measures.

Microwave Oven

I find the microwave to be an essential tool for a variety of tasks, from melting chocolate to reheating anything to bringing refrigerated ingredients like eggs, butter, or milk to room temperature.

Mixers

I use a KitchenAid 5-quart mixer for larger jobs and a handheld mixer for smaller ones. I keep extra sets of beaters for both mixers so that I do not have to wash them between beating a batter and egg whites, for example.

Parchment Paper and Wax Paper

Baker's parchment paper is much cleaner and more reliable than grease on the bottom of cake pans, and it can be used to line cookie sheets as well. Everything from meringues to macaroons releases easily from parchment paper. I still keep wax paper (cheaper than parchment!) in my kitchen for all kinds of miscellaneous tasks that do not require the special characteristics and expense of parchment: for example, as a landing place for sifted flour. Precut parchment paper sheets are easier to use than pieces torn from a roll. Sheets are available from King Arthur Flour (see Sources, page 317).

Pastry Bags and Tips

PASTRY BAGS Pastry bags made of nylon or polypropylene are better than cloth or canvas bags because they wash easily and do not become stiff and cracked or sour smelling. Whipped cream does not weep through these bags either. Disposable plastic pastry bags eliminate the need to wash altogether. A large 16- to 18-inch bag is handy for piping a batch of meringue. A 10- to 12-inch bag is good for smaller quantities. Since pastry bags should not be filled much more than half-full, a bag that is a little too big is better than one that is too small.

PASTRY TIPS Ateco is the universal brand. A useful assortment of tips might include plain round tips varying in diameter from ⅜ to ¾ inch as well as several star tips.

Pastry Brushes

Natural boar's-bristle brushes are the best. Keep separate brushes for sweet and savory dishes, unless you want your desserts to taste of garlic or barbecue sauce.

Rolling Pin

Choose a pin that is comfortable for you: with or without handles, heavy or lightweight. I find that a straight rather than tapered pin works best. Absent a rolling pin, you can improvise with a length of thick dowel or pipe, or a tall bottle.

Scale

Many fine chocolates do not come in premeasured squares, so a scale is really a must. Once you get used to using one, you will wish that all recipes were written by weight instead of cup measures. I like a scale that enables me to put any bowl or pot on it, reset to zero, and weigh the ingredients—without dirtying an extra container. Cookware stores sell a variety of scales, or you can even use a digital postal scale, as I do.

Scissors

Keep a good pair in the kitchen for cutting parchment paper.

Serrated Bread Knife

A knife with a 12-inch blade is ideal for cutting a sponge cake or génoise into horizontal layers, but a shorter blade will also do.

Silica Gel

Silica gel is an inert, nontoxic, granular form of silica, and the highest-capacity absorbent available. Packets of silica are packed in pill bottles and with leather goods, electronics, and myriad other products. Similarly, silica gel can be used to keep cookies crisp in an airtight container and to prevent decorative caramel pieces, caramelized nuts, or praline from becoming sticky from the moisture in the air. Store silica gel in an airtight container. Once saturated with moisture, it can be reactivated (again and again) by baking it in a 250°F oven for 1½ hours. Order silica gel from special cake decorators suppliers, such as Beryl's (see Sources, page 317).

Skewers and Toothpicks

For testing cakes, wooden (barbecue) skewers are cleaner than broom straws and longer than toothpicks. Moist batter and crumbs stick to a wooden skewer or toothpick much better than to a metal cake tester, so that you can see exactly how gooey or dry your cake is within.

Spatulas

RUBBER AND HEATPROOF SILICONE SPATULAS Three sizes will meet every contingency: use the largest for folding meringue into delicate batters and scraping large bowls; a mini spatula teases tiny quantities from small containers; medium handles everything in between. Rubber spatulas melt and discolor if used over heat. Silicone spatulas, on the other hand, are miraculous for cooking everything from custards to caramel; they have replaced both wooden spoons and rubber spatulas in my kitchen.

METAL SPATULAS For frosting cakes, I like a stainless steel spatula with a straight 8-inch-long blade that is rounded at the end. For spreading cake batter in a sheet pan, I like an offset spatula (the blade has a bend in it right after the handle) with a blade at least 8 inches long. For small jobs, I keep straight and offset spatulas with 4-inch blades.

Strainers

I hate cleaning and storing sifters. A large medium-mesh strainer does the job for flour and other dry ingredients. It requires only one hand, and it shakes out and cleans easily. Fine-mesh strainers are best for dusting desserts with powdered sugar or cocoa. I keep on hand a couple of good fine-mesh stainless steel strainers, as well as several inexpensive strainers with plastic rims in a variety of sizes.

Tart and Tartlet Pans

I use a 9½-inch tart pan with a removable bottom, fluted edges, and a shiny reflective surface rather than one made of darkened steel.

I use 3- or 3½-inch (measured across the top) solid-bottom pans ⅝ inch deep for dainty servings; these require a generous ¾ ounce (23 grams) and 1 ounce (28 grams) of dough, respectively, to line them.

Thermometers

INSTANT-READ THERMOMETER Inexpensive instant-read thermometers are available in cookware and hardware stores. These thermometers, which have a range of 0° to 220°F, are perfect for cooking custards, working with chocolate, or checking when eggs, butter, milk, etc., for baking are at room temperature (65° to 70°F). But digital thermometers are quicker and more convenient. I use a combination timer/thermometer with a range of 32° to 392°F. It has a probe attached to a wire that can be inserted into a pot of candy on top of the stove or into a roast or loaf of bread in the oven. The temperature registers on an easy-to-read digital display that sits on the counter, and it can be set to beep when the desired temperature is reached. This is the best thermometer for recipes that require heating and stirring eggs to a particular temperature: just hold the probe in the bowl with one hand and stir with the other until the beeper goes off.

OVEN THERMOMETER Even the best recipes suffer if baked at the wrong temperatures. Use a thermometer to check your oven every now and again to see that it remains accurate. If necessary, either have it calibrated or compensate for any discrepancy yourself until you can get someone to adjust it.

Timer

Whether it's the tick-tick, ding-ding type or a digital buzzer, a timer is a necessity in the kitchen.

Wire Whisks

A whisk is an essential hand tool, and not just for beating. Whisks are better than kitchen forks for mixing dry ingredients together thoroughly or fluffing up flour before it is added to a batter.

Zester (Microplane)

Hate zesting (removing the thin colored top layer of citrus peel)? A Microplane zester is modeled on a fine woodworker's rasp. Rather than "scrubbing" the fruit, and your knuckles, back and forth against a grater, simply draw the zester lightly across the fruit, in one direction, like a violin bow across strings. The Microplane lifts off the thinnest shreds of zest—effortlessly and without any bitter white pith or scraped knuckles. Rather than dreading the task, you will look forward to any recipe that calls for zest.

Ingredients

Baking Powder and Baking Soda

Cakes may be leavened with baking powder or baking soda, or both. Baking powder has an expiration date because it loses its oomph if not fresh and stored in a tightly sealed container. You can check to see if baking powder still has its power by adding a teaspoon or so to about a quarter cup of hot water—if it bubbles vigorously, it's still good. If in doubt, splurge on a new tin.

Butter

I use butter for baking because it tastes better than shortening or margarine. The recipes in this book were tested with regular unsalted butter; salted butter contains ¼ teaspoon of salt per stick, and it will make many butter-rich chocolate desserts taste much too salty. If using salted butter in a recipe where butter is not a major ingredient, subtract ¼ teaspoon of salt for each stick (115 grams) of butter used.

If you are baking for the Jewish holidays and strictly observing dietary laws, for nondairy meals, substitute unsalted pareve margarine for butter. If you must for whatever reason use margarine or shortening instead of butter, avoid tub margarine, butter substitutes, and spreads, which may contain a very high percentage of water. These ingredients are not made for baking, and results will be unpredictable. Do not expect predictable results from substituting vegetable oils for solid fats either.

SPECIALTY BUTTERS Some of the finest French and other butters available in gourmet shops and upscale markets have less water, and thus more fat, in them than the national brands that Americans are accustomed to. In most recipes you can substitute these butters, but you may have some different results.

Chestnuts

If you don't want to roast or steam your own, the best cooked whole chestnuts come in vacuum packages in better supermarkets and gourmet stores. Those in jars are not quite as good, but they are still acceptable. Do not confuse them with sweetened chestnuts or chestnuts packed in syrup. You can also use Faugier chestnut puree (ingredients are listed as chestnut puree, water, corn syrup), which is essentially unsweetened except for the tiny amount of corn syrup. Do not confuse the latter for sweetened chestnut puree, also called chestnut spread, which comes in cans or jars.

Chocolate

See pages 31–42.

Cocoa

See pages 34–36.

Coconut

Sweetened shredded coconut is available in the baking aisle of the supermarket. Unsweetened dried shredded coconut is more often found in specialty or gourmet markets, or in natural or health food stores.

Coffee and Espresso

If a recipe calls for freshly ground coffee beans, use freshly roasted beans from a gourmet coffee purveyor, and grind or crush them yourself if possible. Bypass that big can of ground coffee from the supermarket.

For recipes that call for instant espresso powder, I use Medaglia d'Oro. To substitute regular instant coffee powder or freeze-dried instant for espresso powder, use 25 to 30 percent more than the recipe calls for.

Cream

The freshest, cleanest-tasting cream is simply pasteurized, rather than "ultra-pasteurized" or "sterilized," and it contains no added ingredients. Some ultra-pasteurized and sterilized creams, which have been processed for longer shelf life, no longer taste as cooked or as much like canned milk as they used to, so I am less adamantly against them than I was. But I still buy regular pasteurized whenever possible, and I prefer cream without the stabilizer carrageenan, although the latter does make smoother whipped cream.

Dried Fruits

Dried fruits should be moist, plump, and flavorful. Whole pieces are always better, fresher, and moister than prechopped or extruded pellets. If they are sticky, chop or cut them with an oiled knife or scissors.

Eggs

Use Grade AA large eggs for the recipes in this book. Buy eggs from a source that keeps them refrigerated, and do likewise at your house. When recipes call for eggs at room temperature, remove them from the refrigerator an hour or so ahead, or warm them quickly in a bowl of warm water.

Extracts

Always use pure extracts. Artificial flavorings are not worthy of the time and other good ingredients that you put into your favorite recipes.

Flour

The recipes in this collection were originally developed and tested with bleached all-purpose flour or, when cake flour is called for, bleached cake flour. Since the first edition, I have come to prefer unbleached to bleached all-purpose flour because it tastes better, even though some cookies and cakes may not be quite as tender. I have now made a few adjustments where necessary to ensure that the recipes calling for all-purpose flour will produce good results with *either* bleached or unbleached flour—therefore, you can make the choice. I still use bleached cake flour for those few recipes that call for cake flour.

Liqueurs and Spirits

When recipes call for spirits, such as brandy or rum, it is not necessary to use the finest and most expensive, but choose a brand that you can sip without grimacing, or omit the liquor altogether. If you omit the liquor used as a flavoring, there is no need to substitute another liquid in its place in most recipes. However, omitting the liquor used to flavor truffle centers will make the ganache centers firmer; this can be corrected, if desired, by adding a little extra cream or by using a little less chocolate. I do not use liquor flavorings or extracts, as they taste artificial.

EAU-DE-VIE DE FRAMBOISE Not to be confused with sweet pink raspberry or black raspberry liqueurs such as Chambord, eau-de-vie de framboise is a clear high-proof distilled fruit brandy made exactly the way kirsch is made, but with raspberries instead of cherries. St. George Spirits is my favorite brand.

Nuts

For freshness and flavor, buy nuts raw, rather than toasted, and in bulk from stores that have lots of turnover, rather than packaged from the supermarket. Larger halves and pieces stay fresher longer; it's better to chop them yourself. Nuts keep well in the freezer, packaged airtight.

Fresh nuts are delicious raw, but toasting brings out such rich flavor that almonds and hazelnuts are virtually transformed. Toasted nuts are also extra crunchy. To toast nuts, spread them in a single layer on an ungreased baking sheet. Bake in a preheated oven (350°F for almonds and hazelnuts; 325°F for pecans and walnuts) for 10 to 20 minutes, depending on the type of nut and whether they are whole, sliced, or slivered. Check the color and flavor of the nuts frequently, and stir to redistribute them on the pan. Almonds and hazelnuts are done when they are golden brown when you bite or cut them in half; pecans and walnuts, when fragrant and lightly colored.

To rub the bitter skins from toasted hazelnuts, cool them and then rub the nuts together until most of the skins flake off. When chopped toasted nuts are called for, toast them whole or in large pieces and chop them after they cool.

To pulverize or grind nuts in a food processor without making paste or nut butter, start with a cool (not hot from the dishwasher), perfectly dry processor bowl and blade, and have the nuts at room temperature. Frozen or cold nuts will release moisture that will turn the nuts to paste, as will nuts still hot from the oven. Use short pulses, stopping from time to time to scrape the corners of the processor bowl with a skewer or chopstick. If you observe these rules, there is no particular need to add some of the flour or sugar from the recipe to the nuts to keep them dry, although you may do so as an extra precaution.

Spices

For the best and brightest flavors, use spices that still smell potent in the bottle. For the recipes in this book, I prefer true Ceylon cinnamon (called *canela* in Mexico), which has a more complex, almost citrusy, flavor than the more familiar hot, spicy cassia cinnamon that Americans know best. When you buy cinnamon sticks, you can recognize the variety by color and texture: cassia sticks are reddish brown and as hard as wood, and they are often used as stirring sticks for holiday drinks. Ceylon or *canela* cinnamon sticks are buff-colored rolls of papery bark that are easy to crumble and can be chopped with a heavy knife. Look for Ceylon cinnamon or *canela* in specialty food stores or Latin markets, or order it by mail from Penzeys Spices (see Sources, page 317).

Sugar

I use cane sugar rather than beet sugar for baking and dessert making. Chemically the two substances are exactly the same, yet too many bakers and pastry chefs whom I know have reported differences and disappointments with beet sugar. All of the recipes in this book were tested with C&H pure cane sugar (granulated, golden brown, or dark brown) purchased in the supermarket. After having several cakes fall, I now avoid sugar with added fructose. (Granulated sugar is, by definition, a combination of sucrose and fructose, but when fructose is on the ingredients list, it means that extra fructose has been added.)

Sugars seem to vary in coarseness in different parts of the country. Coarse sugar makes cookies less tender and may cause butter cakes to collapse as well. If your sugar is as coarse as regular table salt and/or your cookies are tough or your butter cakes sometimes sink, switch to "bar sugar," fine granulated sugar, or even superfine sugar—or simply process your regular granulated sugar briefly in the food processor before using it. (Or use C&H bakers' sugar.)

Light (golden) brown and dark brown sugars impart wonderful caramel or butterscotch flavor to desserts. I usually specify my preference for light or dark brown sugar, but you can use them interchangeably. Brown sugar should be lump-free before it is added to a batter or dough, as it is unlikely to smooth after it is added. Soft lumps can be squeezed with your fingers or mashed with a fork. If the sugar is quite hard or has hard lumps, save it for your oatmeal. If you soften the sugar by warming it, the warm sugar may cause a batter to separate or curdle (make applesauce instead). Brown sugar is measured by packing it fairly firmly into the measuring cup.

Vanilla

EXTRACT I use only pure vanilla extract. There are no rules really, but when I want classic vanilla flavor or a subtle backdrop in chocolate desserts, I choose Bourbon vanilla from

Madagascar or Mexican vanilla. When I want a more floral or exotic flavor, I use Tahitian.

POWDER Vanilla powder is a good way to get vanilla flavor without adding any liquid to the recipe. I found it helpful in flavoring a low-fat cheesecake batter without adding unwanted extra moisture. But the seeds from a real vanilla pod or the ground-up pod itself is even purer and more exciting.

BEANS These are slightly more time-consuming to use, but luxurious. Split the bean lengthwise and scrape the seeds into a batter, dough, or custard. In the last case, be sure to steep the whole pod in the liquid as well, then retrieve and discard it later. I also use ground-up whole vanilla beans in cookie dough, cheesecake batter, and ice creams. If you can't find jars of ground vanilla beans (not to be confused with vanilla powder), you can chop a whole bean and grind it as fine as possible in a coffee or spice grinder.

A Chocolate Primer

HOW CHOCOLATE IS MADE

The world's supply of chocolate is produced from cacao culti-vated in a narrow band that encircles the globe, twenty degrees north and south of the equator and in Hawaii. Cocoa beans, the seeds of the cacao tree, are the source of all forms of cocoa and chocolate. The rich, heady, sensual chocolate that we know and love is the result of a complicated processing of these beans, not unlike the miracle of art and science that transforms grapes into wine.

Cacao trees grow only to about twenty feet high. White blos-soms, followed by colorful fruit, form directly on the spin-dly trunks and lower branches, giving cacao groves the exotic appearance of a movie set for a tropical fantasy. The fruit—elongated heavy grooved pods from eight to twelve inches long—may be deep ocher, red, green, or taupe, depending on ripeness and variety.

After harvesting, the pods are split open with a machete to reveal a cluster of twenty-four to forty seeds embedded in a vis-cous white pulp. At this point, the pulp has a fresh, cool, mildly sweet fruity flavor, somewhat reminiscent of that of a fresh lychee nut, while the seeds themselves have very little flavor. The seeds and pulp are scooped out and either heaped on the ground or transferred to boxes; they are then covered with mats or palm or banana leaves (or sheets of plastic) to ferment. This takes about four days, during which time workers frequently turn the heaps with shovels to promote even fermentation. As the pulp ferments, it is converted to alcohol, then acetic acid (vinegar), which in turn transforms the meat of the cocoa beans and creates flavor precursors that later, with care and skilled manufacturing techniques, become the incomparable rich com-plex flavors of the chocolate.

The fermented pulp ultimately drains away, leaving behind the moist fermented beans. The beans are spread out to dry for several more days (ideally in the sun) before they are bagged and shipped to chocolate factories. Proper fermentation and drying are critical to the quality and flavor of the chocolate that will ultimately be produced from the beans. If you have ever sampled chocolate that tastes smoky, for example, it may mean the beans were dried over a fire rather than in the sun. Harsh-flavored chocolate may be a result of inadequate fermentation, while a moldy flavor signals moldy beans from insufficient dry-ing or badly managed fermentation.

Although properly fermented and dried beans, still considered raw, now contain the essential elements for chocolate flavor and quality, at this stage they barely taste of chocolate as we know it. The potential chocolate flavor and quality is realized—or not—at the chocolate factory. Here, in separate batches, beans from different parts of the world, with different flavor profiles, are inspected for quality, cleaned, roasted, and then winnowed to remove their thin shells, or hulls. In the process of winnowing, the roasted beans shatter into fragments called nibs. In tradi-tional large-scale chocolate manufacturing, nibs from differ-ent origins are then blended to produce a specific flavor profile, but artisan and micro-batch chocolate makers these days are likely to use nibs from a single source (or primarily from a sin-gle source) to create single-origin chocolates. Blended or not, the nibs are finely ground to a thick molten paste called choco-late liquor. Chocolate liquor hardened into bars or squares is the unsweetened baking chocolate we buy in supermarkets. It is also the defining ingredient in all other forms of chocolate.

Chocolate liquor—100% pure cacao—has two significant components: fat, called cocoa butter, and nonfat dry cocoa solids. Cocoa butter is a unique fat that is responsible for both the challenges of working with chocolate and the luxurious sensation of eating it. It is the complex crystal structure of cocoa butter that requires that we temper chocolate in order to harden it properly. Even when solid, cocoa butter melts at close to our body temperature, which gives chocolate its most sensual characteristic—it literally melts in our mouths. But, for all of that, cocoa butter is nearly tasteless. Most of the chocolate flavor is in the other component of chocolate liquor, the nonfat dry solids— which you could think of as fat-free cocoa powder.

Although chocolate liquor is the essential and defining ingredient of any kind of chocolate (indeed, each type of chocolate is defined by a minimum level of chocolate liquor), extra cocoa butter is usually added to enhance flavor, fluidity, and smoothness when making sweetened chocolate. Where does the extra cocoa butter come from? Cocoa butter is obtained in the process of manufacturing cocoa, when most of the fat is extracted from the chocolate liquor with a hydraulic press. Then the remaining partially defatted liquor is pulverized into cocoa powder. (Some special-purpose chocolates used by pastry chefs may have extra cocoa powder added instead of extra cocoa butter.)

Cocoa butter, so necessary in manufacturing chocolate, is also an important ingredient in the cosmetics industry. What a chocolate lover may regard as the process of manufacturing cocoa is more accurately a process for extracting cocoa butter, the more valuable commodity. In the larger economic picture, cocoa powder is a by-product of cocoa butter extraction.

Sugar, vanilla, or vanillin and (usually, but not always) a little lecithin are also added to the chocolate liquor to make sweetened

chocolates, including bittersweet and semisweet. Dried or condensed milk or cream is added to make milk chocolate. White chocolate is made similarly to milk chocolate, but starts with cocoa butter only instead of chocolate liquor.

Fine chocolate destined for eating and candy making, and baking too, is then conched: the chocolate liquor, sugar, and other ingredients are mixed and scraped against a slightly rough surface. The friction of the conch heats the chocolate and drives off unwanted volatile flavors and aromas, further improving the taste of the chocolate. Fine chocolate may be conched for twenty-four to forty-eight hours or more—each manufacturer makes a judgment call here. Long conching is a necessary, though costly, step in the manufacture of the finest chocolates, and to a point it improves both flavor and texture. Past that point, though, conching can eliminate desirable flavors and make the chocolate so smooth that it feels slimy on the palate. After conching, the chocolate is tempered, molded, cooled, and packaged.

Blended Versus Single-Origin and Varietal Chocolates

Chocolate manufacturers normally blend cocoa beans from more than one source. Like wine grapes and coffee beans, cocoa beans from different parts of the world, or even from different plantations in the same region, have different tastes. Blending allows the chocolate maker to create a signature flavor that becomes associated with and defines that brand.

Chocolate that is not made from a blend of beans is referred to as varietal or single-origin chocolate. The terms tend to be used interchangeably, although, strictly speaking, a varietal chocolate would be made from only one of the four cacao species, while single-origin chocolate would imply chocolate made with cocoa beans, regardless of species, from a single region, area, or farm. *Varietal* is a questionable term, however, since cacao species are no longer pure or completely distinct from one another; still, cacao from a single region may be the closest thing to a single species that exists today. In any case, the terms are now used to refer to chocolate made with cocoa beans from a single place.

The traditional view (especially in the United States) is that a chocolate made from varietal or single-origin cocoa beans is unbalanced or incomplete and that blending is the real art of chocolate making. The argument is supported by a very practical reality. Cacao is a third world crop subject to weather, soil conditions, farming practices, economics, and local politics; it varies in quality and abundance from season to season. Chocolate makers who blend beans from different sources can adjust their blends and manufacturing process to compensate for the variations in the beans. If beans from one source are more acidic or fruity than usual, a lesser proportion may be used in the blend. If other beans are scarce or the quality is poor, they might be replaced by beans with similar characteristics from another source. The blend is ever-changing as the chocolate maker tries to balance acidity, high and low flavor notes, fruit, spiciness, and the like to produce a relatively consistent, pleasing flavor. On the economic side, blending is also a hedge against price fluctuations.

Meanwhile, the newer generation of artisan and micro-batch chocolate makers focuses on chocolate made exclusively or primarily with cacao from a single region, or even a single farm. And of course prestigious European chocolate companies like Valrhona and Michel Cluizel have been producing varietal chocolates for decades. Varietal wines and single-origin, even single-estate, coffees and teas are well-known to us, but the idea is newer with chocolate. It reflects an increasingly

sophisticated taste and curiosity and an appreciation for intrinsic chocolate flavors, not just sweet candy. It also suggests a growing awareness of *terroir*—the unique contribution of locale, soil, and climate to the flavor, aroma, and texture of food. Single-origin chocolates allow us to taste chocolate flavors that do not otherwise stand alone. Imagine if you were passionate about the symphony and you heard, for the very first time, the solo voice of a cello. Or, if the only wines you had ever tasted were blended from different grapes, how could you resist the chance to taste a chardonnay or zinfandel for the first time? In the same way, single-origin chocolates educate the palate and mind; they broaden our understanding of what chocolate tastes like, making it abundantly clear that there is no single definition of chocolate flavor.

Savvy chocolate lovers are curious and willing to pay a price for interesting and unusual chocolate, and they accept that—as with varietal wines and coffee and estate-grown tea—the flavor and quality of special chocolates may vary from season to season.

The increasing emphasis on single-source or varietal chocolates is improving the quality of cacao, and thus all chocolate, worldwide. Manufacturers dependent on specific cacao sources pay more to ensure quality and availability. When cacao is more profitable, farmers plant more of it, cultivate it more carefully, and give more attention to the critical fermentation and drying processes. A more profitable crop results in better conditions and pay for cacao workers. In the meantime, we may have to let go of the belief that consistency is the paramount value in chocolate and embrace the notion that, like wine, a good varietal chocolate has certain characteristic flavors but cannot taste exactly the same from batch to batch.

TYPES OF CHOCOLATE

These are the various types of chocolate I call for in the recipes in this book and some of the forms they come in.

COCOA OR CACAO NIBS Nibs are roasted (usually), hulled, and broken cocoa beans, the very essence of chocolate. Nibs are comprised of a little more than 50 percent fat (cocoa butter) and a little less than 50 percent dry cocoa solids. Normally nibs are ground to a molten paste (chocolate liquor). Then they are rehardened into squares or bars and sold as unsweetened chocolate, or else they are further processed into all of the sweetened kinds of chocolate. However, nibs are also available to home cooks as an ingredient. They are crunchy and relatively bitter, and have within them deep primal chocolate flavors ranging from toasted nuts to wine to berries, tropical fruit, or citrus, to grass or spice. They encompass every possible nuance of flavor found in chocolate, as well as some flavors normally eliminated in the chocolate-making process. Crushed, ground, chopped, left in their natural form, or infused, nibs add something special to any number of sweet as well as savory recipes.

PREMIUM UNSWEETENED COCOA POWDER Most cocoas, both natural and Dutch-process, vary in fat content from 10 to 24 percent. Premium cocoas, with 20 to 24 percent cocoa butter, are superior in flavor and quality, and these are the cocoas that are called for in this book, even for those recipes that are low in fat. Right now, the only way to tell whether cocoa has 12 percent or 24 percent fat is to look at the nutritional panel on the back of the package. Premium cocoa has 1 gram of fat (instead of 0.5 gram) per 5- to 6-gram serving.

UNSWEETENED CHOCOLATE (100% CACAO), AKA CHOCOLATE LIQUOR Although it contains no alcohol, *chocolate liquor* is the professional term for unsweetened chocolate. On labels, unsweetened chocolate or chocolate liquor may also be called cocoa liquor, cacao or cocoa mass, cocoa beans, or cocoa or chocolate seeds. It is nothing more than ground cocoa nibs— pure roasted and hulled cocoa beans (sometimes with a little vanilla added). Because they are like nuts in structure and in fat content, cocoa nibs become an oily semiliquid paste with the friction and pressure of the grinding process, just as peanuts become peanut butter. Unlike peanut butter, chocolate liquor hardens when tempered and cooled. Home cooks buy it in familiar baking squares or bars labeled "unsweetened baking chocolate." Meanwhile, chocolate liquor is the essential ingredient in any type of chocolate (each type of chocolate is defined by a certain minimum chocolate liquor percentage), from the most intense bar of bittersweet to the sweetest milk chocolate. White chocolate must contain cocoa butter, which is the fat component of chocolate liquor, without the dry solids.

UNSWEETENED COCOA POWDER The cocoa powder that we use to make hot cocoa or desserts is made by removing 75 to 85 percent of the cocoa butter from chocolate liquor (see page 31) and then pulverizing the partially defatted mass that remains. With all of the flavor and a fraction of the fat, cocoa is essentially a concentrated form of cocoa beans. And because cocoa beans are naturally tart and acidic (characteristics that provide fruitiness and complexity in chocolate), those qualities are exaggerated in cocoa powder. The tendency for cocoa to be harsh is exacerbated by the fact that the best cocoa beans are normally reserved for producing chocolate. With some exceptions, cocoa powder is made from beans of lesser quality.

There are two types of cocoa powder: natural (nonalkalized) and Dutch-process (alkalized). Natural cocoa powder is described above. It is bitter and strong. The best-quality natural cocoa is complex and fruity and wonderfully flavorful. Natural cocoa, with its harshness tamed by sugar in the recipes, delivers a strong hit of flavor in American favorites such as brownies and fudge. It also makes flavorful cakes and cookies with a tender crumb, excellent beverages, and remarkable chocolate desserts—potentially with less fat than desserts made with chocolate.

Dutch-processing was developed in an attempt to improve natural cocoa powder. We can't know what cocoa beans were like in 1828, when Conrad Van Houten figured out how to squeeze the fat from them to make cocoa powder in the first place, but we can bet that the results were pretty harsh. He went on to invent the process, still used today, for treating cocoa with chemical alkalis to make it less harsh and acidic. (It was once also believed to render the cocoa more soluble in liquids, but this has turned out not to be true.)

Dutch-processing, or Dutching, gives cocoa an appetizing rich, dark reddish-brown color that we intuitively (if erroneously) associate with deep flavor. While reducing acidity, Dutching strips some of the natural fruit flavors, high notes, and complexity from cocoa. The process also adds a different flavor to the cocoa, whether it is the flavor of the chemical itself or something produced in the marriage of the chocolate with the chemical. Regardless, this flavor, mingled and perhaps confused with chocolate flavor, has developed a following of its own. Extreme Dutching gives cocoa a charcoal black color and the distinctive, although not particularly chocolatey, flavor of an Oreo cookie.

Fans of Dutch-process cocoa appreciate its rich color; toasted, nutty flavor; and coffee notes. Detractors find the taste dull, dusty, chemical, uniform, and lacking in fruit. By contrast, natural cocoa tastes vibrant, fruity, and complex to its admirers (including me) and harsh, bitter, and sour to its detractors.

To learn more about the flavors of natural and Dutch-process cocoa, smell and taste for yourself by doing this: Put some of each type of cocoa into two identical mugs. Close your eyes and have a friend hand you a mug. Cover the mug with your hand and shake it a bit. Keeping your eyes closed, bring the mug up to your nose, uncover it, and sniff. Repeat with the second mug. Without opening your eyes, ask yourself which cocoa smells more like chocolate. Then put a little of each cocoa on a finger and taste it. If you can't tolerate plain cocoa on your tongue, mix up a couple mugs of hot cocoa, sugared to taste. Still with your eyes closed and without knowing which is which, sip and compare. Alternatively, make two batches of the cocoa brownies on page 69.

In recipes, you can often use whichever type of cocoa you prefer. But when recipes include baking powder or baking soda, it is best to stick with the type of cocoa called for, unless specifically given a choice, because these leavenings react with the acidity of the cocoa. In recipes without leavening, I absolutely encourage you to experiment and to choose the cocoa that tastes best to you.

If you roll truffles in cocoa, Dutch-process may look darker and more luscious than most natural cocoas, but I suggest that you close your eyes and put a little cocoa on your tongue before choosing. I used to roll my truffles in Dutch-process cocoa, but tasting converted me to a premium natural cocoa powder. The recipes in this book tell you when you must use a particular cocoa, when you can choose, and what my preferences are.

Dutch-process (alkalized) cocoas may or may not be labeled "Dutch-process," but the ingredient statement should say "cocoa processed with alkali." Natural cocoa is rarely labeled with the word *natural* on the package; the ingredient statement will simply say "cocoa" or "unsweetened cocoa powder." Absent the words *alkalized* or *Dutch-process* on a label, you should be able to assume that the cocoa is natural.

BITTERSWEET, SEMISWEET, AND OTHER DARK CHOCOLATES WITH PERCENTAGES These are the most dynamic and exciting chocolates to eat and bake with, and they were the motivation for writing this book. Although the official definition of bittersweet and semisweet chocolates has not changed in recent years, the chocolates themselves have changed considerably. These chocolates, with varied percentages, are a gift to chocolate lovers and a testimony to changing tastes, but they are a challenge for home bakers or confectioners.

Now that chocolate is labeled with cacao percentages, the words *bittersweet* and *semisweet* are unnecessary, even confusing. The recipes in this revised edition simply call for chocolate by percentage. The percentage tells you how much of the chocolate bar, by weight, is made of pure cacao (cocoa beans) or parts thereof; the rest of the bar is sugar (except in brands that contain small quantities of milk solids, of which up to 12 percent is allowed).

Nevertheless, since the terms *bittersweet* and *semisweet* are still widely used on chocolate labels, and called for in recipes, it's worth explaining them further. The FDA makes no distinction between bittersweet and semisweet chocolates, both of which are defined as sweet chocolate containing a minimum of 35% chocolate liquor (see page 314). (Assuming the additional cocoa butter added to most good chocolate, this might translate to a bar with a total of about 42% cacao.) Savvy chocolate lovers will be surprised at such a low minimum, since most bittersweet or semisweet chocolates today exceed 54%. Regardless of the official minimum (and no official maximum), chocolate makers have been increasing the cacao content of dark chocolate over several decades; this has been done in response to a growing demand for darker chocolate with more chocolate flavor and less sweetness. By the time Scharffen Berger Chocolate Maker, the first of the new American chocolate makers, was founded in 1997, the cacao content of most domestic semisweet and bittersweet chocolate had already climbed to between 54% and 59%, although none had percentages on the label. These 54% to 59% chocolates were the mainstream bittersweet and semisweet chocolates most readily available on the grocers' shelves and most widely used by home cooks. These were the chocolates used to create recipes in cookbooks, food magazines, and newspapers. Since bittersweet and semisweet chocolates had roughly the same amount of cacao and sugar, they were completely interchangeable in recipes.

By 2000, the increasing number of imported and boutique chocolates containing at least a little and often a lot more cacao had effectively, if not officially, redefined bittersweet and semisweet chocolate and significantly changed our experience as nibblers (think of the difference between an old-style cup of American coffee and an espresso) and our experience using these chocolates in recipes. *High-percentage chocolates* was not and is not an official category, but the term is a handy way to describe chocolates with more than the old standard percentages of cacao, less sugar, and no milk solids.

A 70% chocolate behaves differently in recipes than a 55% chocolate. Older recipes, or even new recipes developed with 55% to 59% chocolate, usually need adjustments if higher-percentage chocolates are substituted. Higher-percentage chocolates make cake or torte batters a little thicker, and cakes made with them may be done a little sooner or seem drier than before; ganaches may curdle or separate. A major goal of this book is to explain how chocolates with different cacao percentages affect recipes—and to encourage the use of these chocolates by giving the cook the essential tools. The Chocolate

Notes that accompany most recipes explain how to substitute high-percentage chocolates successfully. For a more comprehensive understanding, see A Dessert Maker's Guide to High-Percentage Chocolates (page 302) in the Appendix.

Is a high percentage of cacao an indication of quality? The answer is not so easy. Chocolate quality is not simply a function of cacao percentage, although the percentage may be an important clue to quality. In dark chocolate, the cacao percentage essentially tells you how much cacao, as opposed to sugar, is in your chocolate. (In milk chocolate the cacao percentage tells you how much cacao is in your chocolate, as opposed to sugar and milk.) We might like to think that chocolate with more of its defining ingredient (cacao) and less sugar is more "the real thing" and thus of higher quality. But cacao content doesn't tell you how good the cacao was to start with or how well the chocolate was made. Furthermore, more cacao means less sugar to hide flaws and off-flavors in bad or mediocre cacao. So it's harder to make good-tasting chocolate with less sugar *unless* the cacao is good to start with.

CANDY MELTS AND COMPOUND COATING Candy melts and compound coatings are made from cocoa and sugar and vegetable fats, but not cocoa butter. The milk and white varieties also contain milk or cream. Because they do not require tempering, they are fun for craft projects, and some pastry chefs use compound coatings for decorations. But these products are not considered real chocolate (they don't taste as good as real chocolate either!), and they are not suitable for recipes in this book.

DARK CHOCOLATE When I refer to dark chocolate in this book, I mean any sweetened chocolate with a cacao percentage over 54% (which effectively excludes milk chocolate and white chocolate). Manufacturers may call dark chocolates "bittersweet,"

"semisweet," "dark," "extra dark," or "extra bitter," but no matter which of these names appears on the label, the percentage that accompanies it—not the name—is the best indicator of how sweet the chocolate is and how it will perform in your recipe. Always shop by percentages rather than names.

MILK CHOCOLATE Made of chocolate liquor (at least 10 percent) mixed with at least 12 percent milk solids (which might be called milk, whole milk, cream, dry milk or cream, milk crumb, or condensed milk), added cocoa butter, and butterfat, milk chocolate is softer and milder than dark chocolate. Depending on the type or processing of the dairy ingredients, milk chocolate may also have pronounced fresh milk, rich cream, or caramel flavors. Today the most flavorful milk chocolates exceed the minimum chocolate liquor requirement considerably, resulting in chocolate with richer chocolate flavor and less sugar. Some of the best milk chocolates today are 35% to 45% cacao. Milk chocolate does not substitute for dark chocolate in recipes, except when chocolate chips are called for. However, milk and white chocolates can usually be substituted for each other.

WHITE CHOCOLATE White chocolate is made of cocoa butter—the fat without the dry cocoa solids contained in chocolate liquor—mixed with sugar, dry milk solids, milk fat, lecithin, and vanilla. Even though white chocolate contains only the fat component of chocolate liquor (and none of its dry cocoa solids), it is now finally recognized and defined by the FDA as a type of real chocolate.

White chocolate is a creamy off-white to buttery yellow or ivory, never stark white. And because cocoa butter melts at body temperature and carries nuances of chocolate flavor, white chocolate has the melt-in-the-mouth texture, the chocolatey aroma, and the quick release of flavor characteristic of all fine chocolate.

Like milk chocolate, white chocolate does not substitute for dark chocolate in recipes, except when chocolate chips are called for. However, milk and white chocolate can usually be substituted for each other.

Finally, keep in mind that real white chocolate should not be confused with "white confectionery coating" (or white compound coating or candy melts). The latter is usually stark white, ultrasweet, and slow to dissolve on the tongue. Instead of cocoa butter, it is made from other tropical vegetable fats such as partially hydrogenated palm kernel, palm, soy, and/or cottonseed oil. White confectionery coating doesn't have a single ingredient derived from cocoa beans.

CHOCOLATE CHIPS, MORSELS, AND CHUNKS Chocolate chips, morsels, and most brands of chocolate chunks are formulated to look, taste, and perform best in cookies or cakes, where it is desirable that they remain intact. They are often made with less cocoa butter than the best bar chocolate, so when they get hot, they hold their shape rather than melt into puddles to burn on a hot cookie sheet. Chocolate chips et al. are often sweeter and coarser than the better bar chocolates.

Like most pastry chefs, I do not recommend substituting chocolate chips/morsels/chunks for bar chocolate in recipes that call for the chocolate to be melted and blended with other ingredients. The very characteristics that make them successful for their intended purpose work against them here. When melted, they are thick and viscous and hard to handle, and they deliver too much sweetness and too little chocolate flavor.

On the other hand, although there is a risk of scorching, I do sometimes use chopped bar chocolate in place of chocolate chips when I want less sweetness and a more sophisticated chocolate flavor. A number of other pastry chefs and

bakers do the same, and, in response, some chocolate manufacturers make chocolate chunks with the same formula as their chocolate bars.

PASTILLES, BUTTONS, PISTOLES, CALLETS, AND RIBBONS You may see these in specialty shops or mail-order catalogs (see Sources, page 317). Not to be confused with chocolate chips, these small drops, wafers, ribbons, or bits of chocolate (white, milk, semisweet, or bittersweet) were designed to be melted. Originally created for chefs and commercial bakers and chocolatiers, they eliminate the step of chopping chocolate before melting it. They are wonderfully convenient, but they vary in type and quality from excellent to ordinary, depending on the manufacturer.

PREMELTED CHOCOLATE IN PREMEASURED POUCHES This product contains cocoa, coconut oil, soybean oil, partially hydrogenated cottonseed oil, TBHQ (whatever that is), and citric acid. I never use it.

STORING CHOCOLATE AND COCOA

Dark and unsweetened chocolate are at their best for at least a year if wrapped airtight and kept cool, away from moisture and odors (*never store packages of chocolate in the cupboard with spices or other aromatic foods*). So long as there is no milk or dairy ingredient on the ingredient statement, dark and unsweetened chocolates will not spoil with longer storage—even after years—but they will lose flavor.

Milk chocolate and white chocolate get stale and develop off-flavors much more quickly. Buy only what you will use within about two months, or divide a larger quantity into portions and freeze the extra, wrapped airtight in foil and/or plastic and then enclosed in an airtight freezer bag. To avoid condensation on the chocolate, thaw it completely before removing it from the freezer bag and unwrapping.

Store cocoa in an airtight container in a cupboard away from herbs and spices or other aromatic substances. The full dimension of cocoa flavors fades over time, so it is best to use it within a few months, or a year at most.

CHOOSING CHOCOLATE (OR COCOA)

Buy chocolate that you like and can afford, of course, but do branch out a little. I wrote this book to inspire chocolate dessert lovers to stray from the more familiar baking chocolates on the supermarket shelves. Good or great chocolate makes better, more complex, and more interesting desserts. Today the distinction between chocolate for eating and chocolate for cooking has become completely blurred, and we have more choices than ever before. Bars of plain chocolate, called bittersweet, semisweet, or just dark, with percentages from 54% on upward without nuts, raisins, bits of toffee, or other distracting embellishments, may or may not be labeled for baking or eating, but they are perfect for either. To decide what chocolate you want to eat or cook with, you owe it to yourself to taste a wide variety.

You can begin to learn your own style and preferences by trying the following highly regarded larger brands: Callebaut, El Rey, Ghirardelli, Guittard, Lindt, Michel Cluizel, Scharffen Berger, and Valrhona. Each manufacturer makes more than one chocolate, often using different bean blends or percentages of cacao; you may like one particular chocolate more than another, even in the same brand. Branch out and try some of the newest artisan and micro-batch chocolates listed on pages 319–320 as well.

Keep in mind that the simplest recipes—those with the fewest ingredients—are the best ones for showing off individual characteristics and nuances of an interesting chocolate. When budget is an issue, use a basic good-tasting chocolate in any recipe with loads of sugar, flour, and fat (cookies, cakes, sweet candies like fudge, and brownies), and save the finest and most complex chocolates for truffles, mousses, sauces, etc.

It is not necessary to buy imported, high-percentage, or hard-to-find chocolate to use this book. Most of the recipes call for chocolates that are easily found in supermarkets—with separate instructions (in the Chocolate Notes) for substituting more specialized or higher-percentage chocolates if you so desire. Don't use chocolate chips or morsels unless they are called for (see page 38), but feel free to use pastilles, buttons, pistoles, callets, etc. (see page 38). Because cacao percentages vary widely among dark chocolates—even those with the same names (bittersweet, semisweet, extra bitter, etc.)—the dark chocolates used in this book are called for by percentages, and you should shop by percentage rather than name. Shopping by percentage will ensure that you are using the right type of chocolate for each recipe.

QUALITIES TO LOOK FOR

APPEARANCE Properly processed and stored chocolate should be glossy with no surface blemishes. Unless the chocolate is Mexican style or for other reasons purposely rustic, the interior, though less glossy, should be dark and evenly colored, without a stratified, grainy, or cakey appearance.

Improper storage, including moisture, heat, or even temperature fluctuations, can cause "bloom"—a dull grayish or mottled appearance, with or without streaks or spots—on the surface of the chocolate. If the chocolate has been jostled or tumbled with other pieces of chocolate, it may become scuffed or scarred; this should not be confused with bloom.

Neither bloom nor scuffing indicates spoilage. But the damage can diminish your aesthetic enjoyment of the chocolate, and severe bloom can change its texture, mouthfeel, and flavor. These flaws are inconsequential, however, if the chocolate is to be melted and made into a confection or dessert, or retempered and molded into a fresh new glossy bar.

The large thick bars of chocolate supplied to chocolatiers and pastry chefs—and often broken up and sold in random weights to home bakers—are sometimes less than perfectly tempered in the center, due to inadequate cooling during the manufacturing process. This is nothing to worry about, though, because the bar is destined to be remelted and transformed into a confection or dessert, or retempered for molding or dipping.

SNAP Good chocolate should break with a crisp "snap." Again, unless it is a purposely rustic chocolate, it should not crumble or break in layers, although this may occur if chocolate is improperly stored. Milk chocolate and white chocolate are a little softer than darker chocolate, but they too should break with a snap.

AROMA Different chocolates smell different from one another, but good chocolate should always have a pleasing natural "chocolatey" aroma, unmarred by the smell of paper or wrapping materials. And, obviously, there should be no rancid or other off or foreign smells.

MOUTHFEEL *Mouthfeel* is the "technical" term for what chocolate (or another food) feels like in your mouth. Cocoa butter has a melting temperature so close to our own body temperature that it increases the sensual appeal of this special food. Chocolate should melt readily as it is warmed by your tongue and palate. It should feel smooth and creamy as it melts, not slimy or greasy, grainy or powdery.

TASTE Of course, taste is subjective but exceedingly important. Chocolates are as varied as wines, coffees, or cheeses. No one can tell you what *you* like. What is divinely fruity and bittersweet to one may be too strong and sour for another. The more you taste and expose yourself to the varieties of chocolate, the more different chocolates you will enjoy. Your own taste criteria may even change over time.

MELTING CHOCOLATE

Rather than using a double boiler, as all cooks are still taught to do, I melt chocolate in an uncovered stainless steel bowl set directly in a skillet of barely (or not even) simmering water—aka an open water bath. (Using a stainless steel bowl is quicker and allows for more control than using a heatproof glass bowl. Glass takes longer to heat up and then stays hot—continuing to heat the chocolate—long after it is removed from the bath. Stainless transfers the heat to the chocolate more quickly and stops transferring heat the moment it is removed from the bath.) The skillet should be several inches wider than the bowl, in order to prevent the edges of the bowl from getting too hot to touch. (White and milk chocolate are handled a bit differently—see page 42.)

Specific steps for melting chocolate are given in each recipe (they can vary depending on what type of chocolate you are melting and whether you are melting the chocolate alone or with other ingredients), so you can skip to the microwave instructions (see page 41) unless you are curious about my reasons for preferring a water bath over a double boiler.

The Advantages of Melting in a Water Bath

Simply stated, a water bath is less likely to scorch chocolate as it's melting. This technique is also more flexible than using a double boiler. With either method, you are meant to see that the water barely simmers and to stir the chocolate frequently. But since the water in a double boiler is covered and out of sight, it is more likely to boil without your even noticing. Practically, unless you lift the bowl and check the water obsessively, your chocolate will be sitting over a closed chamber of steam that is far hotter than boiling water. At the same time, the common technique of creating a makeshift double boiler by setting a bowl over a pot of water poses an additional risk: the sides and rim of the bowl (and thus any chocolate) above the rim of the pot are exposed to scorching heat from the burner flame licking up the sides of the pan.

The open water bath is better: you can turn the heat down (or even turn it off) whenever you see the water bubbling. Although the bowl sits on the bottom of the skillet, there is actually a thin film of water between the bowl and the pan; this layer buffers the heat. The water in the open bath can never exceed the temperature of boiling water, and it's apt to be cooler since you are more likely to notice water bubbling and turn the heat down. In addition, the sides of the bowl don't get too hot if they don't extend beyond the sides of the bath.

The open bath also lets you melt the chocolate in an appropriately sized bowl: a small bowl for a couple of ounces of chocolate, a large bowl if the recipe calls for mixing the rest of the ingredients into the chocolate bowl, and so on. A double boiler, by contrast, limits you to using the insert that came with it, or a bowl at least wide enough to set over a pot.

If you still prefer your double boiler, you can make it safer by letting the water touch the bottom and sides of the upper container so that it is surrounded by hot water instead of scorching steam. And, if you still like your makeshift double boiler (a bowl set over a pot), do likewise, and also make sure that most of the bowl fits into the pot: a wide bowl over a narrow pot is a sure way to scorch the chocolate around the sides of the bowl that extend beyond the pot.

Melting Chocolate in the Microwave

You can melt chocolate in a microwave so long as you do it in stages and stir it after each zap, even if the chocolate does not look melted: never try to melt the chocolate in one longer cooking time. Follow the procedure below.

Chop semisweet or bittersweet chocolate into pieces about the size of almonds; chop milk chocolate or white chocolate very fine. Put the chocolate in a microwave-safe container. Heat dark chocolate on Medium (50%) power and milk and white chocolate on Low (30%, or Defrost). Start with 1 to 2 minutes for amounts up to 3 ounces, or 3 minutes for larger amounts. Then, even if most of the chocolate is unmelted, stir it well before microwaving in increments of 5 to 15 seconds or more, depending on how much of the chocolate is left unmelted each time, stirring after each one. Be conservative: the goal is to melt the chocolate, not cook it.

Here are three essential rules for successful chocolate melting, whichever method you use.

1. AVOID MOISTURE. Unless you are melting chocolate with adequate liquid or some other ingredient such as butter, make sure that the cutting board, knife, melting container, and stirring implements are perfectly dry. Just a little bit of moisture can seize the chocolate (see page 309). Don't cover the container of chocolate while it melts to protect it from steam—this may produce its own moisture in the form of condensation. If you are using a water bath, be careful to avoid inadvertently splashing or dripping water into the chocolate, but don't worry about the

steam drifting up from the skillet. I have never seen rising steam change its mind and dive back down into a bowl of uncovered chocolate just for spite!

2. CHOP THE CHOCOLATE. Because it exposes a lot of surface area, chopping helps you control the melt and prevent burning. Smaller pieces melt faster, over lower heat, and they don't get too hot in the process, as long as you are watching and remove the chocolate as soon as or just before it is melted. How finely you chop depends on your patience and whether you want to spend more time at the front end with the knife, or more time later with the spatula stirring larger pieces over the heat. There are only two circumstances in which I take the time to chop chocolate really fine: I chop white chocolate and milk chocolate very fine because if these chocolates get too hot, they won't melt evenly but will instead thicken, turn gritty, and burn (see An Extra Word About White Chocolate and Milk Chocolate, which follows). Fine pieces ensure a very quick, smooth melt with minimal heat. I also chop chocolate fine when a recipe calls for pouring a relatively small amount of hot cream (or other liquid) over the chocolate in order to melt it. This is simple common sense. If the chocolate is not chopped fine enough, it won't melt before the cream cools, and then you will have to spend time reheating it. In my recipes, I specify finely chopped chocolate only when it's necessary. Otherwise, medium or coarsely chopped chocolate works well. I use a long serrated bread knife or a chef's knife. People who do not mind cleaning food processors can use one to chop chocolate, although the chocolate must first be coarsely chopped to prepare it for the processor. I don't use the processor unless I need a large quantity of very finely chopped chocolate; then it's great.

3. STIR FREQUENTLY, PAY ATTENTION, ADJUST THE HEAT AS NECESSARY, AND PLEASE DIP YOUR FINGER. Stir melting chocolate frequently, whether using a microwave or a water bath.

Frequent stirring melts the chocolate faster and with less heat because it equalizes the temperature in the bowl and allows the warm, fluid chocolate to help melt the remaining pieces. Dip your finger in occasionally so that you will know that the chocolate is warm—not hot.

I often turn the heat off under the bath well before the chocolate is melted and let the hot water finish the job. Even if I have turned the heat off, I try to remove the chocolate bowl from the bath early and stir to finish the melting. Once chocolate is melted, it's best to get it out of the bath because even with the burner turned off, the temperature of the chocolate will continue to rise if it sits in the hot water. If the chocolate cools off too much before you need it, just return it to the bath for a few seconds before using it. All of this becomes second nature once you realize that there is no precision involved and that dipping your finger frequently will tell you what you need to know.

An Extra Word About White Chocolate and Milk Chocolate

Milk chocolate is delicate; white chocolate, even more so. These chocolates need lower heat and more careful treatment and attention, especially with small quantities. They remain most fluid and easy to handle at temperatures below about 115°F. If melting only a small quantity, chop the chocolate very fine, bring a water bath to a simmer, and turn it off. A full minute later, set the bowl of chopped chocolate in it, and melt it with almost constant stirring. For larger quantities, a series of zaps in the microwave on Low (30%) or Medium (50%) power is easier. You can chop the chocolate less fine as long as you stir it frequently between zaps, even when it doesn't look at all melted. Signs of overheating or abuse are thickening and fine grit, although these may also be signs of old or poorly stored chocolate.

About the Chocolate Formulas and Notes

The formulas on pages 304–308 and the Chocolate Notes that accompany almost every recipe in this book grew from the informal notes I began taking in the 1990s as I experimented with European chocolates with higher cacao percentages than our own. Initially with dismay, then with growing interest, I began to realize that my tried-and-true recipes did not always turn out well when I made them with these wonderful but different new chocolates. Some cakes were dry, mousses gummy, ganaches curdled. I was using better chocolate but not always making better desserts.

To solve the problems that arose, I began making adjustments by trial and error, noting the results for each of the high-percentage chocolates I used. Later, when I finally thought to put what I knew about the composition of the chocolates into a kind of chart, the obvious fact that the percentage of sugar decreased inversely as the percentage of cacao increased became even more obvious. But I also realized that as cacao increased, less extra cocoa butter was added to the chocolate to adjust its flavor and fluidity—so the percentage of nonfat dry cocoa solids increased at a greater rate than that of cocoa butter. As a result, using a 70% chocolate in a recipe designed for a 55% chocolate is like adding a lot of cocoa powder and subtracting a lot of sugar from the recipe at the same time: it doesn't just add more chocolate flavor, it drastically changes the taste and texture of the dessert. I ultimately created the formulas at the back of the book to "translate" recipes that were designed for the old standard chocolates with less than 60% cacao into successful recipes using the higher-percentage chocolates. Each formula tells how much less chocolate to use, how much more sugar to add, and how to adjust the butter for an outcome with about the same amount of nonfat dry cocoa solids, total sugar (sugar in the chocolate and granulated sugar combined), and total fat (butter in the recipe and cocoa butter combined) as in the original recipe.

Translating recipes like this generally works. But to my even greater delight, the results are never really identical to the original recipe. Of course, you get the different flavors inherent in the chocolate you've chosen to use. But you also get some unanticipated and very interesting variations because granulated sugar and regular dairy butter affect the texture and melting characteristics of desserts differently than the finely milled sugar in the chocolate and the fat from the cocoa beans. The quartet of brownies on pages 67–68 is a fascinating example of four delicious recipes, each made with about the same amounts of nonfat dry cocoa solids, fat, and sugar, yet each with a different texture, crust, and appearance.

As much as I loved the brownies and what they taught me, there is much more to the story than balancing recipes mathematically. My main interest in using higher-percentage chocolates is to make more distinctive, less sweet, and more flavorful desserts. Formulas are only starting points, and the Chocolate Notes alongside of most recipes will take you far beyond them. I almost always round off the chocolate upward, never add the full sugar adjustment, and only sometimes adjust butter. But you will also see that the notes are not consistent from one recipe to another, because recipes are not equally sensitive to variations in chocolate. Also, some recipes require small changes in technique when using higher-percentage chocolates. Rather than simply doing the math, I have tested and tinkered to get the tastes and textures just the way I want them. Recipes that are more forgiving have fewer notes than recipes where matters of texture are especially delicate. I give the most explicit instructions where it makes the biggest difference. I did not intend to cover every single contingency, but rather, to set you on a well-lighted path with a good map. Common sense fills in the gaps. If a recipe calls for 54% to 62% chocolate, your results with 62%, of course, will be the least sweet. And if the notes call for 5 ounces of 70% or 7 ounces of 62%, you will not go wrong by taking the middle ground, using 6 ounces of 64% chocolate, even if I do not mention it in the notes.

The final key to the Chocolate Notes is this: part of the appeal of high-percentage chocolates is that they have more flavor with less sugar, so wherever possible, the adjustments for high-percentage chocolates yield increasingly bittersweet results as the percentage increases. This means that each recipe allows for a range of sweetness and intensity depending on the chocolate you choose. This scheme captures the richness of my testing and experimentation far better than applying a formula across the board (which I did only for the brownies and a few other recipes). To substitute a high-percentage chocolate for a sweeter chocolate without more bittersweet results, consult the formulas on pages 304–308 instead of the Chocolate Notes.

A NOTE ABOUT THE RECIPES WITH LESS FAT

Recipes with reduced fat are sprinkled throughout the book. They are easily spotted by the simple * beside their titles. The recipes conform to the following self-imposed guidelines: Servings have fewer than 300 calories, fewer than 10 grams of fat, and usually less than 30 percent calories from fat. Because a limited amount of chocolate is used in these recipes, it is worth your while to choose chocolate with superb flavor. Please don't use low-fat or dietetic chocolate. All of the lower-fat recipes were developed with 55% to 60% chocolate, but all are even better with high-percentage chocolates up to and including 72%, although the percentage of calories from fat may slightly exceed 30 percent in some cases. For the story, a few tips, and the philosophy behind these recipes, see pages 152–153.

CHOCOLATE AND THE NECTARINE

The Frog Hollow nectarines I brought home from the Monterey Market that day reminded me of peaches I had bought thirty years before in the Marché St.-Didier, at the height of one Parisian summer. The fruits of memory were so perfectly ripe they teetered on the brink. They were so delicate, in my mind's eye I see myself carrying them home on open palms, like a perfumed offering, although I know I couldn't really have done that and carried the rest of the shopping too. We ate those peaches for dessert, knowing they might not even last the night.

Thirty years later, I was in Berkeley sharing organic nectarines with my daughter, Lucy, who was then thirteen. We sat with the fruit and a paring knife and a plate. On the table there was no Flaky Nectarine Tart or Fresh Nectarine Ice Cream, nothing to suggest Mom was a pastry chef. Just the fruit and the knife. I told her another slice of the Paris story, and that led to talking about perfect simple food. I suggested that putting chocolate, even exquisite chocolate, with a perfect nectarine might ruin both. The suggestion was hypothetical. But when I mentioned chocolate sauce (as another hypothetical example), she did look interested. I thought out loud that it might be possible. It would require the right chocolate, and the right sauce. I got up and mixed three tiny portions of sauce using a new, tart, fruity bittersweet chocolate that we both loved. I made one sauce with cream, one with milk, and one with water. We dipped slices of fruit into each as though sampling olive oil with chunks of good bread. The fruit, with its big, tart, juicy sweetness, made all of the sauces taste bitter, even sour, in comparison. "Ugh," we said.

The least offensive was the sauce made with cream. It was softer and lusher, and the cream buffered the natural tannins and the acidity in the chocolate slightly, so it tasted less sour against the acidic but sweet fruit. I added a little sugar to the sauce hoping to tame it further, but it was only a small improvement. Lucy announced that it was simply the wrong chocolate to go with a nectarine.

So I switched to a Belgian chocolate, which is mellower and has less acidity to start with. I made the sauce with cream. Lucy decided it was a better match with the nectarine, but really boring. I thought the nectarine made the chocolate taste dull and flat. To wake up the chocolate flavor, I would have to back away from the cream. I made the Belgian chocolate sauce twice more, once with milk and once with water. The sauce with milk tasted brighter, and the nectarine tasted better too. But the sauce made with water was better still! Now the nectarine and chocolate both finally tasted delicious. We "sampled" the combination repeatedly, which is always a good sign. I wondered if nectarine juice would be even better than water, but I didn't get around to trying it that day.

Later that afternoon, one of my food magazines arrived in the mail. It's the one that obsessively tests recipes in search of superlatives: the ultimate roast chicken, the most exquisite chocolate brownie, the best lemon bar. The cover of the new issue proclaimed "The Perfect Bittersweet Chocolate Sauce!" Lucy was amused. "Perfect for what?" she wanted to know.

For me the joy of chocolate will always lie in the continuous rediscovery, the endless play, and the ongoing pleasure of tasting and inventing with it.

This book is my journey with chocolate, from the time I was very young until the day of the nectarines and now beyond.

GROWING UP WITH CHOCOLATE

ICE CREAM AND AND BROWNIES

IN PRAISE OF CHOCOLATE ICE CREAM

I grew up in the suburban sprawl of Los Angeles in the 1950s, an unpretentious place and time, on chocolate American style. At our house, chocolate was a treat, not junk food. I liked the shiny dark layer of skin—slightly chewy—on top of the Royal chocolate pudding. We ate Milky Ways directly from the freezer.

When we went to drive-in movies, my dad would buy Hershey bars from the concession stand and toss them in our laps as he climbed back into the car. We each unveiled and nibbled, with a particular private ritual—either breaking off and rationing individual squares or biting right across the divisions. Even today, tearing a wrapper and breathing the mingled smells of foil and chocolate transports me back in time.

On summer evenings, we drove for twenty minutes to get a chocolate ice cream cone or soda—not because the best or only chocolate ice cream was twenty minutes away, but because a drive was a family outing. From our parents' point of view, it was a bonus that we could sustain good behavior long enough to reach that chocolate ice cream. We were partial to Baskin-Robbins in those days, and we preferred the crunchy brown sugar cones to the pale waffled ones that tasted like pleated sweet paper. We didn't care that the ice cream usually melted and leaked from the tip of the cone onto bare legs and car seats. We also ate dainty sundaes, served with macaroons, using tiny long-handled spoons at Wil Wright's ice cream parlor in Pasadena. The parlor was as feminine and frilly as a valentine, and we sat at round marble-topped tables with curvy iron chairs. My mother taught us how to order a chocolate soda properly; that is, with chocolate ice cream. I still do it that way.

At home, we ate gallons of chocolate ice cream. If pints of expensive brands existed then, my mother didn't buy them. We were a family of six, including my grandmother, and ice cream came into our house in multiple half-gallon containers from the supermarket. It was creamy and cold, sweet and satisfying, if not particularly dense or rich. There were other, fanciful flavors loaded with chips and chunks, flecks, ribbons, and ripples and we tried many of them, in between the big cartons of chocolate. We had enormous servings from oversized cereal bowls. I thought everyone ate ice cream this way until I was fifteen and watched my boyfriend's eyes widen as I dished up a bowl for him.

During TV commercials, there was always some maneuvering about who would be the one to get up to spoon out the ice cream for all. Neither my brother nor I wanted to empty the carton and inherit the additional responsibility of having to throw it away. (Today I can't remember why that job was considered so onerous.) My mother used to complain about containers with only a spoonful of ice cream left in them.

And we loved to eat ice cream in movie theaters. You got a "chocolate sundae" with either vanilla or strawberry ice cream. I chose vanilla because I thought it made the chocolate taste stronger—which I believe to this day. The sundae came in a short paper cup covered by a white waxed cardboard circle with a little pull tab folded up against the rim of the cup. Once the cover was removed, there was vanilla ice cream with a well of fudgy sweet chocolate syrup hidden beneath the ice cream. The whole thing was eaten in the dark with a small flat wooden paddle. I did this strategically and with enormous satisfaction, scraping the paddle around the edge of the cup as the ice cream softened and melted there first, taking a detour into the center for a little fudge now and then. The idea was to make the chocolate last as long as the ice cream. The chocolate had an icy texture that made the ice cream seem very smooth by comparison. The whole experience had that unmistakable delicate hint of Popsicle-stick flavor associated with childhood ice cream.

The ice cream I discovered in Paris at eighteen wasn't what we consumed by the bathtubful in my earliest days. It was a costly delicacy. We took our time and made low quiet noises over the tiny scoops from Berthillon on the Ile St.-Louis, only a few doors away from its current location. Its sublime flavors (crème caramel, espresso, coconut, prunes with Armagnac, and chocolate, of course) were worth every franc then (and every euro today!).

Married and living in Paris a couple of years later, I was astonished and captivated by the ritual and the cost of buying *glace à l'emporter,* "ice cream to take out." Fancy pastry shops, not grocery stores, sold ice cream. A typical container held little more than a half pint. The salesperson who rang up your purchase carefully locked the miniature block of ice cream into a thick Styrofoam box, as if placing a frozen gem in a jewel box. I'd always assumed that this was because shopping was done on foot; one could not race home in the car to put the ice cream in the freezer before it melted. Thinking back, I realize that French households in the early seventies did not necessarily have freezers, certainly not large ones. Ice cream was purchased at the very last minute and the container was meant to keep it from melting until that evening, when it would be served. What took our breath away was the cost; we paid around $6 for the equivalent of two normal American-sized scoops in 1972!

The cherry on top of that French year was a little trip to Italy and Yugoslavia. The whole time we were in Italy, I ate gelato three or four times a day, from a different cart every time. Under the certain impression that each purveyor made his own ice cream and no two were alike, I ate nothing but chocolate for several days running. I must surely have tasted over a dozen different chocolate ice creams before I was ready to flirt with strawberry or hazelnut or coffee. My regret in crossing into Yugoslavia was that I had not yet tasted all possible flavors even once.

Years later, I decided to experiment with ice creams myself. Just as I did in Italy a lifetime ago, I focused first on chocolate and then on more chocolate—the white, the milk, and the bittersweet of it.

Seriously Chocolate Ice Cream

Chocolate ice cream should be a natural to make, but in fact, it is tricky to get the flavors and textures right. This is partly because the cocoa butter in the chocolate freezes harder than butterfat and can become grainy in ice cream. Meanwhile, the butterfat and/or egg yolks and sugar that give the ice cream its luxurious texture also lessen the impact of the chocolate flavor. It was a challenge, and quite fun to play with ice cream formulas to get the taste and texture right for recipes using white, milk, and dark chocolate, not to mention cocoa.

Use your favorite chocolates and cocoas and the best natural cream you can find. Organic milks and creams can be especially flavorful. These recipes are simple to make, and they invite variations and flights of fancy. Please do play. I used a simple hand-crank machine with an insert that goes into the freezer for several hours, so no ice or salt is necessary. These ice creams are far from the giant scoops of my childhood. Instead they are the essence of my decades of eating ice cream and my passion for chocolate.

A LESSON FROM ICE CREAM

The ice cream recipes in this chapter were developed and tested using a Donvier ice cream maker. I chose it because it was the smallest, simplest, and least expensive machine (if you can call such a simple device a machine) I could then find. I wanted anyone to be able to make ice cream without a big investment in equipment. I also assumed that if the ice cream came out great using a simple machine, it could only get better with a more sophisticated appliance. How wrong I was. Preparing ice cream

for photographs, I borrowed a big, serious ice cream maker with a self-contained refrigeration unit. It was thrilling at first. But the ice cream was fluffier and less flavorful and creamy than the smaller batches from the Donvier, because the big machine churned the ice cream too quickly. The simplest little machine made the best ice cream of all. Since then, I have produced great ice cream in electric machines that don't spin quite so fast. My favorite electric machine is made by Lello, but you still can't go wrong with the simple Donvier.

OPPOSITE, CLOCKWISE FROM LEFT: Cocoa Nib Ice Cream (page 56); Milk Chocolate Lover's Cinnamon Ice Cream (page 58) with crushed walnut praline (page 203); Bittersweet Chocolate Ice Cream (page 52).

PHOTOGRAPH ON PAGE 51

BITTERSWEET CHOCOLATE ICE CREAM

Different kinds of chocolate affect the taste and texture of ice cream. Ice creams made with unsweetened chocolate or cocoa powder melt more quickly, feel colder and more refreshing, and taste more distinctly of fresh cream than those made with bittersweet or semisweet chocolate. Because the last two add extra cocoa butter to the recipe, the ice cream freezes harder. But if you eat such ice cream soft from the ice cream maker, or after softening it lightly in the microwave, you will find it exquisitely thick, rich, and voluptuous on the tongue. Each has its merits. All are divine. / **Makes about 3½ cups**

SPECIAL EQUIPMENT

Fine-mesh strainer

Instant-read thermometer

Ice cream maker

INGREDIENTS

3½ ounces (100 grams) unsweetened chocolate, coarsely chopped (see Chocolate Notes)

1½ cups heavy cream

1½ cups milk

¾ cup (150 grams) sugar

⅛ teaspoon salt

4 large egg yolks

1 teaspoon pure vanilla extract

DIRECTIONS

• Set the strainer over a medium bowl near the stove for the finished ice cream base. Put the chocolate in a medium bowl next to it. In a 1½- to 2-quart saucepan, bring the cream, milk, sugar, and salt to a simmer over medium heat.

• Meanwhile, in a third medium bowl, whisk the egg yolks just to combine them. Whisking constantly, pour the hot cream mixture slowly over the egg yolks. Scrape the mixture back into the saucepan and cook over medium heat, stirring constantly with a heatproof silicone spatula, sweeping the sides, corners, and bottom of the pan to avoid scrambling the eggs, until the mixture thickens slightly and registers between 175° and 180°F. Strain the mixture into the clean bowl to remove any bits of cooked egg. Stir in the vanilla. Pour just enough of the hot cream mixture over the chocolate to cover it. Stir until the chocolate is melted and the mixture is thick and smooth. Gradually add the rest of the cream mixture, stirring until perfectly blended and smooth. Cover and refrigerate until chilled.

• Freeze according to the instructions for your ice cream maker.

Bittersweet Chocolate Mint Ice Cream   Start early in the day or a day ahead to allow the mint to infuse in the cream and milk. Increase the milk to 1¾ cups. In a bowl, combine the cream and milk with 1½ cups (40 grams) packed coarsely chopped fresh mint; cover and refrigerate for 8 to 12 hours or overnight.

Strain the cream mixture into a saucepan, pressing gently on the mint with a spoon to extract all of the liquid. Discard the mint. Add the sugar and salt and bring to a simmer. Proceed as directed.

Chocolate Vanilla Bean Ice Cream   Normally a nuance in the background, here the vanilla steps forward to become a fragrant partner with the chocolate. Try Bourbon vanilla from Madagascar or the more floral Tahitian bean.

Use a sharp paring knife to split 3 moist vanilla beans lengthwise. Use the knife point to scrape the seeds out of each half into the pan with the milk and cream. Add the scraped bean to the pan, and bring to a simmer. Remove from the heat, cover, and let the vanilla infuse for 10 minutes. Fish out and discard the bean. Add the sugar and salt to the cream, bring to a simmer, and proceed as directed.

CHOCOLATE NOTES

To use cocoa instead of unsweetened chocolate: Substitute ¾ cup (70 grams) premium unsweetened natural or Dutch-process cocoa powder for the chocolate. Put the cocoa in the saucepan and stir in just enough cream to make a smooth paste, then add the rest of the cream and milk.

To use 50% to 62% chocolate instead of unsweetened chocolate: Increase the chocolate to 8 ounces (225 grams) and reduce the sugar to ¼ cup (50 grams).

To use 64% to 66% chocolate instead of unsweetened chocolate: Increase the chocolate to 6½ ounces (185 grams) and reduce the sugar to ¼ cup plus 3 tablespoons (90 grams).

To use 70% to 72% chocolate instead of unsweetened chocolate: Increase the chocolate to 6 ounces (170 grams) and reduce the sugar to ½ cup (100 grams).

MINT CHOCOLATE CHIP ICE CREAM

Don't expect something green with gritty chips. Fresh-mint-infused ice cream with homemade chocolate chunks redefines the genre. / **Makes about 3½ cups**

SPECIAL EQUIPMENT

Fine-mesh strainer

Instant-read thermometer

Ice cream maker

INGREDIENTS

2 cups heavy cream

¼ cup (7 grams) coarsely chopped fresh peppermint

1 cup milk

¼ cup plus 2 tablespoons (75 grams) sugar

⅛ teaspoon salt

4 large egg yolks

Homemade Chocolate Chunks (opposite)

DIRECTIONS

• Combine the cream and mint in a bowl, cover, and refrigerate overnight.

• Strain the cream into a saucepan, pressing on the mint to extract all the liquid; discard the mint. Add the milk, sugar, and salt and bring to a simmer over medium heat.

• Meanwhile, set the strainer over a medium bowl near the stove for the finished ice cream base. In another bowl, whisk the egg yolks just to combine them. Add the hot cream in a thin stream, whisking constantly. Return the mixture to the pan and cook, stirring constantly with a heatproof silicone spatula, sweeping the sides, corners, and bottom of the pan to avoid scrambling the eggs, until the mixture thickens slightly and registers between 175° and 180°F. Strain the mixture into the clean bowl. Let cool, then refrigerate, covered, until thoroughly chilled.

• Freeze according to the instructions for your ice cream maker. Add the chocolate chunks at the end.

HOMEMADE CHOCOLATE CHUNKS

A chopped-up bar of chocolate, even the best brand, feels hard and gritty in your mouth when it's frozen. Manufacturers of chocolate chips for ice cream solve that problem by adding coconut oil to the chocolate to make it melt faster after the initial crunch. But the oil dilutes the flavor of the chocolate. If you want crunchy chocolate shards that shatter and then melt with a big burst of bittersweet flavor even in rich chocolate ice cream, just melt the chocolate, chill it, and chop it. Melting destroys the chocolate's temper and diminishes its ability to harden *except when chilled.* In ice cream, the chocolate is brittle because it is cold, but in the warmth of your mouth it softens and releases flavor more quickly than frozen chunks from a brand-new bar of tempered chocolate. Alternatively, you can make fudgy chunks by adding water—either way, you can't beat homemade chocolate chunks. / **Makes enough for 1 quart of ice cream**

INGREDIENTS

4 ounces (115 grams) 55% to 72% (or even higher-percentage) chocolate, coarsely chopped (see Chocolate Note)

2 tablespoons water (optional)

DIRECTIONS

• Melt the chocolate, with the optional water if you want fudgy chunks, in a medium stainless steel bowl set in a skillet of barely simmering water, stirring frequently. Remove from the heat and pour the mixture onto a piece of parchment paper. Slide the paper onto a small baking sheet and freeze until firm.

• Chop the chocolate into whatever size chunks you desire. Return the chunks to the freezer until needed.

CHOCOLATE NOTE

The higher the chocolate percentage, the more bittersweet the chunks. If making fudgy chunks with the optional water, you must increase the water to prevent the chocolate from seizing when you use chocolate with more than 60% cacao. You can do this by eye. Just stir in a few extra drops, as necessary, to make a perfectly smooth mixture. For example, 66% to 72% chocolate will require at least 1 additional tablespoon of water, if not more.

PHOTOGRAPH ON PAGE 51

COCOA NIB ICE CREAM

This innocent-looking pale-mocha-hued "chocolate" ice cream was a brand-new idea—my most exciting new recipe—even before cocoa nibs were available to home cooks. The base is exquisitely simple: cream infused with bits of roasted cocoa nibs just lightly sweetened, and balanced with milk. Its rich, clean chocolate flavor is somehow both subtle and dramatic. (For more information about cocoa nibs, see pages 248–250). / **Makes about 3 ½ cups**

SPECIAL EQUIPMENT

Fine-mesh strainer

Ice cream maker

INGREDIENTS

1½ cups heavy cream

1½ cups milk

⅓ cup (40 grams) roasted cocoa nibs

½ cup (100 grams) sugar

⅛ teaspoon salt

DIRECTIONS

• Bring the cream, milk, nibs, sugar, and salt to a boil in a medium saucepan over medium heat. Remove from the heat, cover, and let steep for 20 minutes.

• Pour the cream mixture through the strainer into a bowl, pressing on the nibs to extract all the liquid. Discard the nibs. Refrigerate the cream, covered, until thoroughly chilled.

• Freeze the mixture according to the instructions for your ice cream maker.

VARIATION

Double Cocoa Nib Ice Cream Chocolate chip ice cream was never this good. Stir 2 tablespoons (15 grams) fresh nibs (not those used to infuse the cream) or Candied Cocoa Nibs (page 252) into the ice cream in the last stages of freezing. Or, serve the Cocoa Nib Ice Cream with nibs sprinkled over the top.

MILK CHOCOLATE LOVER'S ICE CREAM

Milk chocolate lovers, this is your ice cream. Make it with the milk chocolate that you love most. Then go on to try the variations that follow.

Milk chocolate behaves like white chocolate in ice cream: it can be tricky unless you follow the instructions to the letter and aren't tempted to try shortcuts. For example, experienced cooks may be tempted to streamline the recipe by pouring the hot custard directly over the chopped chocolate to eliminate the melting step, but the extra step produces the smoothest and most sensuous result. / **Makes about 3 ½ cups**

INGREDIENTS

1½ cups heavy cream

1½ cups milk

½ cup (100 grams) sugar

4 large egg yolks

½ teaspoon pure vanilla extract

8 ounces (225 grams) milk chocolate, very finely chopped

SPECIAL EQUIPMENT

Fine-mesh strainer

Instant-read thermometer

Ice cream maker

DIRECTIONS

• Set the strainer over a medium bowl near the stove for the finished ice cream base. In a medium saucepan, bring the cream, milk, and sugar to a simmer over medium heat.

• Meanwhile, in another medium bowl, whisk the egg yolks just to combine them. Whisking constantly, pour the hot cream mixture slowly over the egg yolks. Scrape the mixture back into the saucepan and cook over medium heat, stirring constantly with a heatproof silicone spatula, sweeping the sides, corners, and bottom of the pan to avoid scrambling the eggs, until the mixture thickens slightly and registers between 175° and 180°F. Strain the mixture into the clean bowl. Stir in the vanilla and set aside to cool slightly.

• Meanwhile, place the chocolate in a medium stainless steel bowl and set in a pan of hot tap water for several minutes to melt it gently. Stir with a clean, dry spatula until smooth. Gradually stir the warm cream mixture into the chocolate until completely blended. Let cool, then refrigerate, covered, until chilled.

• Freeze according to the instructions for your ice cream maker.

Milk Chocolate Lover's Hazelnut Ice Cream   Substitute 8 ounces (225 grams) gianduja (milk chocolate to which toasted hazelnut paste has been added; see Sources, page 317) for the milk chocolate.

Mocha Latte Ice Cream   Milk chocolate supplies a rich, creamy background for ice cream with a clear, bright coffee flavor attainable only from freshly roasted coffee beans. Serve this ice cream on its own, or scoop it over hot Budini (page 91), with some caramelized nuts.

Increase the milk to 1¾ cups. Add 3 tablespoons (15 grams) regular (not French- or Italian-roast) coffee beans, coarsely chopped, to the cream, milk, and sugar and bring to a simmer over medium heat. Remove the pan from the stove, cover, and let the coffee infuse for 5 minutes. Strain the cream and return it to the saucepan (discard the coffee beans). Reheat the cream to a simmer, then, whisking constantly, pour it slowly over the egg yolks as directed and continue with the recipe.

Milk Chocolate Lover's Cinnamon Ice Cream (photograph on page 51)   The notes from testing and tasting sometimes make the very best introduction to a recipe. Thus, from Maya Klein via e-mail, "Very cinnamony, very velvety, very good. I don't think anyone is going to make this unless they do like cinnamon, so I think it is OK that the cinnamon level is this high. The slight bitterness of the cinnamon balances out the sweet milk chocolate nicely." Enough said?

Increase the milk to 1¾ cups. Add 1 tablespoon crushed cinnamon stick, preferably *canela* (Ceylon or Mexican) cinnamon, to the cream, milk, and sugar and bring to a simmer over medium heat. Remove the pan from the stove, cover, and let the mixture infuse for 5 minutes. Strain the cream and return it to the saucepan (discard the cinnamon). Reheat the cream to a simmer, then, whisking constantly, pour it slowly over the egg yolks as directed and continue with the recipe.

WHITE CHOCOLATE ICE CREAM

White chocolate is a tricky ingredient in ice cream. If you've ever produced grainy results in the past (as I have), this recipe is especially for you. One caveat: Experienced cooks may be tempted to streamline the recipe by pouring the hot custard directly over the chopped chocolate to eliminate the melting step. Resist that urge! The result will be a superbly smooth white chocolate custard ice cream.

Rich and sweet, this ice cream is spectacular and elegant in small servings. When I scoop white chocolate ice cream, I think of the tiny servings at Berthillon in Paris. One might expect tart and tangy fruit, fresh or cooked, to be a perfect accompaniment. Surprisingly, the most sublime partners are themselves rich in flavor and rather sweet as well. The trick is to find intense flavors with a gentle rather than dramatic contrast of sweetness: rum-soaked raisins, dates, walnut praline topping (see page 203), candied chestnuts, or Blackberry-Raspberry Sauce (page 64). / **Makes a scant quart**

INGREDIENTS

1½ cups heavy cream

1½ cups milk

½ cup (100 grams) sugar

4 large egg yolks

8 ounces (225 grams) white chocolate, very finely chopped

½ teaspoon pure vanilla extract

SPECIAL EQUIPMENT

Fine-mesh strainer

Instant-read thermometer

Ice cream maker

DIRECTIONS

• Set the strainer over a medium bowl near the stove for the finished ice cream base. In a medium saucepan, bring the cream, milk, and sugar to a simmer over medium heat.

• Meanwhile, in another medium bowl, whisk the egg yolks just to combine them. Whisking constantly, pour the hot cream mixture slowly over the egg yolks. Scrape the mixture back into the saucepan and cook over medium heat, stirring constantly with a heatproof silicone spatula, sweeping the sides, corners, and bottom of the pan to avoid scrambling the eggs, until the mixture thickens slightly and registers between 175° and 180°F. Strain the mixture into the clean bowl and set aside to cool slightly.

• Meanwhile, place the chocolate in a medium stainless steel bowl in a pan of hot tap water for several minutes to melt it gently. Stir with a clean, dry spatula until smooth. Gradually stir the warm cream mixture into the chocolate until completely blended. Stir in the vanilla. Let cool, then refrigerate, covered, until chilled. Freeze according to the instructions for your ice cream maker.

VARIATIONS

Rum Raisin–White Chocolate Ice Cream Start at least several hours, or even a day, before you plan to freeze the ice cream.

While the White Chocolate Ice Cream base is chilling, combine ½ cup (70 grams) raisins, ½ cup water, and 2 tablespoons (25 grams) sugar in a small saucepan and bring to a simmer over medium heat. Cover the pan and simmer for 5 minutes. Remove from the heat and chill for at least 2 hours or, preferably, overnight.

When you are ready to freeze the ice cream, drain the raisins, discarding the liquid, and add them to the ice cream base.

White Chocolate Ice Cream with Dates Prepare Rum Raisin–White Chocolate Ice Cream but decrease the sugar to 4 teaspoons (17 grams) and substitute coarsely chopped dates for the raisins.

White Chocolate Ice Cream with Prunes and Armagnac You can use brandy rather than Armagnac, although it doesn't sound quite so magnificent. The prunes are soft and boozy and fantastic. Start the day before you plan to freeze the ice cream.

While the White Chocolate Ice Cream base is chilling, chop 1⅓ cups (8 ounces/225 grams) pitted prunes into pieces the size of almonds. Place them in a bowl with ½ cup Armagnac, ¼ cup (50 grams) sugar, and ½ cup water and refrigerate overnight.

When you are ready to freeze the ice cream, drain the prunes, discarding the liquid, and add the prunes to the ice cream base.

TOASTED COCONUT– WHITE CHOCOLATE ICE CREAM

Toasted coconut is infused in cream and milk and then discarded. The flavored liquid is transformed into the custard base for the ice cream, which is served with more freshly toasted coconut.

The recipe is simple, although it seems to require lots of bowls, straining, and pouring back and forth—just treat it like a little dance with delicious results. The second time you make it, it's much easier. / **Makes about 3½ cups**

INGREDIENTS

½ cup (1½ ounces/45 grams) sweetened shredded coconut

1 cup (3 ounces/85 grams) unsweetened dried shredded coconut

1¾ cups milk

1½ cups heavy cream

4 large egg yolks

3 tablespoons (38 grams) sugar

½ teaspoon pure vanilla extract

8 ounces (225 grams) white chocolate, very finely chopped

SPECIAL EQUIPMENT

Fine-mesh strainer

Instant-read thermometer

Ice cream maker

DIRECTIONS

• Position a rack in the center of the oven and preheat the oven to 350°F.

• Spread the sweetened shredded coconut on a baking sheet and toast in the oven, stirring once or twice, until golden, 5 to 8 minutes; set aside to garnish the ice cream. Toast the unsweetened coconut the same way.

• Set a medium bowl near the stove for the finished ice cream base. Combine the toasted unsweetened coconut, milk, and cream in a medium saucepan and bring to a simmer over medium heat. Remove from the heat, cover, and let steep for 15 minutes.

continued

• Strain the mixture into another bowl, pressing on the coconut to extract all the cream. Discard the coconut and set the strainer over the clean bowl near the stove. Return the cream to the saucepan (keeping the used bowl handy) and bring to a simmer.

• Meanwhile, briefly whisk the egg yolks together in the cream bowl. Whisking constantly, pour the hot cream slowly over the egg yolks. Stir in the sugar. Return the mixture to the saucepan and cook over medium heat, stirring constantly with a heatproof silicone spatula, sweeping the sides, corners, and bottom of the pan to avoid scrambling the eggs, until it thickens slightly and registers between 175° and 180°F. Strain the mixture into the clean bowl. Add the vanilla and set aside to cool slightly.

• Place the chocolate in a medium stainless steel bowl set in a pan of hot tap water for several minutes to melt it gently. Stir with a clean, dry spatula until smooth. Gradually stir the warm cream mixture into the chocolate until completely blended. Refrigerate, covered, until chilled.

• Freeze according to the instructions for your ice cream maker. Serve topped with the reserved toasted coconut.

SICILIAN CHOCOLATE GELATO
ADAPTED FROM MARY TAYLOR SIMETI

Sicilian ice cream! What luck to find something rich and delicious that is also relatively low in fat, at least compared with the ice cream we are accustomed to. Sicilian gelato is made with neither eggs nor cream, only milk with a little cornstarch to provide a satisfying puddinglike thickness. The chocolate flavor will reflect the type and quality of the cocoa that you use; a high-quality natural cocoa has much more complexity and liveliness than Dutch-process, but you can use either.

If you have ice pop or Popsicle molds, Sicilian gelato makes a better Fudgsicle than any you may remember. / **Makes about 1 quart**

INGREDIENTS

¾ cup (70 grams) premium unsweetened cocoa powder (natural or Dutch-process)

3 cups whole milk

⅔ cup (135 grams) sugar

1½ tablespoons cornstarch

½ teaspoon salt

SPECIAL EQUIPMENT

Ice cream maker

DIRECTIONS

• In a medium-large bowl, whisk the cocoa with just enough of the milk to form a smooth loose paste. Set aside, near the stove.

• In a medium saucepan, mix the sugar with the cornstarch and salt. Whisk in enough of the remaining milk to form a smooth paste, then whisk in the rest of the milk. Cook over medium heat, stirring constantly with a heatproof silicone spatula, scraping the sides, corners, and bottom of the pan to avoid scorching, until the mixture thickens and bubbles a little at the edges. Continue to cook, stirring constantly, for 2 minutes longer. Scrape the mixture over the cocoa paste. Whisk until thoroughly blended. Let cool.

• Freeze according to the instructions for your ice cream maker. Because the mixture is slightly thick to begin with, it may take less time than usual to freeze and thicken to the desired consistency.

WALNUT PRALINE AND BLACKBERRY SUNDAE

This elegant, sensuous sundae—a scoop of white chocolate ice cream topped with blackberry-raspberry sauce and chopped caramelized walnuts—entices you with the contrasting temperatures, textures, and sweetnesses.

Look for jam or preserves labeled "100% fruit." These have a particularly intense flavor because they are sweetened with fruit syrup instead of sugar. / Serves 6 to 8

INGREDIENTS

BLACKBERRY-RASPBERRY SAUCE

2 cups (12 ounces/240 grams) fresh or frozen (measured before thawing) blackberries

¼ cup (80 grams) flavorful black raspberry jam or preserves, or more if needed

White Chocolate Ice Cream (page 59)

Praline topping (see page 203) made with walnuts, coarsely chopped

DIRECTIONS

• To make the sauce, puree the berries in a food processor or blender. Strain out the seeds. Stir in the jam. Taste a little of the sauce with a spoonful of ice cream and adjust the sweetness by adding more jam if necessary.

• To serve, scoop the ice cream into bowls. Top with the sauce and sprinkle with the chopped praline.

BROWNIE BINGES

I can close my eyes and still see the stained recipe in my mother's old edition of *Joy of Cooking*. I started making brownies as a child, unwrapping squares of unsweetened baking chocolate and taking seriously the admonition that the melted chocolate must be cooled before the other ingredients are added, lest the brownies turn out tough and dry. (I have since learned to ignore that rule!) I continued to make brownies, and every few years I would go on a brownie baking binge, a flurry of research and recipe testing focused on flavor, texture, sweetness, denseness, crustiness, chewiness, softness.

Brownie binges were never about uncontrolled eating, but a several-week orgy of recipe testing and detailed note taking, which ends with the inevitable cajoling of friends and neighbors to stop by and taste or take brownies home (please!).

It all started when I was in search of the "best" brownie for my chocolate dessert shop in the mid-1970s. A few years later I was in search of a *new* "best" brownie for an article, or at the request of a chocolate manufacturer or another now forgotten reason. When I'm testing, I compare oven temperatures, mixing methods, types of chocolate, etc.: I like details.

When I reviewed my notes from years of brownie research for the first edition of this book, I noticed the following: In two or three generations, brownies had gotten denser, more chocolatey, and less sweet, and they called for less flour than before. Most people said they liked chewy rather than cakey brownies. I suspected that "chewy" was sometimes confused with "moist,

dense, and gooey." If they said they liked especially bittersweet brownies, then what they really meant when they said "chewy" was moist, dense, and gooey. Brownies that are truly chewy in the old-fashioned way require far too much sugar to be really "bittersweet." Moist, dense, and gooey, on the other hand, are qualities achieved by using maximum chocolate, minimum flour, and slight underbaking. And these techniques are perfectly compatible with bittersweet. What had eluded me was chewy and gooey *and* very bittersweet, the best of all worlds.

If I can't have chewy in the old-fashioned sense, I still want a little textural excitement, a little contrast: a crusty or chewy top surface that yields to the melting rich interior of an otherwise soft, not-too-sweet brownie, for example. I don't ask for much.

Two tricks dramatically affect the gloss and/or crackle of the top surface, and one of them seems also to magically provide chewiness, without extra sugar! The first flies right in the face of the brownie-recipe wisdom I grew up with, which warned the cook to let the melted chocolate cool completely before adding the sugar and eggs. Maya Klein, testing the umpteenth version of brownie variations for me, observed that a more beautiful, glossier, and crunchier top resulted from letting the chocolate and butter mixture get relatively hot when you melt it (about 150°F, which feels hot enough that you want to take your finger out of it pretty quickly after dipping) and then carrying on with the recipe without cooling. Indeed, sugar and *cold eggs*, right from the refrigerator, are added immediately, and the batter is beaten vigorously with a wooden spoon (or carefully with

continued

a mixer) until it cools, thickens, and pulls away from the sides of the bowl. (In the days when brownies had more flour in them, we cautioned against overbeating for fear of deadly dry or tough brownies. With significantly less flour, it is now important to beat enough.) In addition, refrigerating the brownie batter in the pan for several hours, or as long as two days before baking, wreaks enormous transformations: it improves the top gloss and crustiness, and it also blends the flavors so that the brownies taste much richer—and the texture is chewier too. One taster said it made the brownies almost too rich! Such a notion led to the intriguing possibility that a not-rich-enough brownie recipe can be made richer simply by refrigerating the batter overnight before baking—an excellent idea for improving low-fat brownie recipes too. And it works!

Later I focused on the differences among brownies made with cocoa, unsweetened chocolate, 55% chocolate, and 70% chocolate. This because my friends used to call late at night: "I'm in my bathrobe making brownies, and the recipe calls for four ounces of unsweetened chocolate; I've got bittersweet and I've got cocoa in the pantry. Do I have to get dressed and go shopping?" I ultimately came up with a single master recipe turned into a quartet of variations compatible with any one of those ingredients.

Different forms of chocolate and cocoa offer different convenience, quality, and flavor choices (and prices). I love choices. Old-fashioned brownie recipes call for unsweetened chocolate, of which there were and still are a limited number of brands widely available. However, there are now myriad dark chocolates with a wide range of percentages. These chocolates produce brownies with fascinating variations in flavor and texture even when the recipe is adjusted to compensate for the differences in sugar, fat, and nonfat cocoa solids in the chocolate. Who would want to miss the experience of tasting all these brownies?

In the meantime, cocoa makes brownies with an almost candy-like crust and the softest interior. This is because the recipe requires more butter to compensate for the small amount of fat in the cocoa (compared with the cocoa butter in unsweetened or bittersweet and semisweet chocolate). Butter is a softer fat and melts at a lower temperature than cocoa butter; therefore, recipes with more butter and less cocoa butter are softer. The top of a cocoa brownie is crusty because the sugar in the brownies is all added granulated sugar rather than the imperceptible ultra-fine particles of sugar in bittersweet and semisweet chocolate. I am not quite sure why granulated sugar particles make more of a crust than finely milled particles, but they do. So, if you use superb cocoa, you will get an all-around superb brownie.

Unsweetened chocolate, the old classic brownie ingredient, also results in some crust, but the interior is a little firmer, so the difference between the two is not as dramatic. However, you can increase the crust-to-interior texture contrast if you employ the ice bath ritual described on page 68.

Finally, dark chocolates with 55% to over 72% cacao make a firm but good brownie with, relative to the other recipes, a glossier crackled crust. And, as mentioned above, for an even crustier surface on any brownie (not to mention a great way to have just-baked brownies at the last minute), make the batter in advance, spread it in the pan, cover, and refrigerate for up to two days before baking.

NEW CLASSIC CHOCOLATE BROWNIES

This recipe makes brownies that are crusty on top and wonderfully gooey within. They are baked at a high temperature for a short period of time, then cooled in an ice bath. Also known as the Steve Ritual (as in Steve Ritual Brownies), this crazy, wonderful method was discovered by Portland educational researcher Steve Klein during his college days; it now has a considerable Internet following. For brownies with a cakier texture, or to use the same basic ingredients but different chocolates, see the variations on page 68. / **Makes 16 large or 25 smaller brownies**

INGREDIENTS

4 ounces (115 grams) unsweetened chocolate, chopped

8 tablespoons (115 grams/1 stick) unsalted butter

1¼ cups (250 grams) sugar

1 teaspoon pure vanilla extract

¼ teaspoon salt

2 cold large eggs

½ cup (65 grams) all-purpose flour

⅔ cup (2⅓ ounces/65 grams) walnut or pecan pieces (optional)

SPECIAL EQUIPMENT

8-inch square baking pan

DIRECTIONS

• Position a rack in the lower third of the oven and preheat the oven to 400°F. Line the bottom and all four sides of the baking pan with parchment paper or foil.

• Place the chocolate and butter in a medium heatproof bowl set in a wide skillet of barely simmering water. Stir frequently until the chocolate is melted and the mixture is smooth and hot enough that you want to remove your finger fairly quickly after dipping it in to test.

• Remove the bowl from the skillet. Stir in the sugar, vanilla, and salt with a wooden spoon. Add the eggs one at a time, stirring until the first one is incorporated before adding the next. Stir in the flour and beat with a wooden spoon or a rubber spatula until the batter forms a shiny, cohesive mass and comes away from the sides of the bowl. It is important that the batter pull together and away from the bowl, so don't stop stirring until it does. Stir in the nuts, if using. Scrape the batter into the lined pan and spread it evenly.

continued

- Bake for 20 minutes, or until the brownies just begin to pull away from the sides of the pan. The surface of the brownies will look dry, but a toothpick inserted in the center will come out quite gooey.

- Meanwhile, prepare an ice bath by filling a roasting pan or large baking pan with ice cubes and about ¾ inch of water.

- When the brownies are ready, remove the pan from the oven and immediately set it in the ice bath. Take care not to splash water on the brownies. Let the brownies cool.

- Remove the pan from the ice bath, lift up the ends of the parchment or foil liner, and transfer the brownies to a cutting board. Cut into 16 or 25 squares. (The brownies can be stored, airtight, for 2 to 3 days.)

VARIATIONS

Classic Chocolate Brownies For cakier brownies, bake at 350°F for 30 to 35 minutes, until a toothpick inserted in the center comes out with some thick, gooey batter still clinging to it. Omit the ice bath; cool on a rack.

Classic 70% Brownies Position a rack in the lower third of the oven. Preheat the oven to 400°F and prepare an ice bath for New Classic Brownies, or skip the ice bath and preheat the oven to 350°F as for Classic Brownies. Combine 6½ ounces (185 grams) 66% to 72% chocolate, 7 tablespoons (100 grams) butter, and 1 cup (200 grams) sugar in a medium heatproof bowl. Proceed as directed for either New Classic or Classic Chocolate Brownies.

Classic 60% Brownies This recipe produces brownies with a beautifully glossy, crackled crust. The batter will be stiffer than you are used to and may require longer and more vigorous stirring to form a smooth, cohesive mass.

Position a rack in the lower third of the oven. Preheat the oven to 400°F and prepare an ice bath for New Classic Brownies, or skip the ice bath and preheat the oven to 350°F as for Classic Brownies. Combine 10 ounces (285 grams) 54% to 62% chocolate, 5 tablespoons (70 grams) butter, and ⅔ cup (135 grams) sugar in a medium heatproof bowl. Proceed as directed for either New Classic or Classic Chocolate Brownies.

BEST COCOA BROWNIES

Cocoa brownies have the softest center and chewiest candylike top "crust" of all because all of the fat in the recipe (except for a small amount of cocoa butter in the cocoa) is butter, and all of the sugar is granulated sugar rather than the finely milled sugar used in chocolate. Use the best cocoa you know for these fabulous brownies. / *Makes 16 large or 25 smaller brownies*

INGREDIENTS

10 tablespoons (140 grams/1¼ sticks) unsalted butter

1¼ cups (250 grams) sugar

¾ cup plus 2 tablespoons (80 grams) premium unsweetened cocoa powder (natural or Dutch-process; see Chocolate Note)

¼ teaspoon salt

½ teaspoon pure vanilla extract

2 cold large eggs

½ cup (65 grams) all-purpose flour

⅔ cup (2⅓ ounces/65 grams) walnut or pecan pieces (optional)

SPECIAL EQUIPMENT

8-inch square baking pan

DIRECTIONS

• Position a rack in the lower third of the oven and preheat the oven to 325°F. Line the bottom and all four sides of the baking pan with parchment paper or foil.

• Melt the butter in a medium heatproof bowl set in a wide skillet of barely simmering water. Add the sugar, cocoa, and salt and stir from time to time until the mixture is smooth and hot enough that you want to remove your finger fairly quickly after dipping it in to test. Remove the bowl from the skillet and set aside briefly until the mixture is only warm, not hot.

• Stir in the vanilla with a wooden spoon. Add the eggs one at a time, stirring vigorously after each one. When the batter looks thick, shiny, and well blended, add the flour and stir until you cannot see it any longer, then beat vigorously for 50 to 60 strokes with the wooden spoon or a rubber spatula. Stir in the nuts, if using. Spread evenly in the lined pan.

• Bake until a toothpick plunged into the center emerges slightly moist with batter, 20 to 25 minutes. Let cool completely on a rack.

• Lift up the ends of the parchment or foil liner, and transfer the brownies to a cutting board. Cut into 16 or 25 squares.

CHOCOLATE NOTE

Natural cocoa produces brownies with more flavor complexity and lots of tart, fruity notes. I think it's more exciting. Dutch-process cocoa results in a darker brownie with a mellower, old-fashioned chocolate pudding flavor, pleasantly reminiscent of childhood.

PHOTOGRAPH ON PAGE 72

MACADAMIA SHORTBREAD BROWNIES

Nuts underneath shortbread batter rather than mixed into it save a toasting step and make an especially crunchy layer. This technique transforms macadamias (which most people love but I find rich and boring) into a quite fantastic, rich, and nutty contrast to the brownies. Try these whether you love macs or not. Or substitute hazelnuts or almonds. / **Makes 25 brownies**

SPECIAL EQUIPMENT

9-inch square baking pan

INGREDIENTS

6 tablespoons (85 grams) unsalted butter, melted

2 tablespoons (25 grams) sugar

¼ teaspoon pure vanilla extract

Pinch of salt

¾ cup (105 grams) all-purpose flour

½ cup (2¼ ounces/65 grams) untoasted unsalted macadamia nuts, chopped medium-fine

1 recipe of any brownie batter on pages 67–69 (without nuts)

DIRECTIONS

• Position a rack in the lower third of the oven and preheat the oven to 350°F.

• To make the crust, combine the melted butter, sugar, vanilla, and salt in a bowl. Stir in the flour to make the dough.

• On a square of wax paper, pat or roll out the dough to a square slightly smaller than the bottom of the baking pan. Sprinkle the dough evenly with the nuts and press them in. Cover with a 12-inch square of foil. Grasping the edges of the wax paper and foil together, lift and flip the dough so that it rests, nut side down, on the foil. Peel off the wax paper. Lift the foil and dough off the tray and into the pan. Press the dough, on the foil, evenly into the bottom, and press the foil up the sides of the pan.

• Bake until the crust is nicely brown all over, 15 to 20 minutes.

• Spread the brownie batter evenly over the hot crust and bake until the edges puff and begin to show fine cracks, 20 to 25 minutes. Let cool completely in the pan on a rack.

• Remove the brownies from the pan by lifting up the ends of the foil, and transfer to a cutting board. Cut into 25 squares with a heavy knife.

BLACK-BOTTOM PECAN PRALINE BARS

PHOTOGRAPH ON PAGE 72

Bittersweet chocolate brownies with a layer of buttery, chewy brown sugar–pecan cookie baked on top.... The perfect marriage? / **Makes 25 bars**

INGREDIENTS

½ recipe of any brownie batter on pages 67–69 (without nuts), made with 1 tablespoon less sugar

¼ cup (30 grams) all-purpose flour

¼ teaspoon baking soda

4 tablespoons (55 grams) unsalted butter, melted

¼ cup plus 2 tablespoons (75 grams) lightly packed brown sugar

¼ teaspoon salt

1 large egg yolk

½ teaspoon pure vanilla extract

1¼ cups (5 ounces/125 grams) coarsely chopped pecans or walnuts

SPECIAL EQUIPMENT

8-inch square baking pan

DIRECTIONS

• Position a rack in the lower third of the oven and preheat the oven to 350°F. Line the bottom and all four sides of the baking pan with parchment paper or foil.

• Spread the brownie batter in a thin, even layer in the bottom of the lined pan. Set aside.

• Mix the flour and baking soda together thoroughly and set aside.

• Combine the melted butter, sugar, and salt in a medium bowl. Stir in the egg yolk and vanilla, then the flour mixture, and finally the nuts. Drop spoonfuls all over the top of the brownie batter (they will spread and cover the brownies entirely during baking).

• Bake until the edges of the topping are well browned and cracked, 20 to 25 minutes. Let cool completely in the pan on a rack.

• Lift up the ends of the parchment or foil liner, and transfer the brownies to a cutting board. Cut into 25 squares.

LACY COCONUT-TOPPED BROWNIES

These extra-bittersweet brownies with a chewy golden-brown coconut macaroon topping put a certain popular candy bar to shame. / **Makes 25 brownies**

INGREDIENTS

1 large egg white

1¼ cups (55 grams) unsweetened dried flaked (not shredded) coconut, also called coconut chips, or 1 cup (3 ounces/85 grams) sweetened shredded coconut

¼ cup (50 grams) sugar

Pinch of salt

¾ teaspoon pure vanilla extract

1 recipe of any brownie batter on pages 67–69 (without nuts), made with 2 tablespoons less sugar

SPECIAL EQUIPMENT

9-inch square baking pan

DIRECTIONS

• Position a rack in the lower third of the oven and preheat the oven to 350°F. Line the bottom and all four sides of the baking pan with parchment paper or foil.

• Combine the egg white, coconut, sugar, salt, and vanilla in a medium stainless steel bowl and set the bowl in a wide skillet of barely simmering water. Stir the mixture, scraping the bottom to prevent burning, until it is very hot to the touch and the egg white has thickened slightly and turned from translucent to opaque, 3 to 4 minutes; a spoonful on a plate will hold a soft shape with no puddle of syrup forming around it. Set aside to let the coconut absorb more of the goop while you make the brownies.

• Spread the brownie batter in the lined pan and set aside.

• Use your fingers to drop lacy clumps of coconut topping over the brownie batter. Bake until the brownies puff at the edges and the shreds of coconut look deep golden brown and crusty, about 25 minutes. Let cool completely in the pan on a rack.

• Lift up the ends of the parchment or foil liner, and transfer the brownies to a cutting board. Cut into 25 squares.

OPPOSITE, FROM LEFT: Black-Bottom Pecan Praline Bars (page 71); Lacy Coconut-Topped Brownies (above); Macadamia Shortbread Brownies (page 70).

THE BLUE PIE

I grew up with very simple food: lots of fresh produce and not much in the way of sauces or fussiness. Yet we cared about how things tasted. Even when my parents were in their eighties, family gatherings always involved tasting and comparing. It happened spontaneously. We might sample new-crop apples in the fall, taste several kinds of smoked fish at breakfast, or sip a trio of single-malt Scotches when all three of us kids showed up for Dad's birthday with a different bottle. This was normal for my family and it still is. We taste, argue, and exchange insults, and a good time is had.

My maternal grandmother, Mabel, hated to cook, but she knew a lot about it. When I was growing up, she was full of opinions about the way things should be done, suggestions, taste memories. Although I rarely saw her do more in the kitchen than boil water for tea, she had a great influence on my cooking because she was so explicit in her understanding of the relationship between quality and simplicity. "Plain is best" was how she put it. Her sister Martha was an enthusiastic and accomplished home baker and cook whose grandsons are the phenomenally successful New York restaurateurs the Bromberg brothers (Eric and Brian), of Blue Ribbon Restaurants. Both Mabel and Martha remember their mother as an extraordinary talent in the kitchen.

My father was an engineer. He was always designing something or figuring something out, so we also learned to enjoy activities that involved "making" something—which, for me, included making food. There was no feeling in our house that you had to be taught things—rather, it was that you could learn or "figure things out" on your own. My early experiments with baking were untutored explorations. When I was a young teenager, my best friend, Linda, and I used food color to tint (a delicate word considering the lurid results) the filling of an apple pie bright blue. It tasted good if you closed your eyes, which we did.

By fourteen, we were far more sophisticated. We undertook to entertain our boyfriends with an ambitious dinner for four. The grand finale was to be a flaming baked Alaska. We assembled the dessert beforehand, complete with plenty of swirly meringue, and stashed it in the freezer. The plan was to pop it casually into a hot oven to brown just before serving, as in "here's a little something we just threw together." We had such a great time that evening that we forgot all about dessert, and the Alaska didn't see a hot oven until the next night. But it held up perfectly and impressed our families so much that they forgot to tease us—about anything. I still love baked Alaska, but when I married and moved to Paris about ten years later, I was ready for the next culinary step.

I was twenty-three when I took cooking classes in Suzanne Bergeaud's cramped and unglamorous kitchen in the 7th arrondissement, in a solidly middle-class apartment not far from the venerable Left Bank department store Le Bon Marché. Friendly yet formidable, Mme. Bergeaud had been teaching for twenty years, and her recipes were collected in a slim limited-edition volume with a red cover, into which I wrote my own notes, mostly in French. (When I visited Madame a few years later, the slim red volume had been replaced by a revised and expanded edition published by Flammarion, touted, right on the cover, as *Le livre le plus clair et le plus simple qui ait jamais été ecrit,*

"The clearest, simplest book ever written!") Her little chocolate cake called Cocolat eventually lent its whimsical name to my dessert shop, although I never used that particular recipe.

During my time with Madame, classes were filled by word of mouth with the wives of Organization for Economic Cooperation and Development staffers and diplomats, some of whom brought their cooks along. We came to learn French cooking from an accomplished home cook who wore a patterned apron, no toque in sight. Everything from *les recettes de famille* to *la grande cuisine* could be learned at Madame's (tiny) stove. My four classmates, none French, and I barely fit into the kitchen. I was the youngest. Within the framework of teaching us about food, Madame was giving us a peep at French culture. She handed a plate of dinner to her husband in the dining room just before class, along with a bowl containing a nice green salad with mustard vinaigrette at the bottom. This was to be tossed and eaten after the main course, naturally. An academic or a writer, he could be glimpsed in his study from time to time. I once heard him described as an *homme de lettres,* which left me with a lasting impression of a mild-mannered, somewhat unworldly scholar. In any case, there in Madame's kitchen I learned to make the simple, rich, low-lying *gâteau au chocolat* that, along with my landlady's recipe for homemade chocolate truffles, changed my future.

The *gâteau* was different from any cake I had ever eaten or baked. It was richer and denser, and it tasted more of chocolate than of sugar. And it had less flour in it than I was accustomed to. It was made with a bittersweet chocolate that was fine enough to eat on its own, rather than what I was used to: cocoa powder or squares of harsh, gritty unsweetened American baking chocolate (which couldn't be found in the neighborhood *épicerie* anyhow). And it was leavened not with baking powder or baking soda, but with folded-in egg whites beaten by hand in a copper bowl.

I went home and made the cake in our tiny flat, on the third floor of a *maison particulière* near the place Victor Hugo. The oven had no thermostat, so I stuck my hand in to gauge the heat, as though I knew what I was doing, extending my fingers the way I knew generations of cooks had done. I still remember serving that cake to friends: the first taste, and the gooey smudge on my plate. That cake was a beginning.

Mme. Bergeaud's cake was not supposed to be light and fluffy like an American cake. It was not a multilayered creation from the Viennese school or a fancy *"opéra"* from the pâtisserie, either. It was a simple thing, my introduction to a family of cakey-yet-gooey chocolate tortes consisting mostly of excellent chocolate and butter, bound by eggs and given texture with perhaps a little flour (or perhaps not) and a handful or three of ground nuts. *C'est tout.* From that cake a whole world of chocolate tortes opened. I found recipes for them in homey French cookbooks, and in the work of Julia Child and Simone Beck, and I got them from friends. The best of the best was surely the luxuriously moist torte with a nuance of almond, regally named La Reine de Saba, or "the Queen of Sheba." A few years later, in Berkeley, I built a business around it.

3

THE QUEEN OF SHEBA

CHOCOLATE TORTES AND VARIATIONS

BAKING WITH THE QUEEN

At twenty-seven, I was working too many hours, overwhelmed by the response to my little chocolate truffle and dessert shop. Newspaper food editors were calling regularly, especially at holiday time, asking for recipes to go along with articles they had written about the shop. I didn't have time to create and test new recipes for every newspaper. In desperation, I typed out the recipe for Queen of Sheba, that classic and gloriously simple chocolate almond dessert from the repertoire of French home cooking, but I substituted walnuts for almonds and rum for brandy, and added minced dried apricots.

After that I was hooked. I developed a series of new chocolate tortes just sitting at the typewriter, knowing they would work. My beloved Reine de Saba was saving my life; it became a dessert for all seasons and all reasons. To meet a deadline, I created an October torte for a seasonal newspaper article, then a November torte and a December torte. When I eventually got around to baking these "new" tortes (long after publication, I admit), I found them delicious, thank goodness.

All these years later, I continue to use the Queen of Sheba format. To show off the flavor and intensity of a particular chocolate, I make the torte with less butter. To accommodate the reduced sugar and higher levels of cocoa and carbohydrates in a 70% chocolate, I decrease the flour a little and/or bake the torte for a shorter period so it remains moist. Sometimes I select fruit and liquor combinations specifically to complement, or contrast with, the flavor of the chocolate that I am using. I might use chestnut flour, semolina, or matzoh meal in place of flour. Or I might use nut pastes—peanut butter, almond butter, even tahini—instead of ground nuts. Sometimes I grind the chocolate instead of melting it. Sometimes I even substitute extra virgin olive oil for the butter.

I have this glorious latitude because this chocolate torte is nothing like most other cakes, and unlike most baking in general. One version may be denser or lighter, creamier or "nubblier," sweeter or more bitter, but there is no precisely correct texture, and the thing almost always looks like a fallen soufflé anyhow. The classic Anglo-American butter cake requires precise measurement, ingredients at the right temperature, patience in creaming the butter and sugar, and an exact choreography of alternately adding wet and dry ingredients thoroughly but carefully so as not to overmix. The sponge cake and finicky génoise are demanding and require technique. By comparison, the chocolate torte is endlessly flexible, wildly forgiving.

As a baker, I love the measured exactness, the precarious interaction of details required for the more formidable classic cakes, but the cook in me loves the torte for its utter lack of rigor, its generous invitation to play. Even the method of mixing used can change the flavor and texture of the exact same ingredients.

Because the torte is more a general idea than a precise recipe, it is a boon to novice bakers and cooks who resist precision. It tolerates both inexperience and uncertain technique, and it thrives on creative impulse and whimsy (which is not to say that good technique and experience cannot raise the dessert to greater heights). If your newest bright idea doesn't taste exactly the way you imagined, a generous dollop of whipped cream usually helps. Then simply try again.

The chocolate tortes that follow are my latest riffs on the Queen of Sheba. Each takes the flavor and texture in a different direction. Each has the ingredients in different proportions. Each is mixed differently. But do not feel bound by the recipes. Vary the ingredients and interchange the methods. Develop your own virtuosity.

A FEW WORDS ABOUT VERSATILITY AND THE ROLE OF INGREDIENTS

This type of torte is essentially an extremely buttery chocolate egg custard given texture with ground nuts and maybe a little flour. The basic ingredients are standard, but the quantity of each is almost infinitely flexible.

- **Eggs**, whether whole or separated, bind the rest of the ingredients lightly and hold them in suspension. Four eggs is the average for an 8-inch torte, but I sometimes use five or three.
- **Flour**, which is used very sparingly, also helps bind the ingredients by affecting the way the eggs cook. Even a small quantity of flour adds a creamy smoothness to otherwise nutty-textured tortes.
- **Nuts** contribute flavor and a pleasantly coarse texture. I have used as little as 3 tablespoons of ground nuts for an 8-inch torte and as much as 1 cup. Nuts may be skinned or not, toasted or raw. The more you use, the heavier and more substantial the torte will be and the nubblier its texture. A torte with a minimal measure of nuts—and flour—has a less cakey texture and is more like a baked mousse or a textured custard.
- **Liqueurs** add flavor. Most of the alcohol is eliminated in the baking. You may omit the liquor if you like; if you do, there is no need to substitute another liquid in its place.
- **Butter** adds richness to both flavor and texture and helps the torte stay moist as well. Butter also softens or mutes the flavor of the chocolate. To make a torte that tastes more chocolatey without adding more chocolate, just reduce the quantity of butter. The classic Queen of Sheba calls for

12 tablespoons of butter. Over the years, I have cut back to 10 or even 8 tablespoons to heighten the chocolate flavor.

In her magnificent *Book of Jewish Food,* Claudia Roden presents a beloved family recipe for a passover chocolate torte. The recipe had been given to her mother by an old friend who realized many years later that she had accidentally left out the butter. Claudia's family had enjoyed the torte without butter for so long that they never corrected the omission. The chocolate torte is nothing if not versatile!

FORMS AND FUNCTIONS

Not only can this one torte be prepared in 1,001 variations, it can also be served in myriad ways. In my bakery, we transformed the shaggy-looking torte into something extremely chic by leveling the uneven edges, inverting it, and applying a sleek and shiny chocolate glaze. In the years since then, I have rarely bothered to level and glaze, preferring to serve the torte like a fallen soufflé. The new look is casual and contemporary, and frankly, chocolate glaze or frosting, though dressy, is really just too much.

To the uninitiated, a baked and cooled torte, still in its pan, looks suspiciously like a baking disaster. How many times have I answered the innocent question "What happened to your cake?" Thank heavens a light dusting of powdered sugar adds a purposeful look of "rustic elegance." I reassure the home cook who might be nervous about offering such a homely creation to guests for the first time that after one taste, everyone will be captivated.

Because the torte itself is exquisitely rich and so delicious, it really needs no accompaniment. But if the lily must be gilded, a little whipped cream, only lightly sweetened, is the finest partner of all. It sets off the flavor of the torte by providing a dramatic contrast, and it looks terrific on the plate.

PHOTOGRAPH ON PAGE 144

THE QUEEN OF SHEBA

If I had not jotted down a few notes occasionally over the forty years or so that I have been making this cake, I might not recognize quite how much it has evolved. Today I like the cake best with stronger chocolate: I often use 66% or 70% chocolate and a little less butter and flour than before. Instead of the original blanched almonds, I now use whole almonds with skins because they have more flavor. Mission almonds, although small and homely to look at, are especially flavorful and worth seeking out.

Making this cake so often, I noticed that this type of batter sometimes cools and stiffens (like cement!), making it difficult to fold in the egg whites. So I changed the mixing procedure to avoid that problem: I beat the egg whites, then fold the flour and nuts into the batter along with the first addition of egg whites.

The cake is rich and magnificent unadorned, although it can be dressed up with chocolate glaze (see pages 192–195). However, I love it best "naked" with a little whipped cream or Cocoa Bean Cream. The former is a dramatic counterpoint that heightens the impact of the bittersweet chocolate; the latter is subtler, more complex, and very sophisticated. / **Serves 12 to 14**

SPECIAL EQUIPMENT

8-by-3-inch springform pan or cheesecake pan with a removable bottom

INGREDIENTS

6 ounces (170 grams) 66% to 70% chocolate, coarsely chopped (see Chocolate Note)

10 tablespoons (140 grams/1¼ sticks) unsalted butter, cut into pieces

3 tablespoons brandy

⅛ teaspoon pure almond extract (optional)

⅛ teaspoon salt

½ cup (2½ ounces/70 grams) unblanched whole almonds

2 tablespoons (15 grams) all-purpose flour

4 large eggs, separated, at room temperature

¾ cup (150 grams) sugar

⅛ teaspoon cream of tartar

Powdered sugar for dusting (optional)

Lightly sweetened whipped cream or Cocoa Bean Cream (page 251)

DIRECTIONS

• Position a rack in the lower third of the oven and preheat the oven to 375°F. Unless you are planning to serve the cake on the pan bottom, line the cake pan with a circle of parchment paper.

• Place the chocolate and butter in a medium heatproof bowl in a wide skillet of barely simmering water. Stir occasionally until nearly melted. Remove from the heat and stir until melted and smooth. Or microwave on Medium (50%) power for about 2 minutes, then stir until completely melted and smooth. Stir in the brandy, almond extract, if using, and salt. Set aside.

• Meanwhile, pulse the nuts and flour in a food processor until the mixture has the texture of cornmeal. Set aside.

• In a large bowl, whisk the egg yolks with ½ cup (100 grams) of the sugar until well blended. Stir in the chocolate mixture. Set aside.

• In a clean, dry bowl, with an electric mixer, beat the egg whites and cream of tartar at medium speed until soft peaks form when the beaters are lifted. Gradually sprinkle in the remaining ¼ cup (50 grams) sugar and beat at high speed (or medium-high speed in a heavy-duty mixer) until the peaks are stiff but not dry. Scoop one-quarter of the egg whites and all of the nut mixture on top of the chocolate batter, and, using a large rubber spatula, fold them in. Scrape the remaining egg whites onto the batter and fold together. Turn the batter into the prepared pan, spreading it level if necessary.

• Bake for 25 to 30 minutes, or until a toothpick inserted about 1½ inches from the edge emerges almost clean but a toothpick inserted in the center is still moist and gooey. Set the pan on a rack to cool. (The cooled torte can be covered tightly with plastic wrap, or removed from the pan and wrapped well, and stored at room temperature for up to 3 days or frozen for up to 3 months. Bring to room temperature before serving.)

• To serve, slide a slim knife around the inside of the pan to loosen the cake. Remove the pan sides and transfer the cake, on the pan bottom, to a platter, or invert the cake onto a rack or tray, remove the bottom and the paper liner, and invert onto a platter. Using a fine-mesh strainer, sift a little powdered sugar over the top of the cake before serving, if desired. Serve each slice with a little whipped cream.

CHOCOLATE NOTE

For a less bittersweet cake, use a 60% or 62% chocolate and increase the flour to ¼ cup (30 grams). Bake for 5 to 10 minutes longer, if necessary.

*FALLEN CHOCOLATE SOUFFLÉ CAKE

This is the slimmer reincarnation of the ever reliable Queen of Sheba (page 80) and remarkable proof, if any were needed, that "the Queen" really can be varied infinitely. Most people cannot tell that I cut all 6 ounces of butter and 2 of the 4 egg yolks, and traded half of the chocolate for a little cocoa. You can emphasize the intensity of the chocolate flavor by topping the dessert with a small dollop of whipped cream, but it is not essential for enjoying this splendid cake. / Serves 10

SPECIAL EQUIPMENT

8-by-3-inch springform pan or cheesecake pan with a removable bottom

INGREDIENTS

¼ cup (1 ounce/35 grams) blanched almonds

3 tablespoons (24 grams) all-purpose flour

3 ounces (85 grams) 66% to 72% chocolate, finely chopped (see Chocolate Note)

½ cup (50 grams) premium unsweetened cocoa powder (preferably natural)

1 cup (200 grams) sugar

½ cup boiling water

2 large eggs, separated, at room temperature

1 tablespoon brandy

2 large egg whites, at room temperature

Scant ¼ teaspoon cream of tartar

2 to 3 teaspoons powdered sugar for dusting

Lightly sweetened whipped cream (optional)

DIRECTIONS

• Position a rack in the lower third of the oven and preheat the oven to 375°F. Unless you are planning to serve the cake on the pan bottom, line the cake pan with a circle of parchment paper. Spray the sides with vegetable oil spray.

• In a food processor or blender, grind the almonds with the flour until very fine. Set aside.

• Combine the chocolate, cocoa, and ¾ cup (150 grams) of the sugar in a large bowl. Pour in the boiling water and whisk until the mixture is smooth and the chocolate is completely melted. Whisk in the egg yolks and brandy; set aside.

• Combine the egg whites and cream of tartar in a medium bowl. Beat with an electric mixer on medium speed until soft peaks form. Gradually sprinkle in the remaining ¼ cup (50 grams) sugar and beat on high speed until stiff but not dry.

• Whisk the flour and almond mixture into the chocolate. Fold about a quarter of the egg whites into the chocolate mixture to lighten it, then fold in the remaining egg whites. Scrape the batter into the pan and level the top if necessary.

• Bake for 25 to 30 minutes, until a toothpick or a wooden skewer inserted in the center comes out with a few moist crumbs clinging to it. Cool in the pan on a wire rack. The torte will sink like a soufflé.

• To serve, slide a slim knife around the inside of the pan to loosen the cake. Remove the pan sides and transfer the cake, on the pan bottom, to a platter, or invert the cake onto a rack or tray, remove the bottom and the paper liner, and invert onto a platter. Using a fine-mesh strainer, sift a little powdered sugar over the top of the cake before serving, if desired. Serve each slice with a little whipped cream, if you like.

CHOCOLATE NOTE

I originally created this recipe using a 60% chocolate and Dutch-process cocoa powder. It was excellent, but it got even better when I switched to natural cocoa powder and a 70% chocolate. If you want to re-create the original, substitute a 54% to 60% chocolate and expect it to take a few minutes longer to bake.

PEANUT BUTTER–CHOCOLATE TORTE WITH STRAWBERRY SAUCE

If you think you are too sophisticated for a French twist on PB&J, you can substitute another nut paste, such as cashew butter or almond butter or even tahini (sesame paste), or any others you can think of. I discovered this variation when I tried making a chocolate torte using nut butter instead of the usual ground nuts. While I was at it, I tried a new mixing method, now dubbed the "frosting method," to eliminate the steps of separating the eggs and beating the egg whites. Essentially everything goes into the bowl at once, and you beat like mad. Child's play. And the ingredients are probably in your pantry. / Serves 12 to 14

SPECIAL EQUIPMENT

8-by-3-inch springform pan or cheesecake pan with a removable bottom

INGREDIENTS

4 ounces (115 grams) 54% to 62% chocolate, coarsely chopped (see Chocolate Notes)

½ cup (100 grams) sugar

2 tablespoons (30 grams) natural peanut butter

⅛ teaspoon salt

6 tablespoons (85 grams) unsalted butter, cut into chunks, slightly softened

4 cold large eggs

1 tablespoon bourbon or other whiskey

1 teaspoon pure vanilla extract

Powdered sugar for dusting (optional)

Mashed or pureed strawberries, sweetened to taste with strawberry jam

White Chocolate Ice Cream (page 59) or vanilla ice cream (optional)

DIRECTIONS

• Position a rack in the lower third of the oven and preheat the oven to 350°F. Unless you are planning to serve the cake on the pan bottom, line the bottom of the cake pan with a circle of parchment paper.

• Place the chocolate in a large heatproof bowl in a wide skillet of barely simmering water and stir occasionally until nearly melted. Remove from the heat and stir until melted and smooth. Or microwave on Medium (50%) power for about 1½ minutes, then stir until completely melted and smooth.

• Whisk the sugar, peanut butter, and salt into the chocolate. Add the butter and beat with an electric mixer at medium speed until smooth and creamy. Beat in the eggs one by one, followed by the bourbon and vanilla. Continue beating at high speed (or medium-high speed in a heavy-duty mixer) for 2 to 3 minutes, or until the batter is fluffy, lightened in color, and the consistency of frosting.

• Turn the batter into the prepared pan, spreading it level if necessary. Bake for 25 to 30 minutes, or until a toothpick inserted about 2 inches from the edge comes out clean but one inserted in the center comes out with moist crumbs clinging to it. Set the pan on a rack to cool. (The cooled torte can be covered tightly with plastic wrap, or removed from the pan and wrapped well, and stored at room temperature for up to 3 days or frozen for up to 3 months. Bring to room temperature before serving.)

• To serve, slide a slim knife around the inside of the pan to loosen the cake. Remove the pan sides and transfer the cake, on the pan bottom, to a platter, or invert the cake onto a rack or tray, remove the bottom and the paper liner, and invert onto a platter. Using a fine-mesh strainer, sift a little powdered sugar over the top of the cake before serving, if desired. Serve each slice with sweetened strawberry puree and a little ice cream, if you like.

CHOCOLATE NOTES

To use a higher-percentage chocolate without overwhelming the other flavors, adjust the recipe as follows.

To use 64% to 66% chocolate: Use 3½ ounces (100 grams) chocolate.

To use 70% to 72% chocolate: Use 3 ounces (85 grams) chocolate, and increase the sugar to ½ cup plus 1 tablespoon (110 grams).

CHESTNUT TORTE

Chestnuts have such a starchy consistency that you don't have to add any flour to this cake batter. I use less chocolate than in other variations to balance the subtle chestnut flavor. In season, roast or steam the chestnuts yourself; otherwise use canned unsweetened chestnut puree or puree the steamed whole chestnuts that come in jars or plastic packages. / Serves 12 to 14

SPECIAL EQUIPMENT

8-by-3-inch springform pan or cheesecake pan with a removable bottom

INGREDIENTS

4 ounces (115 grams) 54% to 62% chocolate, coarsely chopped (see Chocolate Notes)

8 tablespoons (115 grams/1 stick) unsalted butter, cut into pieces

¾ cup (about 6 ounces/170 grams) mashed steamed or roasted chestnuts or canned unsweetened chestnut puree (see page 27)

1 tablespoon rum or brandy

1 teaspoon pure vanilla extract

Pinch of salt

4 large eggs, separated, at room temperature

½ cup (100 grams) sugar

⅛ teaspoon cream of tartar

Powdered sugar for dusting (optional)

Rum- or brandy-flavored whipped cream

DIRECTIONS

• Position a rack in the lower third of the oven and preheat the oven to 375°F. Unless you are planning to serve the cake on the pan bottom, line the bottom of the cake pan with a circle of parchment paper.

• Place the chocolate and butter in a large heatproof bowl in a wide skillet of barely simmering water and stir occasionally until nearly melted. Remove from the heat and stir until melted and smooth. Or microwave on Medium (50%) power for about 1½ minutes. Stir until completely melted and smooth.

• Stir the chestnuts, rum, vanilla, and salt into the chocolate. Whisk in the egg yolks, along with 6 tablespoons (75 grams) of the sugar. Set aside.

- In a clean, dry bowl, beat the egg whites and cream of tartar with an electric mixer at medium speed until soft peaks form when the beaters are lifted. Gradually sprinkle in the remaining 2 tablespoons (25 grams) sugar and beat at high speed (or medium-high speed in a heavy-duty mixer) until the peaks are stiff but not dry. Scoop one-quarter of the egg whites onto the chocolate batter. Using a large rubber spatula, fold them in. Scrape the remaining egg whites onto the batter and fold together.

- Turn the batter into the prepared pan, spreading it level if necessary. Bake for 25 to 30 minutes, or until a toothpick inserted in the center of the pan still has moist crumbs clinging to it.

- Set the pan on a rack to cool. (The cooled torte can be covered tightly with plastic wrap, or removed from the pan and wrapped well, and stored at room temperature for up to 3 days or frozen for up to 3 months. Bring to room temperature before serving.)

- To serve, slide a slim knife around the inside of the pan to loosen the cake. Remove the pan sides and transfer the cake, on the pan bottom, to a platter, or invert the cake onto a rack or tray, remove the bottom and the paper liner, and invert again onto a platter. Using a fine-mesh strainer, sift a little powdered sugar over the top of the cake before serving, if desired. Serve each slice with a little whipped cream.

CHOCOLATE NOTES

To use a higher-percentage chocolate without overwhelming the flavor of the chestnuts, adjust the recipe as follows.

To use 64% to 66% chocolate: Use 3½ ounces (100 grams) chocolate.

To use 70% to 72% chocolate: Use 3 ounces (85 grams) chocolate, and increase the sugar to ½ cup plus 1 tablespoon (110 grams).

GRAPPA, CURRANT, AND PINE NUT TORTE

Grappa is an unaged Italian brandy. Traditionally distilled from the leftover (and not necessarily fresh or first-quality) juice left on the skins after pressing grapes to make wine, grappa bore some resemblance to our moonshine. Today, fine sipping-quality grappas are made from fresh grape skins reserved for the purpose. Some producers even make varietal grappas.

For the most chocolate flavor, make the cake one day ahead. At passover, substitute matzoh cake meal for the semolina flour and margarine for the butter. Voilà! / Serves 16 to 18

SPECIAL EQUIPMENT

9-by-3-inch springform pan or cheesecake pan with a removable bottom

INGREDIENTS

¼ cup grappa

⅓ cup (1⅔ ounces/50 grams) dried currants

¼ cup (1 ounce/35 grams) blanched or unblanched whole almonds

¼ cup (40 grams) semolina flour

9 ounces (255 grams) 70% to 72% chocolate, coarsely chopped (see Chocolate Notes)

14 tablespoons (200 grams/1¾ sticks) unsalted butter, cut into pieces

6 large eggs, separated

1 cup (200 grams) sugar

⅛ teaspoon salt

¼ teaspoon cream of tartar

3 tablespoons (20 grams) pine nuts

Powdered sugar for dusting (optional)

DIRECTIONS

• Position a rack in the lower third of the oven and preheat the oven to 375°F. Unless you are planning to serve the cake on the pan bottom, line the bottom of the cake pan with a circle of parchment paper.

• In a small bowl, combine the grappa and currants. Set aside.

• In a food processor, pulse the almonds and semolina flour until the almonds are very finely ground. Set aside.

continued

CHOCOLATE NOTES

You can use any chocolate from 54% to 72% here, but the higher end of the range balances the grappa. If you serve the torte warm—which is an especially voluptuous experience—be prepared for it to be very boozy. As the torte cools and ages overnight, the chocolate flavor becomes richer and more intense—and the booze recedes. If you use a chocolate at the low end of the cacao range, bake a day ahead of serving so the chocolate is not overwhelmed by the grappa, or use less grappa. Note that the torte made with chocolate at the low end of the range may require up to 10 minutes longer in the oven before it tests done.

• Place the chocolate and butter in a large heatproof bowl in a wide skillet of barely simmering water and stir occasionally until nearly melted. Remove from the heat and stir until melted and smooth. Or microwave on Medium (50%) power for 2½ to 3 minutes. Stir until completely melted and smooth.

• In a large bowl, whisk the egg yolks with ⅔ cup (133 grams) of the sugar and the salt until pale and thick. Stir in the warm chocolate mixture and the grappa and currants. Set aside.

• In a large clean, dry bowl, beat the egg whites and cream of tartar with an electric mixer at medium speed until white and foamy. Gradually sprinkle in the remaining ⅓ cup (67 grams) sugar, beating at high speed until almost stiff. Scrape about one-quarter of the egg whites onto the chocolate mixture, sprinkle all of the almond mixture over the top, and fold together. Fold in the remaining whites. Scrape the batter into the prepared pan. Sprinkle the top with the pine nuts.

• Bake for 20 to 25 minutes or until a toothpick inserted into the cake about 1½ inches from the edge comes out clean. The center of the cake should still jiggle slightly when the pan is jostled and still be gooey if tested. Set the cake on a rack to cool completely; the surface of the cake will crack and fall as it cools. (The cooled cake can be covered tightly, or removed from the pan and wrapped well, and stored at room temperature for 2 to 3 days or frozen for up to 3 months. Bring to room temperature before serving.)

• To serve, slide a slim knife around the sides of the cake to loosen the cake. Remove the pan sides and transfer the cake, on the pan bottom, to a platter, or invert the cake onto a rack or tray, remove the bottom and the paper liner, and invert onto a platter. Using a fine-mesh strainer, sift a little powdered sugar over the top of the cake before serving, if desired.

BUDINI

Budino is the Italian word for "pudding"; *budini,* the plural, are individual servings. This is an easy and luscious hot dessert. Order it in a trendy American restaurant and you get a to-die-for hot bittersweet dessert served in the dish it was baked in.

I once tested a splendid budino recipe from pastry chef Jennifer Millar in order to write it for the home kitchen, and I realized that it was yet another variation on the Queen of Sheba, but without any flour or nuts. Brilliant! The batter was divided among big café au lait bowls, baked, and served hot . . . and, OK, it was also topped with ice cream, caramelized nuts, and caramel sauce. Even in this form, the recipe is just as versatile. You can make the budini in advance, refrigerate them unbaked, and then bake them right before serving, or you can bake them in advance and then reheat.

In my version of budini, just to be perverse, I have added a little semolina flour, but it can be omitted. Feel free to add a handful of chopped or pulverized nuts, or cocoa nibs, or diced candied chestnuts (or drained chestnuts in syrup) to the batter, or just sprinkle any of those on the top of each budino before baking. Or add rum-soaked raisins or crumbled amaretti cookies to the batter. You too can invent new budini. By the way, the liquor is completely optional too. / **Serves 6**

INGREDIENTS

6 ounces (170 grams) 54% to 72% chocolate, coarsely chopped (see Chocolate Note)

8 tablespoons (115 grams/1 stick) unsalted butter

1½ tablespoons brandy or rum (optional)

3 tablespoons semolina flour (optional)

3 large eggs, at room temperature

⅔ cup (135 grams) sugar

Pinch of salt

Cocoa Bean Cream (page 251) or Cocoa Nib Ice Cream (page 56) with a sprinkling of chopped cocoa nibs or Milk Chocolate Lover's Cinnamon Ice Cream (page 58) or lightly sweetened whipped cream or store-bought vanilla or coffee ice cream

continued

SPECIAL EQUIPMENT

Six 8- to 16-ounce ramekins or ovenproof bowls (use the larger size if you plan to top the budini with ice cream)

DIRECTIONS

• If you are going to bake the budini immediately, position a rack in the lower third of the oven and preheat the oven to 375°F.

• Combine the chocolate and butter in a medium heatproof bowl set in a wide skillet of barely simmering water, and stir frequently until completely melted and smooth. Or microwave on Medium (50%) power for about 2 minutes, then stir until completely melted and smooth. Remove from the heat. Stir in the liquor and semolina flour, if using.

• In a large bowl, beat the eggs, sugar, and salt with an electric mixer at high speed until light and fluffy and the consistency of softly whipped cream. Use a large rubber spatula to fold one-third of the eggs into the chocolate mixture, then scrape the chocolate batter over the remaining eggs and fold until blended. Divide the batter among the ramekins or bowls. You can bake the budini now or later in the day. Simply refrigerate, covered, until about 30 minutes before you want to serve them.

• To bake the budini: Place them on a cookie sheet. Bake until puffed, crusted, and deeply cracked but still gooey inside when tested with a toothpick, 15 to 20 minutes, or 25 minutes if they have been refrigerated. Serve hot or let cool, cover, and set aside at room temperature for up to 1 day. The budini will sink as they cool, but they will puff up again when reheated in a 375°F oven for about 10 minutes.

CHOCOLATE NOTE

Budini are as versatile as the Queen of Sheba. Chocolates at the high end of the percentage range will produce a more bittersweet dessert than those at the lower end. The choice is yours.

BREAKING THE RULES

Cocolat, my chocolate dessert shop, emerged entirely out of my imagination. Nothing like it existed either in this country or in France, so there was no standard to measure it against. I was not presuming to copy a French pâtisserie, but rather to take what interested me and leave the rest. I wanted to evoke my own experience of eating chocolate in France.

Later I added selected American chocolate desserts, usually reinvented with lots more dark chocolate and less sugar. I was influenced, naturally, by both my American background and my love of France, but otherwise I made it all up as I went along. Even the name "Cocolat" is not a real French word. It is French baby talk, a word I came across in my teacher Suzanne Bergeaud's recipe collection. I liked the whimsy of it and the lack of pretension.

It seems hardly worth mentioning now, because the practice is commonplace today, but one of the most unusual things we did at Cocolat was to sell every dessert or cake by the slice as well as whole. Imagine! Customers could walk in and see a beautifully decorated cake piled high with chocolate ruffles and ask to buy one slice of it. Or they could buy just a single truffle. At the time, American bakery cakes didn't have chocolate ruffles, and almost no one knew what a chocolate truffle was. The impact was enormous. Our desserts were more expensive than others at the time, so selling slices was a way to introduce them to people who might never have dreamed of paying for a whole cake. And it was a way to make sure that devotees came in often rather than only on special occasions. Some customers even showed up daily, if only for a single truffle or cup of chocolate mousse or slice of cake. But they also showed up to shop for dinner parties, birthdays, weddings, and every other special occasion when desserts or gifts were needed.

If I wasn't presuming to copy a French pâtisserie, I certainly did not aspire to emulate American bakery desserts. At that time, commercial bakeries used commercial ingredients that were economical but often not as good as those a quality-conscious and knowledgeable home cook would buy. Some bakeries even used commercial mixes. The people I hoped to sell to, the people I knew who really cared about good desserts, made desserts at home with recipes from Julia Child or ate them in sophisticated restaurants like the newborn Chez Panisse. I wanted a shop that sold desserts otherwise available only in that sort of restaurant, or from the very best pastry shops in Paris. I wanted to make European-style desserts with homemade quality, but that looked and tasted better than homemade.

Ingredients were a top priority. So I spent hours, days, weeks assembling ingredients. I couldn't find ground blanched almonds, a staple in European pastry kitchens (and available to home bakers there as well), so I decided we would grind our own. We burned out the grinder attachment on my (anniversary gift!) Braun mixer before I finally found a supplier.

But I knew what I wanted. We squeezed fresh oranges and lemons for juice and grated the zest by hand. We whipped fresh heavy cream, without stabilizers; folded in freshly beaten egg whites, these literally by hand; used unsalted butter exclusively; splashed sipping-quality liqueurs over cake layers or poured them into our mousses and fillings. Ingredient heaven!

But the foundation of our desserts was chocolate, and chocolate was our most important ingredient. In batters and mousses and glazes we melted and poured hundreds (ultimately thousands)

continued

of pounds of chocolate good enough to eat; real bittersweet chocolate instead of compound coatings or other substances scooped from bakery-supply-house buckets.

I did not know how to run a business and I had never even worked a day in a bakery. But I knew the cakes and truffles I wanted to make, and what I wanted my customers to experience, and how I wanted things to look in the store. Sometimes the more practical details had to smack me in the face—or my unfailingly practical husband had to intervene.

The memory of opening day in 1976 still makes me smile. Just before the store opened, I ran to the bank to get cash for the register (which the cash register salesman had just shown me how to use). I came back with a bunch of twenty-dollar bills. It didn't occur to me that I needed singles and fives and some change as well!

We had spent nearly a week making enough cakes and truffles to stock the store. We opened late, and then everything we had was sold in three crazy hours. Standing against the back wall, my husband snapped photos of customers four deep in front of the showcase. Then he took my picture after the chocolate dust settled that day. I was wearing flared jeans and a pair of very comfortable (yet French, and quite trendy, I thought) Pierre d'Alby "golf" shoes, with thick blue-and-red squishy soles . . . covered in chocolate glaze. Slumped in a director's chair in the kitchen with a can of beer in one hand and an expression that I cannot describe even from looking at the picture, I remember feeling utter amazed satisfaction. Thank goodness the store would be closed on Sunday and Monday . . . we had two days to replenish the showcases and get ready for Tuesday.

At first, most of what I learned came from simply wading in and doing it. My first employee had worked briefly in the bakery down the block, and she was able to show me a few things about handling equipment and establishing routines. Later I hired some culinary school graduates—I learned from them, and they learned from me. My first recipes were all for making one cake. Before I opened my shop, I'd been baking at home and selling a few cakes at a time to the local charcuterie, so I simply multiplied the recipes I had by four. It never occurred to me that now that I had a bakery I couldn't simply multiply the recipe for one cake up and up and up . . . so that is exactly what I did. Among my memorabilia is a stack of stained and dog-eared handwritten recipe cards for the Queen of Sheba and Gâteau au Chocolat Maison. The earliest cards have recipes for making six cakes at a time, which was the first batch size we made in our used three-deck "pizza" ovens. Farther down in the stack I find recipes for twelve, and then twenty-four, and then thirty-six cakes. Each multiplication was a learning experience, and so it made sense to scale up gradually. Customers were multiplying at the same time, and by the time Cocolat was sold, more than twelve years later, the Queen of Sheba recipe had been neatly typed on the computer by the company secretary in the front office (!) and laminated in plastic for easy cleaning. The recipe made enough batter for 108 Qs of S.

The learning curve was steady. We went from one little bakery and shop to several, and we moved to a larger, separate baking facility. Recipes and procedures were translated to accommodate ever-larger mixers and ovens. Throughout, however, the quality of the desserts and the level of artistry got better . . . one of the things I am most proud of these many years later.

As the kitchen staff grew into a production team, we continued to learn by doing, supplying cakes to seven Cocolat stores, and then ten and fourteen after the business was sold, and I continued to work (briefly) with the new owners. We consulted in the industry occasionally, and other bakers, thank goodness, were generous with their help. But our own experimentation was always critical, because we were still making desserts that no one else made, with ingredients that no one else used in quite the way we did, often using techniques that evolved in our kitchen.

Once, long after Cocolat was sold and then closed, friends and volunteers were in a Boston hotel kitchen helping Flo Braker and me make an eightieth-birthday cake for Chuck Williams, founder of Williams-Sonoma (see the recipe on page 171). I watched as one of them spread batter evenly in a sheet pan and ran a finger neatly around the inside edge of the pan to make a tiny margin of space that would aid in unmolding the layer later. I told him that I had never seen anyone other than a Cocolat baker do that exact thing in that exact way. He grinned and informed me that he had several former Cocolat bakers in his own San Francisco catering kitchen.

Sometime in the first years, James Beard came into the store, escorted by Marion Cunningham. I was mortified because some of my staff were so young that they had no idea who he was! And Marion, of course, had not yet come into her own. A few years later (by this time the bakery was no longer behind the store, and I had enough staff so that I could finally sleep in on a rare Saturday morning), I got an excited call on the phone I kept for staff use only. It wasn't the usual truck breakdown or refrigeration crisis, it was charming Ivan Cousins, calling to say that his sister-in-law, Julia, was in town, and he was bringing her to see the bakery. Out of bed like a shot, I arrived just in time to escort Julia Child and her sister, Dorothy (and Ivan), around the kitchen. Julia chatted with each of the bakers and decorators. I was gratified that when I then drove Julia to the Berkeley store, even the youngest workers knew who she was!

The earliest years were intense and exhausting. But it was a period of extraordinary accomplishment. I would not have missed it, and I am immensely proud, although I also understand today what it cost. I know now that it was thrilling and satisfying, but I don't remember then feeling or enjoying that thrill or satisfaction often. To do what needed to be done required almost impossible tunnel vision—often euphemistically called dedication.

Every few years, cleaning out my office, I again come across my little notebooks and to-do lists from those years. I am amazed and aghast each time. What I had to accomplish in a day and a week makes me simultaneously awed and horrified by that other person I must have been. And no matter how focused I was, I could not have done a fraction of it without the staff, who, for very little money, worked with dedication and, I have to say, love for what we were doing. Many are good friends still. And in those years, when any other marriage I knew would have come apart, my husband provided the most critical support.

My daughter, Lucy, was born in 1989, when I was thirty-nine, shortly before the publication of my first book, *Cocolat*. These two events marked a beginning and an end. Lucy took her central place in our lives. A few months later, the book's reception, and my first James Beard Award for Cookbook of the Year, coincided with the enormous sadness—yet greater relief—I felt at selling a business that had been devouring me alive. The great sense of loss I felt was ameliorated, unexpectedly, by *Cocolat*. In my mind, the book became a beautifully wrapped box tied with a silk ribbon. In it, perfectly preserved, were the best and most important aspects of my life's work and, until Lucy, my only child. To this day, when I think of that book, I see the box. At any moment I can open it and begin to read, picking up and savoring the precious pieces of experience and friendship and accomplishment. The box contains everything positive and radiant, everything that brings a smile to my face (even writing this), everything creative and cherished from my life before Lucy.

It all began with chocolate truffles.

4

COCOLAT

TRUFFLES, MOUSSES, AND MORE

YOUTHFUL FOLLY

I was not a formally trained pastry chef or chocolatier when I started selling truffles in 1974. I had no preconceived notions about what was right and wrong. I went about things my own way rather than the "right" way. While I occasionally went to great trouble just to reinvent the wheel, I also made discoveries because I came to the profession with the innocence and questioning attitude of an outsider.

The chocolate truffles are one good example of naive good fortune. In 1974, most Americans, including my customers, had no idea what chocolate truffles were. I made traditional bite-sized truffles rolled in cocoa, the ones I had learned from Mme. Lestelle, and I also made oversized truffles dipped in chocolate. These, which we later called American chocolate truffles—exuberant and as big as Ping-Pong balls—were born in my home kitchen by accident. I had never intended to make big chocolate truffles. It was just that my earliest attempts at shaping and dipping treacherously soft ganache yielded some very large and exquisitely ugly truffles, which also happened to taste divine. They melted instantly in my mouth with a burst of big chocolate flavor. Shamelessly (in retrospect), I did not hesitate to sell those first results at the charcuterie where I was already selling chocolate tortes and the more traditional small truffles rolled in cocoa.

The response to the big truffles was immediate and ecstatic. They were big and vulgar by European standards, and, looking back, I regard them as something of a youthful folly. But they had an enormous impact. They created a national trend for giant

chocolate truffles and encouraged scores (hundreds?) of small entrepreneurs across the country to start truffle businesses. Later, in order to distinguish among the more than twenty-five flavors in my shop, we decorated each kind of truffle with a little topping or streak or swirl of drizzled chocolate or some other distinctive visual treatment. Imagine my surprise, years later, to see large truffles like mine in Paris and London!

By the time I had mastered truffle forming and truffle dipping, so that they weren't ugly anymore and so I could make them any size I wanted, my audience was hooked on the big ones. Attempts to make them dainty met with the polite equivalent of hissing and booing.

My truffles did not depart from European tradition in size and décor only. Almost everything else about them (including the recipe and technique) was "wrong" as well. They were so highly unorthodox that, to make them as perfect as they could be, I had to keep on breaking the entire string of interrelated chocolatier rules (some of which I didn't even know). If I had done just one thing the "right" way, the whole house of cards would have tumbled, and the truffles wouldn't have worked!

Because my ganache (cream and chocolate) had too much cream in it, my truffle centers were too soft even to hold a shape, much less to be dipped into warm chocolate without melting into a puddle. Rather than reducing the amount of cream to make firmer centers (which, in retrospect, would have been so easy), I froze them to make them firm. And it's a good thing that I was dipping them in melted untempered chocolate (because I didn't know any better at first)—tempered chocolate (see page 310) would have cracked and lost its temper on frozen centers anyway. After dipping, I had to refrigerate the truffles because the untempered chocolate bloomed, turning gray and gritty and less flavorful, when I left them at room temperature for any length of time. Refrigeration prevented all of those bad things and also kept the truffles, with all that extra cream in them, from spoiling.

The result of such blissful ignorance? Incomparable chocolate truffles precisely because of all the broken rules. Extremely soft, creamy centers (because the frozen ganache thaws inside the chocolate coating) dipped in untempered chocolate ultimately set Cocolat truffles apart and kept our clientele coming back, even when chocolate truffles began to crop up everywhere.

Meanwhile, my untempered coating gave me a kind of inferiority complex whenever I met or mingled with professional pastry chefs or "real" European chocolatiers. I knew that I liked my results and so did my customers, but I didn't have the confidence to admit to anyone formally trained that I purposely didn't temper my chocolate, or to discuss it with those to whom it was obvious. It just wasn't done, yet I was doing it. I was also making chocolate ruffles with untempered chocolate and dipping strawberries in it too. Meanwhile, I was mixing cakes in unconventional ways and purposely combining water and chocolate.

Over the years I occasionally sought advice from Terry Richardson, a local chocolate technologist whose usual clients were very big companies both here and abroad. No matter what I asked him, he almost always said, "Alice, you can't do that," to which I almost always replied, "Terry, I *am already* doing that, I just want you to help me do it better!" And sometimes he did.

I gained such a reputation for not tempering chocolate that when I starting teaching tempering classes, people reacted as if I had renounced my faith. As if tempering were a religion.

Cocolat truffles were sensational, but at the time I did not fully understand why. It took me some twenty years to get it. Chilled untempered chocolate melts at a lower temperature than tempered chocolate because the fat is crystallized in a less stable form. This simply means that when you bite into the truffle, the coating melts and releases its flavor the moment it makes contact with the warmth of your mouth. Tempered chocolate requires more heat, thus more time to melt. The speed and temperature of the melting change our perception of flavors and textures. Similarly, ganache that is chilled (or frozen) immediately after it is mixed also becomes softer and melts faster in your mouth. Freezing was my naive solution to firming up the centers, but the bonus result was a soft, luxurious truffle center that felt and tasted like the richest chocolate ice cream. In addition, chilling the ganache ensured against fat separation and other technical flaws that plague classic ganache makers. So my weird method is great for beginners too. How lucky was I, just an innocent young thing who wanted to make chocolate truffles in Berkeley?

TRUFFLES AU COCOLAT

These are the truffles that Mme. Lestelle, my landlady on the rue Copernic, made for my birthday in 1972. A year later, I asked for her recipe as a going-away gift and with it, I started my career, making truffles in my home kitchen in Berkeley and selling them to a local charcuterie. Without this very authentic yet virtually obsolete recipe, I would never have dreamed of opening my own chocolate shop. Bite-sized cocoa-dusted truffles made with butter and egg yolks rather than cream have a unique bittersweet intensity and a smooth, dense texture that is different from that of the cream-based ganache truffles most people know. Every few years I update the recipe for these, my first and still favorite truffles.

I now use a higher-percentage chocolate than before, and I have slightly reduced the amount of butter to create truffles with a heightened chocolate flavor. I have changed the way the egg yolks are handled too; now I heat them first for safety. The result is still an elegant and stunningly easy-to-make confection. No dipping is required; the truffles are rolled directly in good cocoa powder. Choose a fine distinctive chocolate. I like a fruity, not too austere chocolate, such as Scharffen Berger semisweet (62%), Valrhona Le Noir Gastronomie (61%), or E. Guittard Sur Del Lago (65%). Always good after dinner with espresso, port, or Cognac, these truffles also get along surprisingly well with a juicy, fruit-forward red wine with low tannins, such as a syrah or a late-harvest zinfandel.

If you are using fresh farm eggs or are confident about the quality of your eggs, you can skip the egg-heating step: simply add the ½ cup water (cold) to the chocolate and butter before melting them. When the chocolate is completely melted and smooth, add the raw egg yolks and proceed as directed. / *Makes 64 or more truffles*

SPECIAL EQUIPMENT

8-inch square baking pan

Fine-mesh strainer

Instant-read thermometer

INGREDIENTS

1 pound (455 grams) 54% to 62% chocolate, coarsely chopped (see Chocolate Notes)

10 tablespoons (140 grams/1¼ sticks) unsalted butter, cut into small pieces

2 large egg yolks, at room temperature

½ cup boiling water or freshly brewed espresso

½ cup (50 grams) premium unsweetened cocoa powder (natural or Dutch-process)

DIRECTIONS

• Line the bottom and sides of a baking pan with parchment paper or foil. Set aside.

• Place the chocolate and butter in a medium stainless steel bowl in a wide skillet of barely simmering water over low heat. Stir frequently until the chocolate and butter are almost completely melted and smooth. Remove the bowl and stir with a spatula to complete the melting. Set aside. Leave the heat under the skillet on low.

• Place the egg yolks in a small stainless steel bowl and gradually stir in the boiling water. Place the bowl in the skillet and stir constantly with a heatproof spatula, sweeping the bottom of the bowl to prevent the eggs from scrambling, until the mixture registers 160°F on an instant-read thermometer. (You will have to remove the bowl from the skillet to take the temperature unless you are agile enough to stir, hold, and read the thermometer at the same time.) For safety, rinse the thermometer stem in the simmering water to sterilize it after each reading. When the yolk mixture is ready, scrape it immediately over the melted chocolate. Stir gently (without whisking or beating) until completely blended and smooth. Pour the mixture through a fine-mesh strainer into the lined pan and spread it evenly. Cover and chill until firm, at least 2 hours.

• Put the cocoa in a medium bowl. Remove the truffle pan from the refrigerator and use the liner to transfer the truffle sheet to a cutting board. Allow it to soften until you can cut it without it cracking, about 30 minutes if the mixture is very hard. Invert the sheet and peel off the liner. Cut the truffles into squares 1 inch or smaller and toss them in the bowl of cocoa powder. You can leave the truffles square or dust your hands with cocoa and roll them into balls. (Store the truffles tightly covered for up to 2 weeks in the refrigerator or freeze for up to 3 months.) Remove from the refrigerator about 20 minutes before serving to soften slightly.

CHOCOLATE NOTES

To use higher-percentage chocolate, make the following adjustments.

To use 64% to 66% chocolate: Use 12 ounces (340 grams) chocolate, and increase the butter to 12 tablespoons (170 grams/ 1½ sticks). Dissolve 1½ teaspoons (6 grams) of sugar in the hot water before adding it to the egg yolks.

To use 66% to 72% chocolate: Use 11 ounces (310 grams) chocolate, and increase the butter to 12 tablespoons (170 grams/ 1½ sticks). Dissolve 3 to 4 teaspoons (13 to 17 grams) sugar in the boiling water before adding it to the egg yolks.

COLD CREAMY TRUFFLES

With a crisp chocolate shell and a meltingly soft center, these may be the easiest and most sensational chocolate-dipped truffles you will ever make. I've updated and fine-tuned this recipe and procedure so you can enjoy it with a variety of chocolates with different cacao percentages. For the ultimate experience with these truffles, consult the Chocolate Notes. After years of not making them, I was stunned again to find out how good they are, especially with interesting chocolates. At a glance the recipe looks similar to the classic ganache truffle recipes that follow (pages 109–115), but the ratio of ingredients and the way of handling them sidestep all the finicky steps for perfect classic ganache—with dramatic and wonderful results. A high ratio of cream to chocolate not only produces the softest center, it also eliminates any danger that the ganache will separate or break. Unlike ganache for Classic Ganache Truffles (page 109), this one must be mixed gently with a spatula rather than vigorously with a whisk.

Because the chocolate coating is not tempered, you must keep these truffles in the refrigerator to prevent them from discoloring. If you give them as a gift, be sure the recipient knows to put them in the refrigerator. Enjoy them cold, right from the fridge, or let them warm up for half an hour or so, rather like a piece of cheese. But leftovers, if any, should always go back into the fridge. / **Makes about 50 truffles**

SPECIAL EQUIPMENT

Fine-mesh strainer

Miniature ice cream scoop (about 1 inch in diameter) or melon baller

Instant-read thermometer

INGREDIENTS

8 ounces (225 grams) (9 ounces [255 grams] if using the rum) 54% to 61% chocolate, cut into pieces no bigger than almonds

1 cup heavy cream

2 tablespoons rum or other liquor (optional)

12 to 16 ounces (340 to 455 grams) dark, milk, or white chocolate, coarsely chopped, for dipping

About 2 tablespoons (10 grams) premium unsweetened cocoa powder (optional)

DIRECTIONS

• To make the ganache: Place the 8 (or 9) ounces (225 or 255 grams) chocolate in a medium bowl. Set aside. In a small saucepan, bring the cream to a low boil. Pour over the chocolate. Stir gently with a rubber spatula until the chocolate is completely melted and the mixture is smooth; do not whisk or splash the mixture by stirring too briskly, or the texture of the truffles will be cakey and granular instead of smooth and creamy. Stir in the liquor, if using, and mix only enough to blend. To refine the texture, strain the mixture through a fine-mesh sieve into another bowl. Refrigerate, without stirring, until the ganache is firm enough to scoop into balls, at least 4 hours.

• To form the centers: Line a baking pan or a shallow plastic storage container with wax paper or foil. Scrape the ice cream scoop or melon baller across the cold ganache to form a scant 1-inch ball. Place the centers in the lined pan. Repeat with the remaining ganache. Cover the pan with foil or plastic wrap and freeze for several hours, or overnight, until very hard. Leave the centers in the freezer until the moment you are ready to dip them. (The centers can be sealed in an airtight container and kept frozen for up to 2 months.)

• To dip the centers: Melt the 12 to 16 ounces chocolate in a medium heatproof bowl set in a skillet of barely simmering water, stirring frequently. (Be sure that all your utensils are dry and that no moisture is introduced into the chocolate.) Or microwave on Medium (50%) power for about 5 minutes. Stir frequently to hasten the melting. When the chocolate is smooth, melted, and at 100° to 105°F, it is ready to use. Wipe the bottom of the bowl dry if you have used a water bath.

• Place the bowl of chocolate in front of you. Remove one-third (if you are a beginner) or half of the truffle centers from the freezer and place them on a plate to the left of the chocolate (reverse all the instructions as appropriate if you are left-handed). Set a baking sheet, lined with wax paper, parchment, or foil, to the right of the chocolate. If you do not want to dip the truffles by hand, use two plastic spoons (but without tempering the chocolate) as described on page 121; otherwise, dip the truffles by hand as follows: Use your left hand to place a frozen center in the chocolate. Use the middle and index fingers of your right hand to push the center around in the chocolate until it is thoroughly coated on all sides. Leaving the center in the chocolate, wipe excess chocolate from your fingers on the sides of the bowl, then pick up the truffle with the two wiped fingers and your thumb, shake off the excess chocolate, and place the truffle on the lined baking sheet. Repeat, setting the truffles on the baking sheet so that they do not touch one another, and working as quickly as possible to prevent the centers from thawing and melting in the warm chocolate. Don't hold the dipped centers any longer than necessary, or the chocolate will harden and the truffles will stick to your fingers. Wiping your fingers on the bowl and shaking off the excess chocolate prevents the chocolate from forming the puddles called "feet" around the bottoms of the truffles. Practice makes perfect when it comes to dipping without creating feet!

continued

CHOCOLATE NOTES

Perfection in this truffle is a center that melts in your mouth like ultrarich ice cream. This requires the right balance of chocolate and cream. To use higher-percentage chocolate to make truffles that are even more bittersweet while retaining the same creamy texture, adjust the recipe as follows.

To use 60% to 64% chocolate: Use 7 ounces (200 grams) chocolate (with or without the rum) for the centers.

To use 66% chocolate: Use 6 ounces (170 grams) chocolate (with or without the rum) for the centers. Stir 1 tablespoon (13 grams) sugar into the cream before heating it.

To use 70% to 72% chocolate: Use 5½ ounces (155 grams) (6 ounces [170 grams] if using the rum) chocolate for the centers. Stir 2 tablespoons (25 grams) sugar into the cream before heating it. Pour only half of the hot cream and sugar over the chocolate and stir until the chocolate is melted, then add the remaining cream and stir to blend thoroughly.

• When you have dipped all of the centers on the plate, remove more frozen centers from the freezer and dip them likewise until all of the centers are dipped. Sift a little cocoa over the dipped truffles, if you like. Refrigerate the sheet of dipped truffles for at least long enough to harden the coating. Once the coating is hard, peel the truffles from the paper and transfer them to a covered container. Store in the refrigerator for up to 2 weeks, or freeze for up to 3 months.

TROUBLESHOOTING

Since no two chocolates are identical in composition and the fat content of cream varies from region to region, your ganache might not set up exactly as mine does. If it does not get firm enough to scoop and hold a shape after several hours in the refrigerator, freeze it for an hour or two. If that doesn't work, here's the fix: In a microwave on Medium (50%) power or in a wide skillet of almost simmering water, reheat the ganache gently, with minimal stirring, until it is around 110° to 115°F. Add 1 to 2 ounces (30 to 55 grams) of warm melted chocolate and stir gently but thoroughly to incorporate it into the ganache. Return the bowl to the refrigerator until the ganache is firm enough to scoop. (Make a note on the recipe to increase the amount of chocolate next time.)

On the other hand, if your finished truffles are firmer in the center than you would like them to be, reduce the amount of chocolate by ½ ounce (15 grams) each time you make the recipe until you get the texture just the way you like it.

Classic Ganache Truffles

After such rave reviews for cold untempered truffles, why even think about classic truffles? Why worry about making a perfect ganache emulsion, then tempering the chocolate for the coating? Apart from the convenience of having sublime fresh chocolates that do not require refrigeration, I was personally attracted to the challenge, the Zen-like importance of each detail, and the virtuosity involved in mastering the classic techniques. Maybe it's all about overcoming my old complex about not tempering, a way of proving that I can if I want to!

Then there are the subtleties of flavor and texture. Done well, classic ganache truffles are exquisite in an entirely different way from the cold, creamy untempered variety. Untempered truffles made with frozen centers are cold at first, and the melting sensation on your palate is quite exciting. Because the centers are frozen before dipping, these truffles can be made with a higher proportion of cream (one part cream to one part chocolate is excellent), which produces an especially soft creamy center. And because they are dipped frozen, these truffles take on a thicker coat of chocolate, so the contrast between the hard shell and the soft center is dramatic.

Classic ganache truffles dipped in tempered chocolate, on the other hand, are at their best at room temperature. They have a firmer interior consistency and usually a greater intensity of chocolate flavor, because they are made with one part cream to two parts chocolate or three parts cream to five parts chocolate. Rather than cold and creamy, their texture is satin-smooth, like slightly soft butter. Using classic methods, it is possible—in fact, highly desirable—to achieve a very thin coating of chocolate that, when set, offers the barest, audibly crisp resistance to your teeth before you encounter the smooth chocolate center.

This is the type of truffle I make when I am using highest-quality chocolate with unique flavor characteristics that I don't want to hide with too much cream.

So I make both types of truffles, depending on the occasion, the chocolate I am using, etc. Regardless of method, however, I usually prefer small to large truffles, and I gravitate once again to the most traditional presentation of all: unadorned chocolate-dipped truffles rolled in a bed of cocoa or chocolate shavings.

CLASSIC GANACHE IS AN EMULSION

An emulsion is a combination of two substances that normally do not mix together. Oil and vinegar joined to make a salad dressing is an emulsion, as is the perfectly blended mixture of cream and chocolate that we call ganache. In both, tiny droplets of one ingredient are surrounded by and held in suspension within the other. When the emulsion in a salad dressing is formed, two otherwise transparent ingredients become a creamy homogeneous mixture. The emulsion is formed by shaking or whisking the two together so vigorously that the vinegar breaks into microscopic bubbles surrounded by oil; this is called a water-in-fat emulsion. The ganache emulsion is harder to see. In a ganache, vigorous whisking or blending breaks the fat, from both the chocolate and the cream, into tiny droplets, which are then surrounded by the water in the cream; this is called a fat-in-water emulsion.

The ganache emulsion is far more stable than the oil and vinegar emulsion. However, any emulsion can break, or separate. This happens when the little droplets that were suspended in the other ingredient start bumping into one another and combining into bigger droplets, then pools, and then layers, and the heavier ingredient begins to shift and settle. In the oil and vinegar dressing, which is only a temporary emulsion, the two ingredients ultimately separate into distinct easy-to-see layers. A ganache is opaque to begin with and the fat and liquid don't separate quite so completely, but a broken ganache can definitely play havoc with the consistency of your truffles. Take heart, however. Unlike salad dressing, perfectly made ganache can be very stable. And if it is mixed properly and allowed to set without being disturbed, it will solidify into flawlessly smooth classic truffle centers.

This perfection requires chocolate and cream that are not too hot, mixed vigorously and thoroughly together (see Classic Ganache Truffles, page 109). It also requires a certain minimum ratio of cream to chocolate. In any emulsion, there must be enough of the surrounding substance to completely separate and suspend the droplets of the other. Because the dry cocoa particles in chocolate absorb some of the water in the cream, they remove some of what would otherwise be available to surround the fat drops. This means the minimum amount of cream required to form an emulsion with chocolate varies with both the fat content *and* the dry solid content of the chocolate. Luckily, we don't have to attempt to make what would probably be a complicated calculation for all the different chocolates. The percentage of cacao (cocoa butter plus nonfat dry solids) in chocolate is a fairly good indicator of the minimum amount of cream needed for an emulsion. This is true, thank goodness, even though two chocolates of the same percentage do not necessarily have the exact same ratio of dry particles to fat (see Chocolate Components, page 302).

TROUBLESHOOTING: WHAT TO DO WHEN GANACHE BREAKS

A perfectly emulsified ganache pulls itself together before your eyes as the chocolate and cream are blended together. It thickens into a homogeneous mass with a satiny gloss and a puddinglike consistency that shows distinct tracks in the wake of the whisk or blade. If you pour the ganache into another container, it has enough body to hold a soft shape on the surface rather than flow into a completely level mass. It sets at room temperature with an even matte gloss on the surface. It is uniformly firm when pressed with a fingertip and perfectly smooth on the tongue.

If the cream and chocolate are not mixed thoroughly, if you keep mixing after the emulsion is formed, if they are mixed at too hot or cool a temperature (or even if the emulsion is disturbed much later when only partially set), the emulsion will break, and the fat will separate out. How can you tell whether this is happening? You know that ganache is broken when, as you are mixing, it suddenly feels thinner and less viscous and the surface begins to look slightly curdled. Sometimes the change in texture is so slight that you have to lower your head and look closely at the way the light reflects off the surface. Sometimes an emulsion can seem only partially broken: it is mostly thick and emulsified but has fine streaks of oil or oiliness around the edges, and when you tilt it, the ganache slides as though the bowl were oiled. If you whisk harder and faster, hoping to correct or prevent further curdling, the ganache may start to appear stretchy and elastic. Broken ganache gets worse after it sets. The surface may be mottled and dull or marred by streaks or puddles of yellow fat. When pressed it may be soft in some places and firm in others. The texture of a poorly made ganache is grainy rather than smooth. Even the smallest invisible fat puddles will feel like fish scales in your mouth.

When the first signs of curdling appear in a bowl of ganache, instinct tells you to whisk harder and faster or continue to blend with the immersion blender or food processor. After that (usually) doesn't work, there are two fixes to try. If the broken ganache has dropped to a temperature below 90°F, warm it several degrees without stirring, either in a water bath or in a microwave on Low (30%) power, using 5- to 10-second increments. Then whisk or blend again and see whether the emulsion forms as it should. If this doesn't work, and you are using an immersion blender or a food processor, add 2 to 3 tablespoons cream and try blending again. Or, if you are using a whisk, you can fix the ganache using the *mayonnaise method,* which I learned from Jim Graham, one of the very best chocolatiers I know. (No mayonnaise is required, by the way.) Here is how it works: Regardless of the amount of ganache you are trying to fix, bring 3 to 4 tablespoons cream to a simmer. Pour it into a clean bowl and whisk in a few tablespoons of the broken ganache until the mixture looks smooth and thick. Continue to whisk, gradually adding the rest of the broken ganache, as though you were making mayonnaise. I have used this method to repair even fairly large batches of ganache.

TROUBLESHOOTING: WHAT TO DO WHEN GANACHE IS TOO SOFT TO SCOOP OR PIPE

After setting at room temperature for several hours, even perfectly mixed classic ganache may vary in firmness from batch to batch. Once again, this is a fact of life with chocolate. The reasons have to do with differences in the quantity of fat, dry cocoa solids, and sugar among even chocolates of the same percentage. Observe the results and take notes each time you make ganache with a different brand of chocolate, so you'll know whether to increase or decrease the amount of chocolate or cream the next time you make it.

To a certain extent, however, you can also adjust the texture and stiffness of a batch of ganache after it has set. A perfectly firm, smooth, shiny ganache can be formed into truffle centers as is, by scooping or piping it. Or you can lighten its color and flavor by whipping a little air into the ganache before you pipe or scoop. Because whipping also makes ganache stiffer, this technique is useful when your ganache turns out to be softer than you anticipated. Some chocolatiers whip as a matter of course; others do it only for certain flavors or varieties of truffle; others avoid whipping altogether.

If ganache for truffles is whipped, it must first be thoroughly set, so the fat has had a chance to crystallize and form a stable structure. This takes several hours, preferably overnight, at cool room temperature; don't rush this by chilling. (The very light whipped ganache cake filling on page 189 must be thoroughly chilled before whipping, but it is a different ganache altogether.) Disturbing the classic truffle ganache before it is set and stable will break the emulsion. Premature whipping will collapse and curdle the ganache completely; either it will never stiffen or it will stiffen with a grainy texture.

Once the ganache is set, you can whip it by stirring it vigorously with a rubber spatula or beating it with a handheld mixer to lighten and stiffen it significantly. To avoid overwhipped (grainy) ganache, use a rubber spatula. How much you whip is a matter of preference, as long as you don't overwhip. Please note that whipping first softens the ganache—it doesn't stiffen until later, after you've stopped mixing, so you have to learn to anticipate. The color gives you clues; the lighter the color as you whip, the stiffer the ganache will be after it rests. Soft, freshly whipped ganache firms up in a matter of minutes, so if you are forming truffles with a pastry bag, pipe them while the ganache is soft. The piped centers will firm up nicely afterward. If you prefer to scoop the centers, let the whipped ganache firm up first. In either case, remember that the moist surface of truffle centers will dry and crust slightly after they set for an hour or so.

CLASSIC GANACHE TRUFFLES

The key to absolute perfection in these classic truffles is to form a complete and perfect emulsion of the chocolate and cream by mixing thoroughly and taking the time to let the ganache cool, undisturbed, at room temperature, preferably overnight. I always begin at least one day ahead. You can mix by hand with a whisk, but an immersion blender is more foolproof. / **Makes about 48 truffles**

INGREDIENTS

¾ cup heavy cream

10 ounces (285 grams) (11 ounces [310 grams] if using the brandy) 54% to 62% chocolate, coarsely chopped (see Chocolate Notes)

2 to 3 tablespoons brandy or liquor or liqueur of choice (optional)

2 to 4 tablespoons (12 to 24 grams) premium unsweetened cocoa powder, or 1 to 1½ cups (3½ to 6 ounces/ 115 to 170 grams) finely chopped nuts, toasted or raw (optional, for coating truffles without dipping)

1¼ pounds (565 grams) dark, milk, or white chocolate for dipping (optional)

SPECIAL EQUIPMENT

Shallow baking pan (such as a brownie pan) or plastic storage container

Instant-read thermometer

Miniature ice cream scoop (about 1 inch in diameter) or melon baller

Portable fan (optional)

DIRECTIONS

• Line the shallow baking pan with plastic wrap, overlapping two or more sheets as necessary and leaving a generous overhang on two sides (enough to cover the ganache once it is in the pan).

• In a small saucepan, bring the cream to a boil. Remove from the heat and let it cool to 115° to 125°F.

• Place the 10 (or 11) ounces (285 or 310 grams) chocolate in a medium stainless steel bowl in a wide skillet of barely simmering water and stir frequently until most of the chocolate is melted. Remove from the heat and stir until completely melted and smooth. Let the chocolate cool to 115° to 125°F.

• To mix with an immersion blender: Pour the cream and the brandy, if using, into the tall narrow container that comes with the blender, or into a 1-quart glass measuring pitcher or similarly shaped container. Scrape in the chocolate. Blend, keeping the blade beneath the surface and moving it around the bottom and up the sides of the container, until the mixture is perfectly smooth and thickened, like pudding, with a satiny sheen. To mix by hand with a whisk: Pour the cream and the brandy, if using, over the chocolate and whisk briskly, using a circular motion, keeping the whisk in contact with the bottom or the sides of the bowl to minimize splashing (which causes air bubbles), and alternately whisking in the center and around the sides of the bowl, until the cream is thoroughly mixed with the chocolate. Whisk only until the mixture appears completely homogeneous: smooth and thickened like pudding with a satiny sheen. Stop instantly when the ganache looks completely emulsified.

• Immediately scrape the ganache into a puddle in the plastic-wrap-lined pan and let cool at room temperature, without stirring or disturbing it.

• Once the ganache is cool, fold the plastic wrap over it and let set at room temperature for at least several hours, preferably overnight, until firm enough to scoop or pipe. If you are in a hurry, you can refrigerate it to hasten the set, but the texture of the truffles will not be quite as silken. When the ganache has set, however, chilling won't hurt it; you can refrigerate it for a day or two (or freeze it for up to 2 months), until needed. Then let soften at room temperature until pliable enough to scoop or pipe. If piping, you may have to squeeze or knead the plastic-wrapped ganache gently until it is pliable enough.

• If you are rolling truffles in cocoa or nuts (instead of dipping them in chocolate), put 2 tablespoons (12 grams) of cocoa or about ¼ cup (1 ounce/30 grams) of the nuts in a small bowl and have a bowl or storage container at hand. If you are dipping truffles in chocolate or shaping them with a pastry bag instead of a scoop, line a tray or baking sheet with parchment or wax paper.

• To shape the truffles, use the miniature ice cream scoop or melon baller to form ¾- to 1-inch balls of ganache. Smooth the surface with your thumb, or the heel of your hand, before releasing the ganache from the scoop. (If it is difficult to release, between scoops, warm the back of the scoop gently with a hair dryer, or warm it by dipping it in hot water, wiping it dry each time.) Alternatively, scrape the ganache into a large pastry bag fitted with a ½-inch plain tip and pipe rounded mounds on the lined tray.

• For truffles rolled in cocoa or nuts, shape and drop a few truffles into the bowl of cocoa (or nuts). Shake the bowl to coat the truffles; if using nuts, you may need to press some of them on with your fingers. Remove the coated truffles to a storage container. Continue to scoop and coat a few truffles at a time, adding cocoa or nuts to the bowl as necessary, until all of the truffles are finished. Cover and store the truffles.

CHOCOLATE NOTES

To use higher-percentage chocolate, adjust the recipe as follows.

To use 64% to 66% chocolate: Increase the cream by 2 tablespoons.

To use 70% to 72% chocolate: Chocolate at this percentage level requires both more cream and a different mixing method. See Extra-Bittersweet Ganache Truffles (page 113) or Women of Taste Truffles (page 116) for the correct proportions and method.

• For chocolate-dipped truffles, shape and place each truffle directly on the lined tray, slightly apart. Let stand at room temperature, uncovered, until the surface is dry and slightly crusted, at least 2 hours, preferably longer. Be sure that the centers are at a warmish room temperature before dipping them.

• Melt and temper the dipping chocolate (see pages 310–313). Using the techniques on pages 120–121, dip the centers by hand, with a dipping fork, or with two plastic spoons, then finish as desired. Let set at room temperature, ideally in front of a portable fan.

• Truffles rolled in cocoa or nuts will keep for a few days at room temperature or a couple of weeks in the fridge. Chocolate-dipped truffles will keep for up to 10 days at room temperature or for up to a month in the refrigerator; they can also be frozen for up to 3 months. Bring to room temperature before serving.

VARIATIONS

Classic Ginger Truffles Increase the cream by 1 tablespoon. Combine the cream and 3 tablespoons (30 grams) finely chopped candied ginger in a saucepan and bring to a boil. Remove the pan from the heat, cover it, and let the mixture steep for 15 minutes. Line the shallow pan and melt the chocolate as directed. Reheat the cream to about 125°F, then pour it through a fine-mesh strainer onto the chocolate, pressing on the solids to extract all of the cream. Discard the ginger. Mix the cream and chocolate together, proceeding as directed.

Classic Mint Truffles Two days before you plan to make the truffles, in a small bowl, stir ½ cup (15 grams) lightly packed coarsely chopped fresh mint leaves into ¾ cup cold heavy cream. Cover and refrigerate overnight. Strain the cream into a large glass measuring cup and press on the solids to release as much cream as possible; discard the mint. Add enough cream to make ¾ cup. Proceed as directed, substituting the mint-flavored cream for the plain cream.

Classic Jasmine Truffles These subtle, sexy truffles resulted from my collaboration with the artisan natural perfumer Mandy Aftel and artisan distiller Lance Winters of St. George Spirits. The three of us created an experimental sensory "experience" for a Berkeley Symphony fund-raising party at which guests were invited to taste a truffle, sip Lance's natural jasmine-infused vodka, and smell Mandy's jasmine, blood orange, and pink grapefruit perfume. We called it a "symphony of the senses." I used a 62% chocolate for the ganache and coated the truffles with a 70% chocolate for contrast.

continued

Two days before you plan to make the truffles, in a small bowl or jar, combine 1 tablespoon best-quality loose jasmine tea (I use downy pearls) with 1 cup cold heavy cream. Cover tightly and refrigerate overnight to infuse the flavor. Strain the cream into a small saucepan, pressing on the tea to extract all the cream; discard the tea leaves. Substitute the infused cream for the plain cream.

Proceed as directed, adding 1 teaspoon (2 grams) finely grated blood orange zest (organic or unsprayed) and 1½ teaspoons (3 grams) finely grated pink grapefruit zest (organic or unsprayed) to the chocolate with the infused cream.

Melt and temper the chocolate for dipping (see pages 310–313). Follow the instructions on page 120 for double coating and rolling in cocoa. The truffles will keep at cool room temperature in a covered container for up to 10 days, or in the refrigerator for about a month. They can also be frozen for up to 3 months.

EXTRA-BITTERSWEET GANACHE TRUFFLES

The higher the cacao percentage of the chocolate, the more challenging it is to make a perfectly emulsified ganache, especially by hand with a whisk. Higher-percentage chocolate contains less sugar (which normally helps chocolate emulsify with cream) and more dry solids (which hinders emulsification). This makes mixing tricky: ganache made with 70% or more cacao may curdle outright as you mix it, or it may seem smooth to an inexperienced eye but later, after it is cool, develop tiny hard bits of cocoa butter the size and shape of fish scales. You may not be able to see the "fish scales" (my term for these hard bits), but you will definitely feel them on your palate.

I include the method for mixing these truffles by hand, because it *is* possible: the temperature of both the chocolate and the cream is important, as is thorough but not excessive mixing (and, yes, the chocolate must be poured into the cream rather than vice versa). However, I urge you to use an immersion blender or a food processor for perfect results every time. Or, if you double the recipe, you may use the alternative food processor method described on page 116, which skips the step of melting the chocolate altogether. These small truffles are very bittersweet. / **Makes about 48 truffles**

INGREDIENTS

1 cup plus 2 tablespoons heavy cream (1¼ cups if using 66% chocolate)

10 ounces (285 grams) 66% to 72% chocolate, coarsely chopped

2 to 4 tablespoons (12 to 24 grams) premium unsweetened cocoa powder, or 1 to 1½ cups (3½ to 6 ounces/115 to 170 grams) finely chopped nuts, toasted or raw (optional, for coating truffles without dipping)

1¼ pounds (565 grams) dark, milk, or white chocolate for dipping (optional)

SPECIAL EQUIPMENT

Instant-read thermometer

Shallow baking pan (such as a brownie pan) or plastic storage container

Miniature ice cream scoop (about 1 inch in diameter) or melon baller

Portable fan (optional)

DIRECTIONS

• In a small saucepan, bring the cream to a boil. Pour it into a medium bowl. Set aside to cool to 115° to 120°F.

continued

- Line the shallow baking pan with plastic wrap, overlapping two or more sheets as necessary and leaving a generous overhang on two sides (enough to cover the ganache once it is in the pan).

- Meanwhile, place the 10 ounces (285 grams) chocolate in a medium stainless steel bowl in a wide skillet of barely simmering water and stir frequently until most of the chocolate is melted. Remove from the heat and stir until completely melted and smooth. Let the chocolate cool until it is 115° to 120°F.

- To mix with an immersion blender: Pour the cream into the tall narrow container that comes with the blender, or into a 1-quart glass measuring pitcher or similarly shaped container. Scrape in the chocolate. Blend, keeping the blade beneath the surface and moving it around the bottom and up the sides of the container, until the mixture is perfectly smooth and thickened, like pudding with a satiny sheen.

- To mix with a food processor: Scrape the chocolate and cream into the processor. Process for a couple of seconds. Stop and scrape the sides of the bowl and the lid, then process several seconds more, or until the mixture is perfectly smooth and thickened, like pudding with a satiny sheen.

- To mix by hand: Begin pouring the chocolate slowly into the cream, whisking constantly in a circular pattern, in one direction only, keeping the whisk in contact with the bottom of the bowl to minimize splashing (which causes air bubbles). When about half of the chocolate is blended into the cream, stop whisking and scrape in the remaining chocolate. Resume whisking as before, alternately whisking at the center and around the sides of the bowl in order to blend the cream thoroughly and efficiently with the chocolate. Whisk only until the mixture appears completely homogeneous: smooth and thickened slightly, like pudding with a satiny sheen. Stop immediately once the ganache looks completely emulsified.

- Immediately scrape the ganache into a puddle in the plastic-wrap-lined pan and let cool at room temperature, without stirring or disturbing it.

- Once the ganache is cool, fold the plastic wrap over it and let set at room temperature for at least several hours, preferably overnight, until firm enough to scoop or pipe. If you are in a hurry, you can refrigerate it to hasten the set, but the texture of the truffles will not be quite as silken. Once the ganache has set, however, chilling won't hurt it; you can refrigerate it for a day or two (or freeze it for up to 2 months), until needed. Let soften at room temperature until pliable enough to scoop or pipe. If piping, you may have to squeeze or knead the plastic-wrapped ganache gently until pliable enough.

• If you are rolling truffles in cocoa or nuts (instead of dipping them in chocolate), put 2 tablespoons (12 grams) of cocoa or about ¼ cup (1 ounce/30 grams) of the nuts in a small bowl and have a bowl or storage container at hand. If you are dipping truffles in chocolate or shaping them with a pastry bag instead of a scoop, line a tray or baking sheet with parchment or wax paper.

• To shape the truffles, use the miniature ice cream scoop or melon baller to form ¾- to 1-inch balls of ganache. Smooth the surface with your thumb, or the heel of your hand, before releasing the ganache from the scoop. (If it is difficult to release, between scoops, warm the back of the scoop gently with a hair dryer, or warm it by dipping it in hot water, wiping it dry each time.) Alternatively, scrape the ganache into a large pastry bag fitted with a ½-inch plain tip and pipe rounded mounds on the lined tray.

• For truffles rolled in cocoa or nuts, shape and drop a few truffles into the bowl of cocoa (or nuts). Shake the bowl to coat the truffles; if using nuts, you may need to press some of them on with your fingers. Remove the coated truffles to a storage container. Continue to scoop and coat a few truffles at a time, adding cocoa or nuts to the bowl as necessary, until all of the truffles are finished. Cover and store the truffles.

• For chocolate-dipped truffles, shape and place each truffle directly on the lined tray, slightly apart. Let stand at room temperature, uncovered, until the surface is dry and slightly crusted, at least 2 hours, preferably longer. Be sure that the centers are at a warmish room temperature before dipping them.

• Melt and temper the dipping chocolate (see pages 310–313). Using the techniques on pages 120–121, dip the centers by hand, with a dipping fork, or with two plastic spoons, and finish as desired. Let set at room temperature, ideally in front of a portable fan. Store the truffles in a covered container at cool room temperature.

• Truffles rolled in cocoa or nuts will keep for a few days at room temperature or a couple of weeks in the fridge. Chocolate-dipped truffles will keep for up to 10 days at room temperature or for up to a month in the refrigerator; they can also be frozen for up to 3 months. Bring to room temperature before serving.

WOMEN OF TASTE TRUFFLES

The Women of Taste Quilt Show, sponsored by Girls Inc., opened in the spring of 1998 at the Oakland Museum. Fifty luminous quilts were exhibited, each a collaboration between a quilter and a chef. For me it was an opportunity to work with an extraordinary artist, Joan Schulze. For opening night, Alice Waters provided hors d'oeuvres from Chez Panisse, and I made one thousand of these bite-sized chocolate-coated, cocoa-dusted truffles with bitter-sweet 70% chocolate and natural cocoa powder.

This relatively large recipe allows you to streamline the steps. Rather than melting the chocolate and waiting for boiling cream to cool down, you simply pulverize the chocolate as finely as possible in a food processor and then pour boiling cream into it. There is enough hot cream to melt the chocolate thoroughly *and* form the emulsion. This same method is used for the 48 truffles that the recipe for White or Milk Chocolate Truffles (page 118) yields; however, it doesn't work well for a small batch of dark chocolate truffles. These are extra-extra-bittersweet.

Begin at least one day in advance to allow the ganache to set overnight. / **Makes about 144 truffles**

SPECIAL EQUIPMENT

Shallow baking pan (such as a brownie pan) or plastic storage container

Miniature ice cream scoop (about 1 inch in diameter) or melon baller

INGREDIENTS

1 pound 6 ounces (625 grams) 70% chocolate, chopped into small chunks

2 cups heavy cream

2 pounds (910 grams) 70% chocolate for dipping

1 cup (95 grams) (or more) premium unsweetened cocoa powder (natural or Dutch-process)

DIRECTIONS

• Line the shallow baking pan with plastic wrap, overlapping two or more sheets as necessary and leaving a generous overhang on two sides (enough to cover the ganache once it is in the pan).

• Place the 1 pound 6 ounces (625 grams) chocolate in a food processor and process to the consistency of crumbs. In a medium saucepan, bring the cream to a rolling boil. With the processor on, pour the cream through the feed tube, processing for 15 to 20 seconds *including* the time it takes to pour in the cream, or until the ganache has thickened like pudding and has a satiny sheen. Immediately scrape the ganache into a puddle on the plastic-wrap-lined pan and let cool at room temperature, without stirring or disturbing it.

• Once the ganache is cool, fold the plastic wrap over it and let set at room temperature for at least several hours, preferably overnight, until firm enough to scoop or pipe. If you are in a hurry, you can refrigerate it to hasten the set, but the texture of the truffles will not be quite as silken. Once the ganache has set, however, chilling won't hurt it; you can refrigerate it for a day or two (or freeze it for up to 2 months), until needed. Let soften at room temperature until pliable enough to scoop.

• To shape the truffles, use the miniature ice cream scoop or melon baller to form ¾- to 1-inch balls of ganache. If necessary, smooth the surface with your thumb, or the heel of your hand, before releasing the ganache from the scoop. (If it is difficult to release, warm the back of the scoop gently with a hair dryer, or warm it between scoops by dipping it in hot water, wiping it dry each time.) Place the centers slightly apart on a tray lined with parchment or wax paper. Let stand at room temperature, uncovered, until the surface is dry and slightly crusted, at least 2 hours, preferably longer. Be sure that the centers are at a warmish room temperature before dipping them.

• Melt and temper the dipping chocolate (see pages 310–313). Use the Ultrathin Hand-Dipping Method on page 120, and finish with cocoa powder as described. Let set at room temperature in a cool place. Store the truffles in a covered container at cool room temperature for up to 10 days or in the refrigerator for up to a month; they can also be frozen for up to 3 months. Bring to room temperature before serving.

WHITE OR MILK CHOCOLATE TRUFFLES

This recipe gives proportions and a simple food processor method for making plain milk choco-late or white chocolate truffles, to which you can then add any flavorings you like. Another way to vary the truffles is to dip the truffle centers into a contrasting chocolate, milk or white or dark, or to skip the dip and roll the truffles in chopped nuts. / **Makes about 48 truffles**

SPECIAL EQUIPMENT

Shallow baking pan (such as a brownie pan) or plastic storage container

Miniature ice cream scoop (about 1 inch in diameter) or melon baller

Portable fan (optional)

INGREDIENTS

12 ounces (340 grams) (13 ounces [370 grams] if using the rum), white or milk chocolate, chopped into small chunks

2 to 3 tablespoons rum or liquor or liqueur of choice (optional)

½ cup heavy cream

1 to 1½ cups (115 to 170 grams) finely chopped nuts, toasted or raw (optional, for coating truffles without dipping)

1¼ pounds (565 grams) white, milk, or dark chocolate for dipping (optional)

DIRECTIONS

• Line the shallow baking pan with plastic wrap, overlapping two or more sheets as necessary and leaving a generous overhang on two sides (enough to cover the ganache once it is in the pan).

• Place the 12 (or 13) ounces (340 or 370 grams) chocolate in a food processor and process to the consistency of crumbs. Add the liquor, if using.

• Bring the cream to a boil in a small saucepan. With the food processor on, pour the cream through the feed tube, processing for a total of 20 to 30 seconds, until the chocolate is melted and the mixture is perfectly smooth.

• Scrape the ganache into a puddle on the plastic-wrap-lined pan and let cool at room tem-perature, without stirring or disturbing it.

• Once the ganache is cool, fold the plastic wrap over it and let set at room temperature for several hours, preferably overnight, until firm enough to scoop or pipe. If you are in a hurry, you can refrigerate it to hasten the set, but the texture of the truffles will not be quite as silken. Once the ganache has set, however, chilling won't hurt it; you can refrigerate it for a day or two (or freeze it for up to 2 months), until needed. Then let soften at room temperature until pliable enough to scoop or pipe. If piping, you may have to squeeze or knead the plastic-wrapped ganache gently until it is pliable enough.

• If you are rolling truffles in nuts (instead of dipping them in chocolate), put about ¼ cup (30 grams) of the nuts in a small bowl and have a bowl or a storage container at hand. If you are dipping truffles in chocolate or shaping them with a pastry bag instead of a scoop, line a tray or a baking sheet with parchment or wax paper.

• To shape the truffles, use the miniature ice cream scoop or melon baller to form ¾- to 1-inch balls of ganache. Smooth the surface with your thumb, or the heel of your hand, before releasing the ganache from the scoop. (If it is difficult to release, warm the back of the scoop gently with a hair dryer, or warm it between scoops by dipping it in hot water, wiping it dry each time.) Alternatively, scrape the ganache into a large pastry bag fitted with a ½-inch plain tip and pipe rounded mounds on the lined tray.

• For truffles rolled in nuts, shape and drop a few truffles into the bowl of nuts. Shake the bowl to coat the truffles; you may need to press some of the nuts into the surface with your fingers. Remove the coated truffles to a storage container. Continue to scoop and coat a few truffles at a time, adding nuts to the bowl as necessary, until all of the truffles are finished. Cover and store the truffles.

• For chocolate-dipped truffles, shape and place each truffle directly on the lined tray, slightly apart. Let stand at room temperature, uncovered, until the surface is dry and slightly crusted, at least 2 hours, preferably longer. Be sure that the centers are at a warmish room temperature before dipping them.

• Melt and temper the dipping chocolate (see pages 310–313). Using the techniques on pages 120–121, dip the centers by hand, with a dipping fork, or with two plastic spoons, and finish as desired. Let set at room temperature, ideally in front of a portable fan. Store the truffles in a covered container at cool room temperature for up to 10 days, or refrigerate for up to a month. They can also be frozen for up to 3 months. Bring to room temperature before serving.

VARIATIONS

White Chocolate–Lemon Truffles White chocolate is at its best when that sweet edge is offset with a crisp or tangy flavor with a little acidity. Lemon is perfect. Dip these in white or bittersweet chocolate. If you like, garnish each with a sliver of candied lemon peel.

Add 1 teaspoon (2 grams) finely grated lemon zest and 3 to 4 teaspoons fresh lemon juice to the chocolate before adding the cream.

Gianduja Truffles Substitute 4 ounces (115 grams) gianduja (milk chocolate to which toasted hazelnut paste has been added; see Sources, page 317) and 8 ounces (225 grams) milk chocolate for the 12 ounces (340 grams) white or milk chocolate.

DIPPING AND FINISHING TRUFFLES

Here are four methods for dipping and finishing truffles refer-
enced in the truffle recipes on pages 100–118. You can mix and
match the methods with any of the truffles except Cold Creamy
Truffles, which has its own dipping method. The first turns out
truffles with a paper-thin, crisp chocolate coating, cocoa-coated
and irregular like the authentic fungus for which chocolate
truffles were named. The centers are coated twice very thinly
(between chocolate-covered palms) and then rolled in a bed of
cocoa, finely chopped nuts, or chocolate shavings. (If you have
taken a shortcut and chilled the mixture for the Classic Ganache,
Extra-Bittersweet Ganache, Women of Taste, or any white or
milk chocolate truffles, the double-coating method mitigates
the problem of cracking that occurs when you dip a cold center
into tempered chocolate: the first coat will crack, but the second probably will not. In any case, the cocoa hides a multitude
of sins.)

The second method uses a dipping fork and yields smooth
chocolate-dipped truffles, which can be sprinkled with cocoa
or topped with other ingredients that go with the flavor of the
truffle. The third method is similar to fork dipping, but it is
done with your fingers. The fourth method, using two plastic
spoons, is great for anyone who does not want to get her or his
hands into the chocolate but has difficulty dipping with a fork.
Ordinary disposable plastic spoons are easy to use, and best
because they are not as cold as metal, so the chocolate does not
harden up on them so quickly.

**ULTRATHIN HAND-DIPPING METHOD: DOUBLE COATING, WITH
OR WITHOUT COCOA** Melt and temper the chocolate (see pages
310–313) for the coating. If using cocoa (or nuts or shavings),
spread it on a baking sheet in an even bed about ¼ inch deep.
Line another baking sheet with wax or parchment paper. Use
your fingertips to smear about a teaspoon of chocolate onto the
centers of both palms. Pick up a truffle center and roll it gently
between your palms to coat it very thinly with chocolate, and
put it down on the lined baking sheet. Repeat with the remaining centers, dabbing more chocolate onto your palms as necessary. Work quickly so the chocolate on your hands doesn't
harden. When all the truffles are lightly coated, start over again
with the first one. Coat it lightly, as before, but once it is coated,
place it in the bed of cocoa (or return it to the lined tray if you
are skipping the cocoa). Repeat with 2 or 3 more truffles, then,
as the coating is just beginning to set, use a spoon to push the
first truffle across the bed of cocoa, rolling it over and over and
leaving gentle wrinkles on its surface. Repeat with the remaining coated truffles. Continue to coat a few truffles at a time and
roll them in the cocoa. As you get faster, you can increase the
number you coat before rolling them. As the cocoa-covered
truffle coatings set, or when the cocoa bed gets too crowded,
transfer the truffles to a plate or another tray.

FORK-DIPPING METHOD: WITH GARNISHES OR SPRINKLING Line
a baking sheet with parchment or wax paper. Have ready any
garnishes or toppings, such as slivers of candied ginger or candied citrus peel, chopped nuts, dried fruit, chopped chocolate
or chocolate shavings, or cocoa. Melt and temper the chocolate for the coating (see pages 310–313). One at a time, place
each truffle center in the tempered chocolate and submerge it
by pushing it under the surface with the tines or the loop of the
dipping fork. Slip the fork or loop under the center and lift it out
of the chocolate. Quickly, with a little upward jerking motion, lift
the fork up and down several times, touching the truffle lightly
against the surface of the chocolate, to drain excess chocolate
back into the bowl. If the fork has tines, wipe them against the
edge of the bowl before sliding or rolling the truffle onto the
lined sheet; if the fork has a loop, hold the loop close to the lined

pan and flip it over to turn out the truffle. Before the chocolate sets on the truffles, top them with the chosen garnish. Place the truffles in front of a fan to set.

THREE-FINGER-DIPPING METHOD This is just like fork dipping, but it is done with your fingers. Prepare a baking sheet, garnishes, and tempered chocolate as for fork dipping. Place a truffle center in the tempered chocolate and use your middle and index fingers to submerge and push the center around in the chocolate until it is thoroughly coated. Leaving the center in the chocolate, wipe the excess chocolate from your fingers on the side of the bowl. Using a little upward jerking motion, pick up the truffle with the two wiped fingers and your thumb, shake off the excess chocolate, and place the truffle on the lined baking sheet. Garnish as desired and place the truffles in front of a fan to set.

PLASTIC-SPOONS METHOD Prepare a baking sheet, garnishes, and chocolate as for the fork-dipping method. Use two plastic spoons. Drop a truffle into the chocolate and push it under with one of the spoons. Lift the truffle from the chocolate and pass it back and forth between the spoons two or three times (quickly) to remove excess chocolate. Each time you pass the truffle from one spoon to the other, scrape excess chocolate from the empty spoon using the back of the spoon holding the truffle. Place the truffles on the lined baking sheet. Garnish as desired and place the truffles in front of a fan to set.

REDISCOVERING CHOCOLATE MOUSSE

The bar of plain dark *chocolat à croquer* ("eating chocolate") from the *épicerie* tasted pretty good to me in the early 1970s. It was nicely bittersweet, and I, like everyone else in France, bought it for both eating and cooking. A basic recipe for chocolate mousse was printed on the wrapper.

Chocolate mousse was a classic dessert served in simple French restaurants and cafés and frequently made at home as well. Americans thought it very elegant, but chocolate mousse was the chocolate pudding of France, savored by children and adults alike. *Mousse* simply means "foam." I recall my delight in discovering that shaving cream was called *mousse à raser,* that the curving ripple of froth at the edge of the surf was also *mousse,* and that sparkling wines were described as *mousseux* ("foamy" or "bubbly"). Linguistic discovery was one of the simple pleasures of learning French in France.

Chocolate foam, then. Creamy and smooth, but foamy. A mousse could be dense foam or light fluffy foam, but foam it was. Not pudding, not cream, not custard. Foam—it was supposed to have tiny air bubbles in it. The recipe on the chocolate wrapper had only four ingredients, with instructions to melt the chocolate with coffee or water (it was OK to add some brandy too), whisk in egg yolks, and then, to lighten it, fold in egg whites, beaten *en neige* ("into snow"). Divide among dessert glasses, chill, and serve. Top with whipped cream (*crème chantilly*) if desired. Grandma, if yours was French, used to make it. It didn't have butter in it, or cream (unless you count the topping), and I don't recollect

adding sugar. All the flavor and sweetness of the mousse came from the perfectly satisfactory bar of dark chocolate.

What happened to that minimal but delicious old-fashioned chocolate mousse?

In France, chocolate mousse got more complex when it began keeping fancier company. It appeared as the signature of a new, more modern school of pâtisserie, at the vanguard of which were Le Nôtre in Paris and Yves Thuriès in Cordès, in the form of a filling for very elegant multilayered desserts. Mousse has a lighter texture but deeper chocolate flavor than classic buttercream, and chefs could pile it higher. At least one venerable establishment was accused (by jealous competitors?) of discovering how to sell "air" at a high price, as foamier fillings edged out denser creams and custards. Then came the many and sometimes splendid variations on the simple mousse. Additions of butter and/or cream multiplied the flavor and texture possibilities enormously.

What happened to chocolate mousse in America was less sublime. Sweeter chocolate, more and more sugar, and the frequent and frightful addition of gelatin destroyed the poetry of a simple but magnificent bittersweet chocolate dessert-in-a-dish.

Then, even as the American palate began to appreciate better and more intense chocolate, the specter of salmonella raised havoc. Culinary classics that contained uncooked eggs were abandoned (or went underground). Real chocolate mousse and real Caesar salad took a big hit. Magazines refused to publish recipes using uncooked eggs; book publishers and cookbook authors hedged by printing disclaimers. Some chefs tried to salvage recipes by pouring a little hot sugar syrup over the eggs, although this does not usually heat them adequately. Valid or not, such revisions made recipes more complicated and often sweeter. My own early attempts to reinvent a chocolate mousse recipe required thirty-eight steps (or so it seemed), an eagle eye, and the hands of a surgeon. Even I didn't enjoy making mousse very much anymore. The simplest and best chocolate dessert had become a real pain in the neck.

Now some people have returned to eating uncooked eggs, although there is a lingering belief that they are not entirely safe for young children, the elderly, or people with immune deficiencies. I still taste raw batter and I will eat an authentic Caesar salad if the right person makes it with good farm eggs, but I hesitate to serve uncooked eggs to unknowing guests or the public.

However, I so missed simple old-fashioned chocolate mousse, especially with chocolate becoming ever more interesting and extraordinary. I was back in the kitchen trying once again to make a simple egg-safe chocolate mousse when my brother, Albert, arrived. And it was his birthday. Imagine a former ice cream lover who had recently developed a severe lactose intolerance. I had a new mousse idea ready to test when I realized that the cream in it was going to be a problem for the birthday boy. So I tried something else. I made the mousse by replacing the cream with water. I ate mine with whipped cream on top; Albert didn't. Both of us loved the superb light texture and the clean deep chocolate flavor of mousse made with water! I should have known. After all, what had I done but accidentally rediscover (and reorganize) *mousse au chocolat à l'ancien*: old-fashioned French chocolate mousse. Again I was reminded that the simplest things are often the best, that the flavor of chocolate is truest when it is not mixed with dairy products. The cream on top? A perfect way to accentuate the bittersweet chocolate flavor.

With Albert's "water mousse," I returned to square one, back to the most basic chocolate mousse. From there, I tried new variations made with cream, and even crème fraîche, and with butter. Each affects the flavor and texture in various pleasing ways, offering the cook and chocolate lover room to play.

Meanwhile, the breakthrough that eliminated thirty-six (forgive the exaggeration) of thirty-eight "safe-egg" mousse-making steps was the realization that the eggs did not need to be separated and the whites and yolks heated separately. It is easier to heat whole eggs, with water and sugar added, to 160°F. They are less likely to scramble, and they whip to a foam sturdy enough to fold into melted chocolate without deflating.

The recipes for Albert's Mousse (page 124) and Chocolate Marquise (page 128) include the heated safe-egg technique, but if you have fresh farm eggs or are confident in the quality of your eggs, you can skip that step. Just beat the eggs with the sugar and salt (omit the water) for 4 to 5 minutes at high speed until they have the texture of softly beaten whipped cream. Or, do it the classic way: Separate the eggs and whisk the yolk into the chocolate base with the salt. Whip the whites (with ⅛ teaspoon cream of tartar) until they hold a soft peak when the beaters are lifted, then beat in the sugar to make a stiff-but-not-dry meringue. Then carry on with the recipe.

Once I'd developed the new mousses, Maya Klein asked, "Have you tried baking them yet?" Voilà, warm mousse, exquisitely pure and elegant. And the whole egg-heating step was eliminated!

I still love chocolate mousse, whether it's simply spooned from a little dessert glass or layered into an elegant dessert. The recipes that follow include the "safe-egg" method where appropriate (you will need a thermometer), with an option for fresh farm eggs.

PHOTOGRAPH ON PAGE 144

ALBERT'S MOUSSE

This is a lovely light (and nondairy if you want it to be) chocolate mousse with intense chocolate flavor. It is the lightest mousse of all if you make it with water or coffee. Milk or cream adds a little body. Either way, you can top it with whipped cream, unless you are serving Albert himself. If you are using fresh farm eggs or are confident about the quality of your eggs, you can use the fresh-egg method instead of the heated (egg-safe) procedure. / **Makes about 4 cups; serves 6 to 8**

SPECIAL EQUIPMENT

Instant-read thermometer

Six to eight 4- to 6-ounce ramekins or dessert cups

INGREDIENTS

6 ounces (170 grams) 54% to 62% chocolate, finely chopped (see Chocolate Notes)

¼ cup water, coffee, or milk, or ½ cup heavy cream

1½ tablespoons brandy, rum, or liquor of choice (optional)

3 large eggs, at room temperature

3 tablespoons (38 grams) sugar

Pinch of salt

3 tablespoons water

Lightly sweetened whipped cream or Cocoa Bean Cream (page 251; optional)

DIRECTIONS

• Place the chocolate and the ¼ cup water (or liquid of your choice) in a medium stainless steel bowl in a wide skillet of barely simmering water. Stir frequently until the chocolate is nearly melted. Remove the bowl and stir until completely melted and smooth. Stir in the liquor, if using, and set aside.

• For the heated (egg-safe) method: In a medium stainless steel bowl, whisk the eggs with the sugar and salt until well blended. Whisk in the 3 tablespoons water. Set the bowl in a skillet of barely simmering water and stir with a heatproof silicone spatula, sweeping the bottom and sides of the bowl continuously, to prevent the eggs from scrambling. Continue until the eggs register 160°F on an instant-read thermometer. (You will have to remove the bowl from the skillet to check the temperature unless you are agile enough to both stir and hold and read the thermometer at the same time!) For safety, rinse the thermometer in the hot skillet water between readings. Remove the bowl and beat with an electric mixer at high speed for 3 to 4 minutes, until the eggs have a texture like softly whipped cream.

- For the fresh-egg method: Whip the eggs, sugar, and salt—without the water or heating step—at high speed for 4 to 5 minutes, until the eggs have a texture like softly whipped cream.

- Fold about one-quarter of the eggs into the chocolate. Scrape the chocolate mixture onto the remaining beaten eggs and fold just until evenly incorporated. Divide the mousse among the ramekins.

- Chill for at least 1 hour, or until set, before serving. If you are not serving the mousse within a few hours, cover the ramekins with plastic wrap.

- Serve topped with the whipped cream, if desired.

CHOCOLATE NOTES

To use higher-percentage chocolate, adjust the recipe as follows.

To use 64% to 66% chocolate:
Use 5 ounces (140 grams) chocolate. Increase the sugar to ¼ cup (50 grams). If you are using water, milk, or coffee, add 1 tablespoon (14 grams) unsalted butter in the melting step.

To use 70% to 72% chocolate:
Use 4½ ounces (130 grams) chocolate, and increase the sugar to ⅓ cup (65 grams). If you are using water, milk, or coffee, add 2 tablespoons (30 grams) unsalted butter in the melting step.

WARM BITTERSWEET MOUSSE

Baking transforms chocolate mousse in wonderful subtle ways, deepening its flavor and making it more melt-in-your-mouth. It also allows you the luxury of eating warm chocolate mousse straight from the cup it was baked in, garnished with whipped cream or Cocoa Bean Cream, fresh berries, or nothing at all. Baking eliminates the egg-heating step, and the extra three tablespoons of water necessary to accomplish it, but otherwise these two recipes are the same!

The mousses can be prepared ahead and refrigerated for as long as overnight before baking. And the baked mousses are also delicious served cold. / Makes about 4 cups; serves 6 to 8

SPECIAL EQUIPMENT

Six to eight 4- to 6-ounce ramekins or dessert cups

Instant-read thermometer

INGREDIENTS

6 ounces (170 grams) 54% to 62% chocolate, finely chopped (see Chocolate Notes)

¼ cup water, coffee, or milk, or ½ cup heavy cream

1½ tablespoons brandy, rum, or liquor of choice (optional)

3 large eggs, at room temperature

3 tablespoons (38 grams) sugar

Lightly sweetened whipped cream or Cocoa Bean Cream (page 251; optional)

DIRECTIONS

• If you are planning to bake the mousse right away, position a rack in the lower third of the oven and preheat the oven to 325°F. Put a kettle of water on to boil.

• Place the chocolate and water (or liquid of your choice) in a medium stainless steel bowl in a wide skillet of barely simmering water. Stir frequently until the chocolate is almost completely melted and smooth. Remove the bowl from the skillet and stir to finish melting the chocolate. Stir in the liquor, if using. Set aside.

• In a medium bowl, whisk the eggs with the sugar until well blended. Beat with an electric mixer at high speed for 3 to 4 minutes, until the eggs have a texture like softly whipped cream. Fold one-quarter of the eggs into the chocolate. Fold in half of the remaining eggs until nearly blended. Add the rest of the eggs and fold just until evenly incorporated. Divide the mousse among the ramekins. (The mousse can be prepared to this point, covered with plastic wrap, and refrigerated for up to 24 hours before baking; bake right out of the fridge.)

• To bake, place the ramekins in a large baking pan. Pull out the oven rack, put the pan on the rack, and carefully pour in enough boiling water to come about halfway up the sides of the ramekins. Slide the rack back in and bake until the center of the mousses registers 155°F on an instant-read thermometer (this will be about 3 minutes after it registers 140°F), 14 to 16 minutes. Remove the pan from the oven and remove the ramekins with tongs. Let the mousses cool for at least 10 minutes before serving hot, or let cool and refrigerate until chilled. If you are not serving the mousse within a few hours, cover with plastic wrap.

• Serve topped with the whipped cream, if desired.

CHOCOLATE NOTES

To use a higher-percentage chocolate, adjust the recipe as follows.

To use 64% to 66% chocolate: Use 5 ounces (140 grams) chocolate. Increase the sugar to ¼ cup (50 grams). If you are using water, milk, or coffee, add 1 tablespoon (14 grams) unsalted butter in the melting step.

To use 70% to 72% chocolate: Use 4½ ounces (130 grams) chocolate, and increase the sugar to ⅓ cup (65 grams). If you are using water, milk, or coffee, add 2 tablespoons (30 grams) unsalted butter in the melting step.

CHOCOLATE MARQUISE

A richer chocolate mousse that includes butter, Chocolate Marquise is excellent on its own and positively glamorous with Caramel Shards (page 202) and Spun Sugar. Because it sets firm enough to slice, it is also perfect for filling a ladyfinger-lined mold or spreading between cake layers. Or top with two contrasting mousses to make Triple Mousses (page 137). If you are using fresh farm eggs or are confident about the quality of your eggs, you can use the "fresh egg" method instead of the heated procedure. / **Makes about 4½ cups; serves 8 to 10**

SPECIAL EQUIPMENT

Instant-read thermometer

Eight to ten 4- to 6-ounce ramekins or dessert cups

INGREDIENTS

8 ounces (225 grams) 54% to 62% chocolate, coarsely chopped (see Chocolate Notes)

8 tablespoons (115 grams/1 stick) unsalted butter, cut into pieces

4 large eggs, at room temperature

¼ cup (50 grams) sugar

Scant ⅛ teaspoon salt

¼ cup water

Lightly sweetened whipped cream or Cocoa Bean Cream (page 251; optional)

Spun Sugar (page 202; optional)

DIRECTIONS

• Place the chocolate and butter in a medium stainless steel bowl in a wide skillet of barely simmering water. Stir frequently until the chocolate is nearly melted. Remove the bowl from the heat and stir until completely melted and smooth. Set aside.

• For the heated (egg-safe) method: In another medium stainless steel bowl, whisk the eggs with the sugar and salt until well blended. Whisk in the water. Set the bowl in the skillet of barely simmering water, and stir with a heatproof silicone spatula, sweeping the bottom and sides of the bowl continuously, to prevent the eggs from scrambling. Continue until the eggs register 160°F on an instant-read thermometer. (You will have to remove the bowl from the skillet to take the temperature unless you are agile enough to both stir and hold and read the thermometer at the same time!) For safety, rinse the thermometer stem in the hot skillet water between readings. Remove the bowl from the skillet and beat the eggs with an electric mixer at high speed for 3 to 4 minutes, or until they have a texture like softly whipped cream.

OPPOSITE: Spun Sugar (page 202) atop Chocolate Marquise.

• For the fresh-egg method: Whip the eggs, sugar, and salt—without the water or heating step—at high speed for 4 to 5 minutes, until the eggs have a texture like softly whipped cream. Fold one-quarter of the eggs into the chocolate.

• Fold in half of the remaining eggs until nearly blended. Add the rest of the eggs and fold just until evenly incorporated. Immediately, before the mousse can begin to stiffen and set, divide it among the ramekins, or use it to fill a cake or other dessert. Chill for at least 1 hour, or until set.

• Serve with whipped cream or Spun Sugar, if desired.

CHOCOLATE NOTES

To use a higher-percentage chocolate, adjust the recipe as follows.

To use 64% to 66% chocolate: Use 6½ ounces (185 grams) chocolate. Increase the sugar to ¼ cup plus 1 tablespoon (60 grams), and the butter to 9 tablespoons (130 grams).

To use 70% to 72% chocolate: Use 7 ounces (200 grams) chocolate. Increase the sugar to ⅓ cup plus 1 tablespoon (80 grams) and the butter to 9 tablespoons (130 grams).

*BITTERSWEET DECEPTION

Although it is not really a mousse, *cake* doesn't begin to do justice to this dense, moist, melt-in-your-mouth bittersweet chocolate dessert. I served bite-sized pieces of it at the James Beard Awards gala one year. I waited until each person tasted before announcing that it was low in fat. Every single guest thought I was either lying or making a predictable joke. Make it at least one day before serving. / Serves 10 to 12

SPECIAL EQUIPMENT

8-inch round cake pan
(not a springform)

INGREDIENTS

5 ounces (140 grams) 54% to 72% chocolate, finely chopped
(see Chocolate Note)

½ cup (50 grams) premium unsweetened cocoa powder (natural or Dutch-process)

2 tablespoons (16 grams) all-purpose flour

1 cup (200 grams) sugar

Pinch of salt

¾ cup plus 2 tablespoons water

1 tablespoon rum or Cognac

1 teaspoon pure vanilla extract

2 large eggs, at room temperature

1 large egg white, at room temperature

Powdered sugar for dusting (optional)

Lightly sweetened whipped cream (optional)

Raspberry puree or fresh raspberries (optional)

DIRECTIONS

• Position a rack in the lower third of the oven and preheat the oven to 350°F. Grease the sides of the cake pan and line the bottom with a round of parchment paper. Put a kettle of water on to boil.

• Place the chocolate in a large bowl and set aside.

• Combine the cocoa, flour, ½ cup (100 grams) of the sugar, and the salt in a small heavy saucepan. Whisk in enough of the water to form a smooth paste, then whisk in the remaining water. Cook over medium heat, stirring constantly (especially around the edges of the pan) to prevent scorching, until the mixture begins to simmer. Simmer very gently, stirring constantly, for 2 minutes. Immediately pour the hot mixture over the chopped chocolate. Stir until the chocolate is completely melted and smooth. Whisk in the rum and vanilla.

- In a medium bowl, beat the eggs, egg white, and the remaining ½ cup (100 grams) sugar with an electric mixer at high speed until nearly doubled in volume, 5 to 6 minutes. The eggs will be very foamy but still liquid rather than thick. One-third at a time, fold the eggs into the chocolate mixture. Scrape the batter into the cake pan and smooth the top.

- Set the cake pan in a large baking pan at least 2 inches deep. Pour enough boiling water into the baking pan to come halfway up the sides of the cake pan. Bake until the cake rises and crusts slightly on top and the surface springs back when gently pressed, about 30 minutes. The cake will still jiggle in the center, like very firm Jell-O, and the interior will still be quite gooey. Remove the cake pan from the water and cool completely on a rack. Cover with plastic wrap and refrigerate overnight before serving. (The cake can be refrigerated for up to 2 days or frozen, wrapped airtight, for up to 2 months.)

- To unmold, run a thin knife around the edges to release the cake from the pan. Cover the top with wax paper and an upside-down plate, invert the cake onto the plate, and peel off the parchment liner. Invert onto a serving platter and remove the wax paper. Refrigerate.

- At serving time, using a fine-mesh strainer, sift a light dusting of powdered sugar over the top, if desired. Serve unaccompanied or with a dollop of whipped cream and/or raspberry puree or fresh raspberries.

CHOCOLATE NOTE

I prefer a bittersweet in the 70% range here, as it delivers the most flavor, but you can use what you like.

BITTERSWEET SEMIFREDDO WITH ROSE CREAM AND SESAME CRUNCH

Lying somewhere between mousse and ice cream (*semifreddo* is Italian for "half frozen"), this creamy dark chocolate concoction topped with rose-scented whipped cream and a sparkly handful of crunchy crushed sesame candy is simple, but sophisticated enough for a holiday dinner party. For a sensational but less exotic dessert, lose the rose water and replace the sesame candy with peanut or almond brittle, toffee, or homemade praline. For the smoothest and creamiest texture, whip the cream far less than you think it should be whipped, fold it quickly (and just until blended) into the chocolate, and get it into the mold without hesitation! / Serves 12 to 14

SPECIAL EQUIPMENT

6-cup loaf pan

Instant-read thermometer

Fine-mesh strainer

INGREDIENTS

FOR THE SEMIFREDDO

10 ounces (285 grams) 70% or 72% chocolate, chopped medium fine (see Chocolate Notes)

1 cup whole milk

5 large egg yolks, at room temperature

½ cup (100 grams) sugar

Scant ⅛ teaspoon salt

1½ cups heavy cream

FOR THE TOPPING

1½ cups heavy cream

¾ teaspoon rose flower water, or more as needed

2½ teaspoons (10 grams) sugar

16 to 18 pieces (100 grams) sesame honey crunch candy, crushed, or about 1 cup (100 grams) crushed purchased nut brittle or toffee or homemade Praline (page 203)

DIRECTIONS

• Spray or wipe the loaf pan with oil and line it with a piece of plastic wrap long enough to overhang the ends.

• Put the chocolate in a medium bowl with a fine-mesh strainer set over it.

• Bring the milk to a simmer in a heavy medium saucepan.

• Meanwhile, whisk the yolks with the sugar and salt in a medium bowl. Very gradually at first, whisk the hot milk into the yolk mixture. Scrape the mixture back into the saucepan and cook over low heat, stirring with a heatproof silicone spatula, sweeping the sides, corners, and bottom of the pan continuously to avoid scrambling the eggs, until the mixture thickens very slightly and registers between 165° and 170°F on an instant-read thermometer.

• Immediately pour the custard into the strainer over the chocolate. Rap the strainer against the rim of the bowl to release as much of the custard as possible without pressing on any bits of cooked egg that might be left behind. Whisk the custard until the chocolate is completely melted and smooth. Set the bowl aside for a few minutes until the mixture is just cool, not cold.

• Whip the cream in a chilled bowl only until it is thickened and barely beginning to hold a shape—when you tilt the bowl, the cream should flow to one side, fluffy but still pourable and not at all stiff. Scrape the cream onto the chocolate mixture and fold carefully but quickly until incorporated. Immediately scrape the mixture into the lined mold. Fold the overhanging plastic wrap over the chocolate and freeze at least until solid, or up to a week ahead.

• Prepare the topping when you're ready to serve: Whip the cream with the rose water and sugar until it thickens. Adjust the sweetness and flavor, adding rose water (if necessary) by the drop, to keep the flavor very subtle. Continue whipping the cream until it holds a good soft shape. Transfer to a serving bowl.

• Unmold the semifreddo on a serving platter. Serve ½- to ¾-inch slices with a dollop of cream and a generous scatter of crushed candy.

CHOCOLATE NOTES

You may simply substitute a lower-percentage chocolate to produce a sweeter dessert, or adjust the recipe as follows.

To use 55% to 60% chocolate:
Decrease the sugar by 2½ tablespoons (31 grams).

To use 62% to 66% chocolate:
Decrease the sugar by 1½ tablespoons (19 grams).

WHITE OR MILK CHOCOLATE MOUSSE

This mousse has the consistency of extra-thick whipped cream rather than the more aerated structure of even the richest classic chocolate mousse. After waxing rhapsodic about the taste and texture of classic chocolate mousse made with eggs, and the use of milk or water instead of cream, why am I backsliding with this eggless recipe loaded with cream? Because white and milk chocolates taste and behave quite differently from dark chocolate in recipes. Years ago I tried a dozen recipes for white and milk chocolate mousses. In recipes that called for eggs, I found the flavors less clean, and I didn't like the sticky, slightly elastic texture caused by the eggs. Cream interfered less with the flavors of the chocolate and improved the texture.

On the face of it, the recipe is no more than whipped cream folded into chocolate, but there are critical details that ensure that the mousse turns out with a perfectly smooth rather than grainy texture. Melting the chocolate first with water (or another liquid) to loosen it is essential, and then you must positively restrain yourself when whipping the cream: it must be so soft that you are certain it can't be right—but it is.

Made with white chocolate, this mousse is perfect with tart sweet berries or stone fruits. Both the white and milk chocolate versions invite simple flavor variations, including infusions, and experimentation. Serve the mousse in dessert glasses, or use it as a filling for cakes and desserts. If you want to use the mousse to fill cake layers, or as an element in a composed dessert, have everything else ready, then prepare the mousse immediately before you need it to assemble the finished product. The mousse begins to set very quickly and the texture is damaged if you spread or stir or move it after it has begun to set. / Makes 4 cups; serves 6 to 8

INGREDIENTS

9 ounces (255 grams) white or milk chocolate, finely chopped

6 tablespoons water (or half water and half eau-de-vie, brandy, or other liqueur)

1½ cups heavy cream

DIRECTIONS

• Place the chocolate and water in a medium stainless steel bowl. Bring 1 inch of water to a simmer in a wide skillet. Turn the burner off (if your stove is electric, remove the skillet from the burner) and wait for 30 seconds, then set the bowl of chocolate in the hot water. Stir constantly until the chocolate is melted and smooth. White chocolate is especially fragile and burns easily; do not turn the heat on again under the skillet unless absolutely necessary. Remove the bowl of chocolate from the hot water. Or, melt the chocolate with the water in a microwave on Low (30%) power for about 3 minutes. Stir until completely melted and smooth.

• Let the chocolate cool to about 85°F (a small dab on your upper lip should feel slightly cool, not cold). If the chocolate mixture is too cold, the mousse may turn out grainy; if necessary, set the bowl in the pan of warm water for a few seconds before the next step.

• Whip the cream in a medium bowl only until it is thickened and barely beginning to hold a shape—when you tilt the bowl, it should flow to one side, fluffy but still pourable and not at all stiff. Scrape the cream into the bowl of chocolate and fold carefully but quickly just until the two are incorporated. The mousse should seem too soft; it will firm up later. Immediately, while the mousse is still soft, divide it among dessert glasses or spoon into a serving bowl. Cover and chill until set, at least an hour; longer if it is in a single large dish.

VARIATIONS

Gianduja Mousse   Make the mousse with 9 ounces (255 grams) gianduja (milk chocolate with toasted hazelnut paste; see Sources, page 317) and reduce the water to ¼ cup. Top with lightly sweetened whipped cream and chopped toasted hazelnuts.

Mocha Mousse   Make the mousse with milk chocolate and substitute freshly brewed espresso for the water, or add 4 teaspoons instant espresso powder to the water. Top each serving with an espresso bean.

White Chocolate Mousse with Fresh Mint   Start a day ahead.

Stir ¾ cup (20 grams) lightly packed coarsely chopped unsprayed mint leaves into the cream. Cover and refrigerate overnight. Strain and reserve the cream, pressing gently on the leaves in the strainer to release as much cream as you can; discard the leaves. Proceed with the recipe.

White Chocolate-Citrus Mousses Citrus zest adds welcome sparks of flavor to sweet white chocolate. Use organic, or at least unsprayed, fruit if possible. You can play around by combining flavors as marmalade makers do, using a mélange of several fruit peels. A combination of pink grapefruit and blood orange is lovely, for example. Citrus peels are most aromatic in their season, which is winter and early spring. My first inclination was to use a little of the acidic fruit juice, as well as the zest, just as I do in White Chocolate-Lemon Truffles (page 119). The truffles are successful, but citrus juice curdles the whipped cream in the mousse and ruins its texture. So I've resorted to liqueur instead!

Orange or Blood Orange: Use white or milk chocolate. Substitute ¼ cup Grand Marnier or Cointreau for ¼ cup of the water and add 1 teaspoon lightly packed finely grated orange zest.

Lemon, Lime, or Grapefruit: Use white chocolate. Substitute ¼ cup white rum, vodka (try one infused with citrus), tequila, or gin for ¼ cup of the water and add 1 teaspoon lightly packed finely grated zest.

TRIPLE MOUSSES

It's fun to play with three mousses in one dessert. The key to greatness, whether it is an individual serving or a large cake, is to use much more of the darkest, most intense chocolate mousse as an anchoring flavor on the bottom, and top it with lesser amounts of the two lighter, sweeter mousses. I like the dark layer to have a different texture from the others. Here, bittersweet Chocolate Marquise is topped with layers of Gianduja Mousse and White Chocolate–Orange Mousse. But you could substitute Mocha Mousse or Milk Chocolate–Orange Mousse for the gianduja and use plain White Chocolate Mousse for the top, and so forth. Prepare each mousse just before using it.

Instead of individual desserts, you can make one large dessert. A full recipe of each mousse will fill a chocolate-lined pan, as for Strawberry Celebration Cake (page 167), or simply an 8-inch springform pan lined with a plastic strip, also described in the Celebration Cake recipe.

/ **Makes 8 to 10 servings**

INGREDIENTS

2 ounces (55 grams) of the same (or any other) chocolate used for Chocolate Marquise, finely chopped, if using dessert rings

½ recipe Chocolate Marquise (page 128)

⅓ recipe Gianduja Mousse (page 135)

⅓ recipe White Chocolate–Orange Mousse (page 136)

Ruffled chocolate fans (see page 196), chocolate cigarettes (see page 199), strips of candied orange peel (store-bought), or caramel-glazed hazelnuts (see page 203) for decoration

SPECIAL EQUIPMENT

Eight to ten 2-inch dessert rings (see Note) or 5- to 6-ounce martini glasses or parfait glasses

DIRECTIONS

• If using dessert rings, melt the chocolate in a medium stainless steel bowl set in a wide skillet of barely simmering water, stirring frequently until the chocolate is almost completely melted and smooth. Remove from the heat.

• Meanwhile, cut ten 3-inch squares of foil and trace a 2-inch circle on each; lay the foil on a cookie sheet. Divide the melted chocolate among the foil squares, spreading it to cover each traced circle. Set a dessert ring over each chocolate circle. Refrigerate to harden the chocolate. If not using rings, set out martini or parfait glasses.

continued

• Prepare the Chocolate Marquise. If using rings, fill each one almost half full—there is no need to make an even layer. (Leftover marquise can be refrigerated and nibbled on later.) If using glasses, divide all of the marquise evenly among them. Refrigerate the rings or glasses.

• Prepare the Gianduja Mousse. Spoon it neatly into the rings, leaving room for the final mousse. (Scrape any extra mousse into the bowl with the leftover marquise.) If using glasses, divide all of the mousse equally among them, on top of the marquise.

• Prepare the White Chocolate–Orange Mousse. Fill the rings, heaping the mousse slightly above the top, then use a metal icing spatula to spread the mousse level in each ring. (Add any leftover mousse to the others.) If using glasses, simply divide all of the mousse among them, on top of the gianduja. Refrigerate for at least 1 hour, or until set, before serving.

• The mousses are served in their glasses, or unmolded from the rings as follows: Pick up one dessert ring and peel off the foil. Set it on a serving plate. Warm the ring carefully with a hair dryer, or wrap a wrung-out hot wet washcloth around it, then pull the ring off the mousse. Repeat until all of the mousses are unmolded.

• Serve each mousse topped with a chocolate fan or cigarette, a strip of orange peel, or a caramelized hazelnut, if desired.

Note: Rings this size hold ½ cup mousse; if your rings are larger, count on fewer servings. You can figure out how much mousse you need for any size ring by lining one with foil and measuring how much water it holds filled to the top. Multiply by the number of rings you want to fill, and consult the yield of each mousse recipe.

LOOKING FOR THE PERFECT CHOCOLATE MERINGUE

I've always liked plain white, crisp, light meringue. I like to treat it in ways that offset its extraordinary sweetness, either by contrasting it with fillings or sauces or by adding something to the meringue to make it flavorful and interesting even before it is filled.

For years I looked for the perfect chocolate meringue. Every now and then I'd try adding different amounts of cocoa or comparing natural versus Dutch-process cocoa. But I never was happy with the results, so I always returned to plain meringue, to which I'd sometimes add nuts or powdered espresso.

Finally I realized that the perfect chocolate meringue would be plain white meringue with loads of ground bittersweet or semisweet chocolate in it. Use your favorite dark chocolate. Try the nutty variation too.

Some bakers make meringues with powdered sugar or with half powdered and half granulated sugar. I use only granulated sugar, because I do not like the flavor or texture of the cornstarch in the powdered sugar. This is also why I do not add cornstarch to my nutty meringues, as some do. To ensure that meringues made with granulated sugar (and without starch) will be tender rather than hard or tough, it is essential that some of the sugar remain undissolved. Yes, undissolved. If the meringue is beaten long enough for all of the sugar to dissolve—as cookbooks sometimes instruct—the results can be as hard as china plates. Folding a portion of the sugar in by hand after the meringue is beaten stiff is a simple way to ensure that some of the sugar remains undissolved. In the recipes that follow, the tenderizing sugar is folded in with the chocolate. Easy.

Good meringues are a dessert maker's secret stash. Make layers in advance and store them airtight (they keep for at least two months). Then, for a fast, easy dessert, fill them with whipped cream and berries, or buttercream, or ice cream, or use them to make an elaborate pâtisserie-style dessert by stacking them between layers of liqueur-moistened génoise and buttercream. You pick the flavors and build the layers as high as you like.

CHOCOLATE MERINGUE

The secret to great chocolate meringue is chocolate—finely ground with some of the sugar and folded into plain meringue. The results are far more flavorful than meringue made with cocoa, and you can choose any chocolate you love, of any percentage, including unsweetened chocolate (though you might want to use a bit less of it). Milk chocolate is delicious too. If there are interesting or exotically flavored bars (lavender, coconut, espresso, curry, citrus, chiles . . .) that you love out there, don't hesitate to try them! / **Makes two 9-inch meringues, three 7-inch meringues, or twenty-four 2½- to 3-inch meringues**

INGREDIENTS

5 ounces (140 grams) dark or milk chocolate, coarsely chopped (see Chocolate Note)

⅔ cup (135 grams) sugar (see Note)

3 large egg whites, at room temperature

⅛ teaspoon cream of tartar

⅛ teaspoon salt

1 to 2 tablespoons (6 to 10 grams) premium unsweetened cocoa powder (optional)

SPECIAL EQUIPMENT

Large pastry bag fitted with a ⁷⁄₁₆- to ⅜-inch plain tip (Ateco #5) (optional)

DIRECTIONS

• Position a rack in the center of the oven and preheat the oven to 200°F. Line a large baking sheet with parchment paper and use a heavy pencil to trace two 9-inch circles or ovals on the paper. (Or, if you want to make a smaller but taller dessert, trace three 7-inch circles. For about a dozen individual desserts, trace 24 or more 2½- to 3-inch circles.) Turn the paper over so that the pencil marks cannot transfer to the meringue.

• Pulse the chocolate with about one-third of the sugar in a food processor, until it looks like fine crumbs. Set aside.

• In a clean, dry bowl, beat the egg whites, cream of tartar, and salt on high speed (medium speed if using a heavy-duty stand mixer) until soft peaks form when the beaters are lifted. Gradually beat in the remaining sugar, taking 1 to 1½ minutes. The meringue should stand in very stiff dull peaks when the beaters are lifted. (Remove the bowl if using a stand mixer.)

• Pour all of the ground chocolate mixture over the meringue and fold it in with a large rubber spatula just until incorporated. If you are using a pastry bag, scrape the meringue into the bag. Starting at the center of one of the traced circles, pipe an ever-widening spiral of meringue

CHOCOLATE NOTE

No alterations are necessary for different percentage chocolates. The ground-up chocolate remains in the form of tiny flecks rather than mingling or melting into the other ingredients, so you can make your choice based on flavor alone. I like to use 70% chocolate since the meringue is so sweet.

(counterclockwise if you are right-handed) to cover the entire circle. Or, scrape half of the meringue (or one-third if making 3 layers, or a dollop if making small meringues) into the center of each traced circle and spread it evenly with a spatula. Use a fine-mesh strainer to sprinkle the tops of the meringues lightly with cocoa, if desired.

• Bake for 2 hours. Turn off the oven and let the meringues cool completely in the turned-off oven. Store in an airtight container for up to 2 months.

Note: The granulated cane sugar that I use (C&H) is visibly finer than ordinary table salt, and I have not found it necessary to use extra-fine or special bakers' sugar for making meringues. However, you can substitute either of those with confidence, or you can process regular granulated sugar in a food processor for a few seconds if it seems too coarse.

VARIATIONS

Nutty Chocolate Meringue   Reduce the chocolate to 4 ounces (115 grams). Pulse the chocolate (without any sugar) to the size of crumbs. Scrape into a bowl. Pulse ½ cup (1¾ ounces/50 grams) walnut or pecan halves or pieces with one-third of the sugar until fine. Add to the ground chocolate. Proceed with the recipe.

White Meringue   Sometimes plain is still best. Properly made plain white meringue is lighter and stiffer than chocolate meringue, so it holds tall, dramatic, or sharply defined shapes with ease. Use it for Carmen Meringay (page 183) or other inventive meringue shells, or whenever crisp classic meringue is needed.

Omit the chocolate and the food processor step. Set aside one-third of the sugar. Beat the remaining sugar into the egg whites as directed. Fold in the reserved sugar and proceed as directed in the recipe.

CHOCOLATE MERINGUES WITH BERRIES AND CREAM

These are always delightful and simple as can be. If you use the Nutty Chocolate Meringue, try walnuts with strawberries, or toasted hazelnuts with blackberries.

Although you should assemble this dessert within an hour of serving, you can have all of the elements ready: Rinse and pat the berries dry, and whip the cream and sugar in advance. Keep berries and cream in the fridge until needed, and give the cream a few strokes of the whisk just before using to reincorporate any liquid that has separated. / Serves 12

INGREDIENTS

2 cups heavy cream

2 tablespoons (25 grams) sugar, or more to taste

1 teaspoon pure vanilla extract

Chocolate Meringue (page 141) or Nutty Chocolate Meringue (page 142): twenty-four 2½- to 3-inch meringues to make 12 individual desserts or two 9-inch meringues to make one large dessert

2 pints berries, rinsed and patted dry

Powdered sugar for dusting (optional)

SPECIAL EQUIPMENT

Large pastry bag fitted with a medium star tip, such as Ateco #856 (optional)

DIRECTIONS

• Whip the cream with the sugar and vanilla until almost stiff. Cover and refrigerate until ready to use.

• Set aside the best-looking meringue(s) for the top. Spread or pipe about two-thirds of the cream over the other meringue(s) and distribute most of the berries over it. Spread or pipe the remaining cream over the berries and top with the remaining meringue layer(s). Scatter the extra berries on top and sieve a little powdered sugar over them, if you like.

VARIATION

Strawberry Chocolate Meringues with Cinnamon Ganache Substitute Whipped Mexican Cinnamon Ganache Filling (page 190), chilled but not yet whipped, for the heavy cream, sugar, and vanilla. Use sliced or quartered strawberries. With an electric mixer, beat the chilled ganache until it stiffens to the consistency of very thick, stiff whipped cream. Proceed with the recipe.

MERINGUES GLACÉES WITH THE WORKS

If you are one who dismisses meringues as too sweet, too old-fashioned, or too boring, you have never eaten meringues glacées with whipped cream and chocolate sauce. Nothing quite compares. Imagine light and rich, warm and cold, smooth and crunchy, sweet and tart, all at the same time. The first time I tried one, I had just eaten cassoulet in a small town renowned for that dish and was so full I had no business even looking at dessert. But there it was on the plate. Melting. It appeared unassuming—it wasn't even served with chocolate sauce—and I didn't expect much. That was more than forty years ago, and I still remember it.

Here's a new twist, with ice cream and chocolate sauce, and berries too. / Serves 12

INGREDIENTS

1 quart ice cream (vanilla, chocolate, coffee, or any favorite)

Chocolate Meringue (page 141) or Nutty Chocolate Meringue (page 142): twenty-four 2½- to 3-inch meringues to make 12 individual desserts or two 9-inch meringues to make one large dessert

Lightly sweetened whipped cream

Alice's Chocolate Sauce (page 241), warmed

1 to 2 pints berries, rinsed and patted dry

DIRECTIONS

• Soften the ice cream in the refrigerator for 15 to 20 minutes, or in the microwave with 10-second bursts. It should be just pliable but not melting.

• For individual meringues, spoon 3 to 4 tablespoons of ice cream over the top of one meringue and level it with a spatula, then press a second meringue gently on top. Immediately place on a baking sheet in the freezer. Continue until you have used all of the meringues. For one large dessert, spread all of the ice cream onto one meringue and top with the second layer. To avoid breakage, rotate the top layer gently to seat it rather than pressing it.

• Freeze the meringue(s) for several hours, until firm. Pipe whipped cream around the sides or on top and serve with warm chocolate sauce and berries.

OPPOSITE, CLOCKWISE FROM CENTER: Meringues Glacées with the Works; slices of Queen of Sheba (page 80); Mendiants (page 297); Albert's Mousse (page 124); Chocolate Marquises (page 128).

GÂTEAU DIANE

In the very earliest days at Cocolat, we made a classic dessert called Gâteau Diane. It was just two spiraled layers of tenderly crunchy white meringue sandwiched with buttercream. The sides were encrusted with toasted sliced almonds and the top stenciled with a design in cocoa and powdered sugar. It was simple, rich, and sweet, and it had a small but passionate following. One customer, Mr. R, placed an order for Gâteau Diane most weeks when we offered it and went away looking forlorn when we didn't.

Here it is with bolder flavors and lots more texture. It's still rich and sweet, but even better. I think Mr. R, wherever he is, would approve. / **Serves 10 to 12**

SPECIAL EQUIPMENT

Stencil (optional)

INGREDIENTS

Nutty Chocolate Meringue (page 142): two 9-inch meringues

½ recipe Whipped Chocolate Ganache Filling (page 189), chilled but not whipped

About ½ cup (2 ounces/55 grams) chopped or sliced nuts or chocolate shavings (optional)

Premium unsweetened cocoa powder and powdered sugar for dusting (optional)

DIRECTIONS

• Set the better-looking meringue aside for the top. Beat the chilled ganache with an electric mixer on medium speed just until it stiffens but can still be easily spread. Do not overbeat.

• Immediately spread two-thirds of the filling between the layers, then spread the sides of the cake with the remaining filling and press the nuts into it. Refrigerate to firm the filling.

• For a crunchy dessert, serve within the hour. Otherwise, cover and refrigerate for up to 2 days, allowing the meringue to soften and merge with the filling. If you like, dust the dessert with cocoa or powdered sugar before bringing it to the table.

OPPOSITE, CLOCKWISE FROM TOP LEFT: Raspberry-Laced Chocolate Cupcakes with Marbled Glaze (page 219); Bittersweet Pavé (page 160); Strawberry Celebration Cake (page 167); Tribute Cake (page 171); Gâteau Diane.

ON FLAVORINGS

From making my first chocolate truffles, I learned that the simplest recipes demand the best chocolate. Because they are made with so few ingredients, truffles let the chocolate reveal itself, for better or worse!

As soon as new and more interesting chocolate became available, truffles became even more exciting. Suddenly you could make a dozen batches of "plain" chocolate truffles, each with a different chocolate, and end up with a dozen different truffle "flavors," simply because each chocolate maker selects, roasts, blends, and carries out the process of making chocolate a little differently.

In my cooking classes, we frequently taste and talk about the different flavors in different chocolates. The flavors are often described in terms of other familiar foods, such as almond, toasted nuts, cherry, coffee, vanilla, honey, spices, citrus, and so forth, or with adjectives like *grassy, tannic,* or *fruity.* I am always careful to clarify that I am talking about the natural tastes inherent in the chocolate, flavors that have been nurtured and developed by the farmer and the chocolate maker, rather than those that come from added extracts, oils, or essences. If I am not specific about this, I am sure to be misunderstood, because so many people confuse flavors with flavorings.

Flavorings, in the form of liquids and powders and pastes, are pervasive in the food industry. They are used to "enhance" everything from coffee beans to snack foods, but they are also found in dairy products and natural and organic foods. Whether the flavorings are "natural" or artificial, the food often ends up tasting like a caricature of the real thing. Flavorings corrupt the palate. They distance us from the pure taste of real food made only from real ingredients. Cheese powder comes to mind. How many people mistake the flavor of cheese powder for Cheddar because they were raised on macaroni and cheese from a box?

Years ago I discovered that people who are passionate about chocolate love chocolate first and chocolate with other flavors second, if at all. Of the twelve truffle flavors (rotated each month from a list of more than fifty) always offered at Cocolat, the most popular was plain Dark on Dark: bittersweet ganache dipped in bittersweet chocolate (see Cold Creamy Truffles, page 102). These were never rotated off the menu. But other flavors were also essential to keep our clientele excited and interested.

We flavored truffles in a very simple, rather expensive way. We added good sipping-quality liqueurs and spirits such as Grand Marnier, Myers's rum, and the exquisite high-proof fruit brandies called eaux-de-vie, made by the California craft distiller St. George Spirits. I avoided the bottled extracts, flavorings, compounds, and pastes that were being used increasingly in Europe and even more widely here. I didn't think much about it at the time: they simply didn't taste good enough to me.

Almost a decade after I sold my business, I had an opportunity to see the direction that "fine" chocolates had taken, especially in the hands of large companies. I spent two years tasting and selecting chocolates for a monthly chocolate club. I opened hundreds of boxes and ballotins of fancy filled chocolates and chocolate truffles, looking for the best among them. I found that too many reeked of their flavorings. The aroma of chocolate, if it was there at all, was secondary. I didn't have to take the first bite (although I did) to know that the flavorings would also dominate the taste of the chocolates in an unpleasant way. Most of the commercial filled chocolates and chocolate truffles you buy today are made with flavorings. Even natural flavorings are unnaturally strong, and it is apparently hard to use them with finesse!

Only a small handful of the very best artisan chocolatiers flavor their truffles with pure, real ingredients, yet there is no reason in the world that a home cook can't do the same. In addition to liquors or liqueurs, I like to use freshly grated citrus peel, fresh fruit purees, coffee beans, teas, herbs, even rose petals. One of the most exciting ways to flavor ganache, or any cream-based mixture, is with aromatic ingredients, real ones rather than extracts, steeped in the cream and then removed before the cream is mixed with the chocolate. Some flavors are best when infused overnight in cold cream; others are better steeped in hot liquid. The results are incomparable. Fresh mint from the garden, cold-infused, makes an unforgettable mint truffle. You would have to go far to find something as good in a shop. Freshly grated citrus zest (from organic fruit) added to ganache or steeped in the hot cream, depending on the desired effect, adds a flavor that cannot be matched by even the highly touted citrus oils. These same techniques are used throughout this book

to flavor sauces, mousses, and ice creams with chiles, toasted coconut, vanilla beans, cocoa nibs, and more.

The difference between chocolates or desserts flavored with natural ingredients and those containing artificial flavorings, or even prepared natural flavorings, is the difference between edible poetry and barely palatable advertising jingles. Flavorings and extracts from a bottle are more convenient, but once you've tasted real flavors from real ingredients, convenience doesn't seem so important anymore. Your own truffles can be far better than 99 percent of what can be bought in the marketplace. This I know.

LESS IS MORE

SOUFFLÉS AND OTHER CONFECTIONS

MAXIMIZING THE MINIMUM

If you want great attendance at a healthy cooking class, ask a known chocolate dessert chef to teach it. Before I was invited to do that many years ago, I had never considered making chocolate desserts with less fat or less of anything. When customers asked for something "lighter," I regularly told them to eat a smaller piece. I said that a tiny piece of rich chocolate torte made with superb ingredients would be more satisfying than a big piece of something made of compromises.

At the time, commercial low-fat desserts were unbearably sweet and filled with weird fat "replacers" from industrial food laboratories, modified food starches, and artificial flavors to camouflage it all. Meanwhile, home cooks were learning to replace as well—prune puree for butter, egg whites for egg yolks, dietetic chocolate or nonfat cocoa for the good stuff, and heaven-knows-what for sugar. Results were dismally dry or rubbery.

With the exception of foods inherently low in fat, like fresh fruit, sorbet, or meringues, low-fat dessert choices were more like punishment than pleasure. I wondered if I could make superb chocolate desserts with superb ingredients, but less fat and no compromises. I knew I could at least do better than the current offerings.

I knew I was on the right track after the second class when I saw students oohing and aahing as though they were tasting decadent desserts! And they were excited about serving the new desserts without a disclaimer or even mentioning that they were lower in fat. My lighter desserts were fooling people, including my friends and customers accustomed to the richest fare.

I was hooked. I spent the next two years working on *Chocolate and the Art of Low-Fat Desserts,* for which I won the James Beard Cookbook of the Year Award. Most satisfying, the award was not for the best low-fat book of the year, but for the best cookbook! Almost better still, the work taught me about tasting and flavor, lessons that would change and improve all of my cooking—both lean and rich.

I'd always known, as everyone does, that fat enhances flavors and textures. What I had not known until I worked with a limited fat budget was how fat can also dull and blur flavors and how subtracting some fat can add flavor. What began as a set of strict "takeaways" (less fat) and limitations (fewer calories) turned into positive techniques for creating bigger and better flavors in desserts.

The most important lessons from the low-fat experience are summarized below. If you consider them without limiting your thinking to low-fat recipes, they will enhance your understanding and the quality of everything you cook or bake.

• Quality ingredients are essential in all fine cooking. They are especially important in low-fat recipes. You can't hide any flaws. Bad flavors, poor balance, artificial flavors—all these show up more in a dish with less fat. So if you cut down on fat, you need ingredients with the most and best flavor: good dairy products, fresh nuts, sipping-quality liqueurs (if you use them), and real flavor ingredients. If chocolate, which is inherently high in fat, is to be the starring ingredient, you must choose one with lots of flavor, intensity, and complexity, because you will be limited in how much you can use.

• When too much fat or all the fat is eliminated, a dessert no longer tastes or feels indulgent. (That's when your guests feel like leaving your table and immediately going out for hot fudge sundaes.) You can cut some fat without replacing it, but cut wisely. Most rich chocolate desserts are conveniently loaded with other high-fat ingredients, so you have lots of choices. Different recipes require different strategies, of course, but in general, the idea is to cut the rich ingredients that contribute the least flavor and texture to the dessert.

• Contrast is also a valuable tool. Where and how you use a particular fat in a dessert can make an enormous difference. For example, I like to serve a little dab of real whipped cream as a final touch on my Fallen Chocolate Soufflé Cake (page 82). It's great without the cream, but astonishing with it. This illustrates something valuable to know about chocolate desserts, regardless of how rich or lean they are. Through sheer contrast of color, flavor, and texture, even a little whipped cream intensifies the flavor of chocolate. The impact of this contrast can be more dramatic than using three times the amount of cream blended into the dessert itself. (I use this trick even when I am not intentionally creating reduced-fat desserts.)

• Flavor layering, the opposite of contrast, can add a perception of richness. To reinforce and deepen a flavor, use more than one ingredient to make the statement. Forced to cut down on chocolate, I may add cocoa. I also get different effects by combining different brands of chocolate with different cocoas (both natural and Dutch-process), because all have different flavors.

• Watch out for upstaging the chocolate when creating low-fat chocolate desserts with other assertive flavors. To keep chocolate in the starring role, make sure that other potentially strong notes such as liqueurs, citrus zest, or mint are kept sotto voce or eliminated.

• Finally, desserts made with less fat are less forgiving. Check your oven temperature and pay attention to timing, because these desserts will overbake and dry out faster. Measure carefully (especially dry ingredients) to prevent heavy desserts.

This book is lightly sprinkled with lower-fat desserts (indeed, there is only one in this chapter), but it is even more liberally laced with the lessons about flavor that I learned in creating them. By the time I turned my attention to better-quality chocolates with more distinctive flavors, those lessons were so fully integrated into my baking that I sometimes forgot how effective they can be.

*CHOCOLATE-FLECKED COCOA SOUFFLÉS

I like chocolate soufflés to be more rich and chocolatey than light and ethereal. These push the limits with flavor and richness, even though each has less than 7 grams of fat and only 180 calories. Individual dishes work better than a single large soufflé here; that way each guest gets to enjoy the contrast of crunchy sugared edges and gooey interior without having to share. These come with a do-ahead feature: You can cover and refrigerate the unbaked soufflés for up to a day. Preheat the oven toward the end of the meal, then pop the soufflés in the oven for less than 15 minutes. Voilà! / Serves 8

SPECIAL EQUIPMENT

Eight 4- to 5-ounce ramekins

INGREDIENTS

About 2 tablespoons (25 grams) sugar for coating the ramekins (optional)

½ cup (50 grams) premium unsweetened cocoa powder (natural or Dutch-process)

2 tablespoons (16 grams) all-purpose flour

¾ cup (150 grams) sugar

½ cup 1% milk

2 large eggs, separated

1 teaspoon pure vanilla extract

Pinch of salt

2 large egg whites

⅛ teaspoon cream of tartar

3 ounces (85 grams) 70% to 72% chocolate, finely chopped (see Chocolate Notes)

Powdered sugar for dusting

DIRECTIONS

• If baking immediately, position a rack in the lower third of the oven and preheat the oven to 350°F. Lightly butter the sides and bottom of the ramekins. If you are sugaring them, pour the sugar into one ramekin. Hold it over a second ramekin to catch any spills, and tilt and rotate the sugar-filled ramekin until the bottom and sides are coated with sugar. Tap the excess sugar into the second ramekin. Repeat until all the ramekins are coated, adding more sugar if necessary. Set on a baking sheet.

• In a small saucepan, combine the cocoa, flour, and ½ cup (100 grams) of the sugar. Stir in enough of the milk to form a smooth paste, then stir in the remaining milk. Heat slowly, stirring constantly, until the mixture bubbles slightly around the edges. Continue to cook and stir, scraping the bottom and sides of the pan to prevent scorching, for about 2 more minutes, until the mixture is slightly thickened. Scrape into a large bowl. Whisk in the egg yolks, vanilla, and salt. Set aside.

• In a large clean, dry bowl, beat the egg whites and the cream of tartar with an electric mixer at medium speed until soft peaks form when the beaters are lifted. Gradually add the remaining ¼ cup sugar (50 grams), and continue to beat at high speed until the eggs whites are stiff but not dry.

• Fold about one-quarter of the egg whites into the batter to lighten it. Scrape the remaining egg whites into the bowl and fold just until the egg whites are partially blended. Sprinkle in the chopped chocolate and fold until the egg whites and chocolate are blended. Divide the mixture among the ramekins, filling them nearly full. (The soufflés can be covered with plastic wrap and refrigerated overnight before baking.)

• Place the ramekins on a baking sheet. Without wiping the sugar from the rims, run a fingertip (or a Q-tip) around the inside edges of the cups about ¼ inch into the batter so that the soufflés will rise high and straight. Bake for 15 to 16 minutes (cold soufflés will take a minute or two longer to bake), until the soufflés puff up above the rim of the ramekins and crack on top and a toothpick inserted in the center of each emerges with thick, creamy batter still clinging to it. Do not overbake.

• Using a fine-mesh sieve, sift powdered sugar over the tops, and serve immediately.

CHOCOLATE NOTES

I use natural cocoa, but you can use Dutch-process, if you prefer it.

For the chopped chocolate, you will get the most flavor from 70% or 72% (or even higher) chocolate, but it's OK to choose a lower percentage for a sweeter result. Chocolate chips are acceptable as well, just not as wonderful.

WHEN CHOCOLATE SPEAKS

I used to lead a "chocolate tour" class at the Sur La Table store nearest my house. After my brief lecture on the history of chocolate and the cultivation of cacao, we took a private tour with one of the owners of the original Scharffen Berger Chocolate Maker factory in Berkeley, California. When we returned to the kitchen, I demonstrated three "minimalist" desserts, each made with one of the Scharffen Berger chocolates.

At the outset, I always asked if anyone ever plunked down a small fortune to buy sensational extra virgin olive oil. Many hands would shoot up and there would be smiles and murmurs of pleasure. (I knew my Berkeley audience well.) I would then ask if anyone ever whisked that precious green-gold elixir with mustard and honey and Worcestershire sauce and twenty-seven different herbs and spices to make salad dressing. That is the cue for knowing chuckles and head shaking, because in this rare corner of the world, people understood that such divine oil needs only a splash of good vinegar or a squeeze of citrus, a judicious sprinkling of sea salt, and a grind or two of the pepper mill. We save more complicated recipes for lesser oils. The same is true for chocolate: good distinctive chocolate begs not to be crowded by too many ingredients or overwhelmed with an excess of sugar, butter, or cream.

If, as I originally learned by making chocolate truffles, the simplest recipe calls for the best chocolate, then the reverse is also true: the best chocolate requires the simplest recipe.

A "minimalist" recipe, like the simplest vinaigrette, lets the inherent qualities of the ingredients shine. Sure of myself in this regard, I was unprepared for what happened one day and rudely awakened when the concept was played out to its logical conclusion.

At the end of a class, amid oohs and aahs produced by the Intensely Bittersweet Soufflés (opposite) made with Scharffen Berger chocolate and topped with Cocoa Bean Cream (page 251), one brave woman admitted that the soufflés tasted too tart and bitter. Her daughter, sitting next to her, agreed. My spirits sagged like their two half-eaten soufflés; I could no longer hear the sighs and moans of delight all around me. Someone hadn't loved my dessert? I asked the traitors (very politely) if they had enjoyed the chocolate by itself. They said it was too tart, too bitter. Then I realized that my dessert had not failed: I meant to create a recipe that revealed the chocolate, and I had done it well enough that someone who didn't like the chocolate had not liked the dessert either. (I wanted to shout "Aha!" Actually I did shout "Aha.") I suggested that the two women go home and try the recipe, using *their* favorite chocolate. I knew that the recipe would deliver the flavors they loved best in the chocolate that they loved best. I had made my point after all.

INTENSELY BITTERSWEET SOUFFLÉS

This recipe is positively a showcase for the chocolate you make it with, so you must use a chocolate of distinction. Choose one that you adore eating, one with flavors that beg to be savored rather than masked with excess butter, sugar, or cream. Such a chocolate inspired the recipe in the first place, which, as it has evolved, reads more like mousse (no flour) than a classic soufflé. No matter; it produces a dessert that acts and tastes like a soufflé, and it is easier to make. I make these a day or so ahead and refrigerate them, unbaked, until shortly before I want to serve them. Preheat the oven toward the end of dinner, then bake the soufflés while you clear the table and make the coffee. Expect big chocolate flavor and extravagant praise. / **Serves 8**

INGREDIENTS

About 2 tablespoons (25 grams) sugar for coating the ramekins

8 ounces (225 grams) 70% chocolate, finely chopped (see Chocolate Note)

1 tablespoon unsalted butter

⅓ cup milk

3 large eggs, separated, at room temperature

1 large egg white, at room temperature

⅛ teaspoon cream of tartar

⅓ cup (65 grams) sugar

FOR THE TOPPING

1 cup heavy cream

½ teaspoon pure vanilla extract

1 tablespoon (13 grams) sugar

Powdered sugar for dusting (optional)

SPECIAL EQUIPMENT

Seven or eight 5- to 6-ounce ramekins

DIRECTIONS

• If you are baking the soufflés right away, position a rack in the lower third of the oven and preheat to 375°F. Lightly butter the sides and bottom of the ramekins.

• Pour the sugar into one ramekin. Hold it over a second ramekin to catch any spills, and tilt and rotate the sugar-filled ramekin until the bottom and sides are coated with sugar. Tap the excess sugar into the second ramekin. Repeat until all the ramekins are coated, adding more sugar if necessary.

continued

This is a remarkably versatile recipe. You can substitute a lower-percentage chocolate if you prefer a sweeter, less intense chocolate flavor; or reduce the sugar to ¼ cup (50 grams) to partially compensate for the sweeter chocolate, if desired. There is no need to make other changes in the recipe.

• Place the chocolate, butter, and milk in a large stainless steel bowl in a large skillet of barely simmering water. Stir until the chocolate is melted and the mixture is smooth. Remove the bowl from the water bath and whisk in the egg yolks. (Don't worry if the mixture stiffens slightly or is less than perfectly smooth at this point.) Set aside.

• In a medium dry bowl, beat the egg whites and cream of tartar with an electric mixer on medium speed until soft peaks form when the beaters are lifted. Gradually sprinkle in the ⅓ cup (65 grams) sugar and beat at high speed until the whites are stiff but not dry. Fold one-quarter of the egg whites into the chocolate mixture to lighten it, then fold in the remaining egg whites.

• Divide the mixture evenly among the prepared ramekins, filling each at least three-quarters full. (The soufflés can be prepared to this point, covered, and refrigerated for up to 2 days. Bake directly from the refrigerator.)

• Place the ramekins on a baking sheet. Without wiping the sugar from the rims, run a fingertip (or a Q-tip) around the inside edges of the cups about ¼ inch into the batter so that the soufflés will rise high and straight. Bake until they rise and crack on top and a wooden skewer plunged into the center emerges very moist and gooey (but the centers should not be completely liquid), 14 to 16 minutes, perhaps a minute or so longer if the soufflés have been refrigerated.

• Meanwhile, make the topping: Beat the cream with the vanilla and sugar until it holds a soft shape (or stiffer, if you like it that way). Transfer to a serving bowl and refrigerate until ready to serve.

• When they are done, remove the soufflés from the oven, and serve immediately, with a little powdered sugar sifted over the top, if you'd like. Pass the whipped topping separately.

VARIATION

Intensely Bittersweet Soufflés with Cocoa Bean Cream   Sometimes I top the soufflés with lightly sweetened Cocoa Bean Cream (page 251) instead of plain whipped cream. The effect is sensual and subtle, as opposed to the sharp dramatic contrast with plain whipped cream. It's hard to choose which is better; you will have to try both.

BITTERSWEET ROULADE

Thin flourless chocolate soufflé layers have always been among my favorite and most use-ful "building blocks," whether I am making this simple roulade or the most intricate ten-layer extravaganza. This version was designed especially for 70% chocolate. It yields an intensely flavorful layer (slightly cakey because of the higher percentage of cocoa solids—although there is still no flour in the recipe!) that is not so sweet as what we used to make. / Serves 12

INGREDIENTS

FOR THE BITTERSWEET CHOCOLATE SOUFFLÉ SHEET

6 ounces (170 grams) 70% chocolate, coarsely chopped (see Chocolate Notes)

⅓ cup water or freshly brewed espresso, or 1 teaspoon instant espresso powder (such as Medaglia d'Oro) dissolved in ⅓ cup hot water

1 teaspoon pure vanilla extract

6 large eggs, separated, at room temperature

¼ teaspoon cream of tartar

¾ cup (150 grams) sugar

1 to 2 tablespoons (6 to 12 grams) premium unsweetened cocoa powder

1 cup cream or Cocoa Bean Cream (page 251), chilled but not whipped, with 2 to 3 teaspoons (8 to 12 grams) sugar, or ½ recipe Whipped Chocolate Ganache Filling (page 189)

Premium unsweetened cocoa powder and/or powdered sugar for dusting

SPECIAL EQUIPMENT

11-by-17-inch or 12-by-17-inch jelly-roll or half sheet pan

DIRECTIONS

• Position an oven rack in the lower third of the oven and preheat the oven to 375°F. Line the baking sheet with parchment paper.

• Place the chocolate and water in a large bowl set in a wide skillet of barely simmering water and stir frequently until the chocolate is completely melted and the mixture is smooth. Or microwave on Medium (50%) power for about 1 minute and 15 seconds, then stir until smooth. Stir in the vanilla and set aside.

• Place the egg whites and cream of tartar in a large dry bowl and beat with an electric mixer on medium speed until soft peaks are formed. Gradually sprinkle in the sugar and continue to beat at high speed until the whites are stiff but not dry.

continued

CHOCOLATE NOTES

For this recipe you can substitute a lower-percentage chocolate and simply let the sweetness of the chocolate determine the sweetness of the soufflé sheet. However, you must adjust the amount of water in the recipe (because chocolate with more cacao absorbs more water) and, for the sweeter option, adjust the baking time and temperature.

To use 64% to 66% chocolate: Use ¼ cup water.

To use 54% to 62% chocolate: Reduce the water to 3 tablespoons. Bake the sheet for 10 minutes, then reduce the oven temperature to 350°F and bake for another 5 to 7 minutes, or until the surface of the sheet seems firm to the touch.

• Whisk the yolks into the melted chocolate mixture. Fold one-quarter of the egg whites completely into the chocolate mixture to lighten it. Add the remaining egg whites and fold in gently but completely. Spread the batter evenly in the prepared pan.

• Bake until the cake springs back when pressed lightly with your fingertips and a toothpick inserted into the center comes out moist but not gooey, 8 to 10 minutes. Cool completely in the pan on a rack. (The soufflé sheet can be covered tightly and refrigerated for up to 2 days or frozen for up to 3 months.)

• To unmold, first run a small knife around the inner edges of the pan to release the cake. Using a fine-mesh strainer, sift the 1 to 2 tablespoons cocoa over the surface. Cover with a sheet of foil. Holding the foil and the pan edges together at both ends, invert the pan onto the counter. Remove the pan and peel off the parchment liner.

• Whip the cream or cocoa cream with sugar to taste until nearly stiff. Or, whip the ganache until nearly stiff. Spread the filling evenly over the cake. Starting at one short edge and using the foil to help you, roll up the cake. At first the pastry will crack severely, but the cracking will get less severe as the roulade gets fatter; a little cracking on the finished roulade ends looks like tree bark and is quite appetizing. Wrap the roulade tightly in the foil and refrigerate it for up to a day.

• To serve, unwrap the roulade and transfer it to a platter, seam side down. Using a fine-mesh strainer, sift on a little more cocoa and/or a little powdered sugar.

VARIATION

Bittersweet Pavé (photograph on page 147)   For a dressier cake, cut the soufflé sheet into 6 equal layers and construct a rectangular layer cake with any of the fillings. Omit the cocoa. Glaze or frost with Bittersweet Chocolate Glaze (page 193) or Sarah Bernhardt Chocolate Glaze (page 194).

MELTING CHOCOLATE MERINGUES

Deceptively light and delicately crusted, these cookies are moist and meltingly bittersweet within. Without butter or egg yolks, they are the soul of simplicity, and a nice way to use a distinctive chocolate. / *Makes about thirty 2-inch cookies*

INGREDIENTS

6 ounces (170 grams) 54% to 62% chocolate, coarsely chopped (see Chocolate Notes)

2 large egg whites, at room temperature

⅛ teaspoon cream of tartar

½ teaspoon pure vanilla extract

¼ cup (50 grams) sugar

¾ cup (1⅞ ounces/75 grams) chopped walnuts

DIRECTIONS

• Position the racks in the upper and lower thirds of the oven and preheat the oven to 350°F. Line two cookie sheets with parchment or wax paper.

• Melt the chocolate in a medium heatproof bowl set in a wide skillet of barely simmering water, or in the microwave on Medium (50%) power for 3½ to 4 minutes. Stir frequently until the chocolate is almost completely melted, then remove from the heat or microwave and stir to complete the melting. Set aside.

• In a large bowl, beat the egg whites with the cream of tartar and vanilla until soft peaks form when you lift the beaters. Gradually add the sugar, continuing to beat until the eggs whites are stiff but not dry. Pour the nuts, then all of the warm chocolate, over the egg whites and fold in with a rubber spatula until the color of the batter is uniform. *Do not let the batter wait.*

• Drop tablespoonfuls of the batter at least 1 inch apart onto the cookie sheets. Bake for 8 to 10 minutes, rotating the sheets from front to back and top to bottom about halfway through the baking period. The surface of the cookies should look dry and feel slightly firm but still gooey inside when you press them. Slide the paper pan liners onto racks to cool. Let cool completely before storing. (The cookies are best on the day they are baked, but still delectable for another 2 to 3 days; store in an airtight container.)

CHOCOLATE NOTES

To use a higher-percentage chocolate, adjust the recipe as follows.

To use 64% to 66% chocolate: Use 5 ounces (140 grams) chocolate.

To use 70% to 72% chocolate: Use 4½ ounces (130 grams) chocolate, and increase the sugar to ⅓ cup (65 grams).

RICH HOT CHOCOLATE

You may be surprised that a chocolate recipe labeled "rich" calls for water and milk rather than for all milk or even half milk and half cream. But it's all about the flavor. My goal was to show off the chocolate. Less milk, less creaminess, and less fat allow us to taste more of the complex and subtle flavors that make one chocolate distinct from another. Try this with your favorite chocolate and you will see what I mean. Or, if you want a creamier drink, or one so thick your spoon stands up in it, you can make the obvious changes. If you insist on cream, try serving it whipped on top, rather than stirred in; the contrast will be dramatic and satisfying, and it won't diminish the chocolate flavor.

I often make this in advance—it thickens and becomes more flavorful as it stands—and reheat it using the steamer of my espresso machine. Delicious, and foamy too. / Serves 6 to 8

INGREDIENTS

6 ounces (170 grams) 54% or more chocolate, coarsely chopped (see Chocolate Note)

1½ cups boiling water

1½ cups milk

DIRECTIONS

• Place the chocolate in a small saucepan. Pour about half of the boiling water over the chocolate and stir until the chocolate is melted and smooth. Stir in the rest of the boiling water and the milk. Heat over medium heat, whisking continuously, until hot but nowhere near boiling (the texture and flavor are both best if the hot chocolate never exceeds 180°F). Serve immediately, or set aside and reheat just before serving.

CHOCOLATE NOTE

The chocolate you choose will determine how sweet or intense your results will be. I like it with 70% chocolate. It's always possible to stir in a little sugar to taste or add a little milk or cream if you go overboard with the chocolate percentage!

VARIATIONS

Mocha Hot Chocolate   The recipe invites variations. Make it mocha using only ¾ cup water and adding the other ¾ cup espresso or strong coffee with the milk.

Ancho Chile Hot Chocolate   Dried ancho chiles are also called *pasillas*. They are deep chocolate red and heady with an earthy musk. After seeing the 2001 film *Chocolat* a friend and I came directly home for hot chocolate. From drawers and cupboards, little jars of dried ground chiles were unearthed from past bouts of Indian and Mexican cooking. Between sips of chocolate, we began to inhale from each jar. The anchos beckoned, and we stirred pinches into our cups—just enough to feel the heat. Try it.

Spiced Hot Chocolate   Following the sniffing ritual described above for Ancho Chile Hot Chocolate, experiment with other spices, such as anise, cinnamon, nutmeg, Chinese five-spice, ground vanilla beans, pieces of dried citrus peel, or grated fresh citrus zest. One spice blend will suggest another to you, as they do to me.

GLITZ AND GLAMOUR

GRAND CAKES, FILLINGS, AND GLAZES

DESSERTS WORTH CELEBRATING

The heart and soul of Cocolat were the chocolate truffles and the sleek-looking bittersweet chocolate tortes, exemplified by the Queen of Sheba, beautifully glazed and encrusted with toasted shaved almonds. But there was glitz and glamour on the menu too: special-occasion desserts with complex multiple layers and contrasting textures of génoise and sponge cake, ganaches and glazes, mousses, and meringues. The most memorable were variously wrapped in chocolate, enveloped with halos of spun sugar, topped with ruffled chocolate fans, or gilded with gold leaf. Dream desserts.

Hardly a week goes by without someone in the grocery store, at a party, or on the street reminding me that I (we) made the cake for their wedding, anniversary, or birthday, or all of the above!

From the beginning, however, I never liked cake decorating in the traditional sense, and I still don't. But I did love to design desserts, to choose and plan the construction of the layers, flavors, and textures so that when everything is put together, the result looks spectacular and tastes even better. The engineer and architect buried somewhere in me is still enthralled with the pastry chef's craft—the special effects and fancy feats—and the ingenuity involved in putting it all together.

So, while I normally serve simple desserts at home, I'm still a show-off. I think every cook needs a dramatic, spectacular dessert up his or her sleeve, to pull out on special occasions. One of my favorite pastry chef tricks—because it looks much harder than it is—involves assembling the elements of the dessert in a pan that has been lined with a band of chocolate spread on a plastic strip (see page 169). Once the chocolate liner is in the pan, the assembly is easy. You fill the lined pan with cake layers, fruit, and cream, or layers of cake and mousse, or three different mousses, or ice creams with meringues and sauce; it's entirely up to you. Top the whole affair with a bouquet of ruffled chocolate fans or an arrangement of thin abstract (meaning not so perfect) attempts at ruffled chocolate fans or simple chocolate curls, or just handfuls of fresh berries. When the dessert is unmolded and the plastic strip peeled away to reveal a shiny wall of chocolate, you may gasp involuntarily at the perfection of your own work (as I still sometimes do). The dessert can be prepared ahead, and the whole thing screams for invention. Having done it once, you will do it again and again, perhaps differently each time. Use the mousses and fillings and cake bases and meringues and ices creams from this book as you like, or use favorite components from your own repertoire. Now you are designing desserts and thinking like a pastry chef.

STRAWBERRY CELEBRATION CAKE

PHOTOGRAPH ON PAGE 147

This celebration cake is a chocolate shell filled with rum-splashed cake, ripe strawberries, and whipped mascarpone and cream. But, for the latter, you could use Whipped Mexican Cinnamon Ganache Filling (page 190), crème fraîche, Albert's Mousse (page 124), or Chocolate Marquise (page 128). You could substitute blackberries for the strawberries or omit them altogether. Once you learn the method for lining the pan with chocolate and assembling the layers, you can go wild with flavors and textures. Master the technique for shaving chocolate off a cookie sheet, and you will be in great demand whenever a show-off dessert is needed. / *Serves 14 to 16*

INGREDIENTS

3 ounces (85 grams) 54% to 72% chocolate, chopped medium-fine (see Chocolate Note)

FOR THE SOAKING SYRUP

⅓ cup (65 grams) sugar

⅓ cup water

⅓ to ½ cup rum

2 cups (480 grams) mascarpone cheese

1 cup heavy cream

¼ cup (50 grams) sugar

2 teaspoons pure vanilla extract

Chocolate Génoise (page 187)

About 2 pints ripe strawberries, rinsed, patted dry, and hulled

Ruffled chocolate fans or chocolate ruffles (see page 196)

Powdered sugar for dusting (optional)

SPECIAL EQUIPMENT

26-by-3-inch strip of plastic shelf liner or .005 (or thicker) Mylar or Dura-Lar (see Note)

8-by-3-inch springform pan or cheesecake pan with a removable bottom

Instant-read thermometer

DIRECTIONS

• To line the pan with chocolate: Fit the plastic strip around the inside of the cake pan. Mark and then trim the ends so that it fits exactly, with the ends butted together: it should not overlap at all, nor should there be a gap. Tear off a sheet of wax paper longer than the plastic strip and place it on the counter. Place the plastic strip on the wax paper, with the smoother side facing up.

continued

• Melt the chocolate in a small heatproof bowl set in a wide skillet of barely simmering water, stirring frequently until melted and smooth. Or microwave on Medium (50%) power for about 2½ minutes, stirring once or twice. The chocolate should be 115° to 120°F. If you used a water bath, wipe the bottom of the chocolate bowl dry.

• Pour all of the chocolate in a thick band down the center of the plastic strip from one end to the other. Spread the chocolate evenly with an offset spatula, covering the plastic completely and allowing the excess to run over onto the wax paper. Use the point of a paring knife to locate and lift one end of the chocolate-coated strip. Slip your hand under the strip and hold it by the edges about a quarter of the way from one end. Slide your other hand under the strip and hold it by the edges about a quarter of the distance from the other end. Lift the strip and carefully fit it into the pan, chocolate facing the inside, ends butted together. Repair any gaps in the chocolate caused by your fingers with a little additional chocolate applied with your fingertips or a spatula. Refrigerate the chocolate-lined pan until needed.

• To make the soaking syrup: Combine the ⅓ cup (65 grams) sugar and water in a small saucepan. Stir just to moisten all the sugar, then bring to a simmer for about 2 minutes to dissolve the sugar. Let cool, then add rum to taste.

• Combine the mascarpone, cream, ¼ cup (50 grams) sugar, and vanilla in a large bowl and whip until the mixture holds a good shape—almost stiff peaks.

• Use a serrated knife to cut the chocolate génoise horizontally into 2 layers. Fit the bottom layer, cut side up, into the chocolate-lined pan. Brush the layer with about 3 tablespoons of the rum syrup. Spread half of the cream evenly over the cake layer. Arrange and press the strawberries, lying on their sides, into the cream with a little space between them. Spread enough of the cream between and over the berries to just cover them. Spread a little extra cream about ½ inch up the sides of the pan.

• Moisten the second génoise layer lightly with about 2 tablespoons syrup and fit it, moist side down, in the pan. Press it into place. Moisten the top of the génoise with the remaining syrup and cover with any remaining cream. Cover the pan and refrigerate for several hours or overnight.

continued

CHOCOLATE NOTE

To line the pan and make the ruffles for decoration, you can use an even higher percentage chocolate than called for, but be sure you taste it first so you know what you are getting into. You could even create a variation with white or milk chocolate.

• Remove the sides of the springform pan, or set the pan with the push-up bottom on a canister and pull the sides down and off the cake. (If, as is occasionally the case, there was little or no mascarpone filling left to spread on the top génoise layer, you can either beat a little extra whipping cream and spread it on, or melt 2 ounces bittersweet or semisweet chocolate with 3 tablespoons unsalted butter or cream and spread the cake with the resulting glaze, then add the chocolate sheets or fans.) Set the cake on a serving dish. Carefully peel the plastic strip off the cake. Arrange overlapping chocolate sheets or ruffles on top of the cake to cover the cream, extending beyond the sides of the cake. Refrigerate until ready to serve.

• If desired, using a fine-mesh strainer, sift a little powdered sugar over the top to highlight the chocolate just before serving. Cut with a sharp serrated knife dipped in hot water and wiped dry between slices.

Note: Plastic shelf liner is a flexible plastic sheet with a ribbed side and a smooth side. It is sold on a roll, like Con-Tact paper, in the housewares section of most hardware stores. An 8-inch pan requires a length of at least 26 inches, but if you think that you will make larger chocolate-banded cakes, buy 36 inches instead. The liner is wide enough so you will have some left over in case you don't cut it quite right the first time, with plenty left to cut longer or shorter or wider strips to fit other pans. The strips are reusable. Mylar, which may go by the brand name Dura-Lar, is sold in art supply stores.

TRIBUTE CAKE

Some years ago I collaborated with my friend Flo Braker, a wonderful baker and cookbook author, on an eightieth-birthday cake for Chuck Williams, founder of Williams-Sonoma. The party was a hearty family-style luncheon in Boston, where three hundred members of the American Institute of Wine and Food were gathered for a conference. Flo and I describe the cake we made as "Flo's cake with Alice's goops": four thin layers of Flo's sensational devil's food cake, filled with my light whipped ganache and glazed with my Sarah Bernhardt Chocolate Glaze. Each serving had a handmade fan-shaped chocolate ruffle anchored by a little chocolate medallion with Chuck's name on it.

That cake for three hundred took us days to make and decorate in the bowels of an unfamiliar and not too luxuriously appointed hotel kitchen. We missed a number of the conference activities because we were up to our ears in, well, Flo's batter and my goops. We came up from the depths each day for a stiff drink and a giggle about the adventures below. But when it was finally served, Chuck looked touched, and Julia Child stood up spontaneously to pay her respects. We were thrilled.

Let me try to convey the true brilliance of this cake. The individual elements were excellent, but the idea of putting them together was pure Flo Braker genius. There were three (four, if you count the ruffled chocolate fans) different textures and intensities of chocolate, and they were perfection together. It was very chocolatey but not heavy; rich and yet light. It was a poem. I loved it, and I continue to make it for all kinds of special occasions.

The cake inspired me. I love to take good ideas and use them as a springboard for new and different desserts. But there was one problem here. Flo's cake is the best devil's food I have ever eaten. It is sweet and tender and moist in the best American cake tradition without the equally traditional flavor of overalkalized cocoa (a taste I do not like) that results from too much baking soda. And it happens to go perfectly with the less-sweet European-style fillings and chocolate glazes I like. I admit I tried to improve on the cake, but I just wasn't able to. So I asked Flo if I could publish our cake.

Here it is, with her blessing, the way I make it at home, with three layers to serve 14 to 16 rather than 300. You can prepare the ganache up to four days in advance, and you can assemble the cake up to two days before glazing and serving it. / **Serves 14 to 16**

continued

SPECIAL EQUIPMENT

Three 9-inch round cake pans

9-inch cardboard cake circle

Instant-read thermometer

Decorating turntable or lazy Susan (optional)

INGREDIENTS

FOR THE CAKE

2 cups (200 grams) sifted (before measuring) cake flour

1 teaspoon baking soda

¼ teaspoon salt

½ cup (40 grams) sifted premium unsweetened natural cocoa powder

½ cup lukewarm water

½ cup buttermilk, at room temperature

½ cup water

2 teaspoons pure vanilla extract

2 large eggs, at room temperature

8 tablespoons (115 grams/1 stick) unsalted butter, at room temperature

1 cup (200 grams) sugar

1 cup (170 grams) lightly packed light brown sugar

Whipped Chocolate Ganache Filling (page 189), chilled but not whipped

Sarah Bernhardt Chocolate Glaze (page 194), cooled to frosting consistency

1 ounce (30 grams) white chocolate, melted, for piping the greeting

Ruffled chocolate fans (see page 196) (optional)

3 (unsprayed) roses (optional)

DIRECTIONS

• Position a rack in the lower third of the oven and preheat the oven to 350°F. Line the bottom of the cake pans with rounds of parchment paper.

• In a medium bowl, mix together the flour, baking soda, and salt, then sift onto a sheet of wax paper. In a small bowl, whisk together the cocoa and lukewarm water; set aside to cool. In a glass measure, combine the buttermilk, the remaining ½ cup water, and the vanilla. In a small bowl, whisk the eggs briefly to combine the whites and yolks.

• In a large bowl, beat the butter with an electric mixer for a few seconds, until creamy. Gradually add the sugars and beat until light and fluffy, 6 to 7 minutes. With the mixer on medium, slowly add the eggs, taking about 2 minutes in all. Continue to beat, scraping the bowl as necessary, until the mixture is fluffy and velvety.

• Stop the mixer and scrape in the cocoa mixture, then beat on medium speed just until combined. Stop the mixer, add one-third of the flour mixture, and beat on low speed only until no flour is visible. Stop the mixer and add half of the buttermilk mixture, and beat only until the liquid is absorbed. Repeat with half of the remaining flour, then all of the remaining buttermilk,

and finally the remaining flour. Scrape the bowl as necessary, and beat only enough to incorporate the ingredients after each addition.

• Pour the batter into the pans and spread it level. Bake until the layers spring back slightly when lightly pressed with your fingers and a toothpick inserted in the centers comes out clean, about 20 minutes. Cool the layers on a rack for about 5 minutes before unmolding to cool completely, right side up, on the rack.

• To assemble the cake: Beat the chilled ganache with an electric mixer on medium speed just until it stiffens and holds its shape like very thick whipped cream but can still be easily spread. Do not overbeat.

• Place one cake layer, upside down, on the cardboard cake circle. Spread with half of the ganache. Place the second cake layer upside down on the ganache and press into place. Spread with the remaining ganache and top with the third layer of cake (upside down). Chill the cake for at least 1 hour, or up to 2 days, before glazing it.

• Spread a very thin layer of the cooled glaze over the top and sides of the cake. This layer is called the crumb coat; it is just to smooth the surface, glue on any crumbs, and fill any cracks. Chill the cake for a few minutes to set the crumb coat.

• Set the bowl of the remaining glaze in a pan of barely simmering water and reheat very gently, stirring with a rubber spatula, until it is fluid and shiny; it should be no warmer than 90°F. Center the cake on the turntable or lazy Susan. Have a clean, dry, metal icing spatula ready. Pour all of the glaze over the center of the cake. Working quickly, using just 3 or 4 strokes and rotating the turntable, spread the glaze over the top of the cake so that it runs down to coat the sides. If there are any bare spots left uncoated, use the spatula to scoop up excess glaze and touch it to those spots, but don't spread it: spreading the glaze as it begins to set will make it look dull. Refrigerate the cake immediately, and save the excess glaze.

• After the glaze is set, write a birthday greeting on top of the cake with the melted chocolate and attach the optional chocolate fans to the sides of the cake with the reserved glaze or more melted chocolate. Decorate the cake with the roses, if desired. Refrigerate the cake until about 1 hour before serving.

VARIATIONS

It's hard *not* to play with even a great cake. Whipped ganache is a perfect vehicle for infused flavors: ideas and recipes follow.

Gianduja: Fill the cake with Whipped Gianduja Ganache Filling (page 190) or Gianduja Mousse (page 135). Decorate with toasted hazelnuts (see page 28), shards of toasted hazelnut praline (see page 203), or caramel-glazed hazelnuts with stems (see page 203) instead of chocolate fans.

Espresso: Fill the cake with Whipped Mocha Ganache Filling (page 190) and glaze it with Glace à l'Eau (page 195) made with espresso. Top the cake with Mendiants (page 297) decorated with cocoa nibs.

Canela: Fill the cake with Whipped Mexican Cinnamon Ganache Filling (page 190). Garnish with chocolate cigarettes (see page 199) dusted with cocoa and ground cinnamon to look like cinnamon sticks, or use real cinnamon sticks, dipped halfway in chocolate. Accompany the cake with sliced strawberries or a sauce of pureed strawberries.

Raspberry: Embed ½ pint (4.5 ounces/130 grams) fresh raspberries in the filling between each layer.

JULIA'S CAKE

This is another stunning adult birthday cake. Crème fraîche and eau-de-vie de framboise add an extra dimension and plenty of sophistication to everyone's favorite raspberry-and-chocolate combination. The cake is a kissing cousin to the one that I made on the PBS series *Baking with Julia*. But in this version, instead of a chocolate wrapper and a crown of ruffles, the cake is cloaked with a chocolate glaze. It remains an elegant and dramatic presentation yet tailored enough to serve as a man's birthday cake, especially with deep red roses and your best chocolate script. / Serves 12 to 14

SPECIAL EQUIPMENT

8-by-3-inch springform pan or cheesecake pan with a removable bottom

Instant-read thermometer

Decorating turntable or lazy Susan (optional)

INGREDIENTS

FOR THE SOAKING SYRUP

⅓ cup (65 grams) sugar

⅓ cup water

⅓ cup eau-de-vie de framboise (not sweet raspberry liqueur), or ⅔ cup Chambord (or other sweet raspberry liqueur)

2 cups (480 grams) crème fraîche, chilled

1½ teaspoons pure vanilla extract

One 8-inch Chocolate Génoise (page 187)

3 tablespoons boiling water

4 ounces (115 grams) 60% to 62% chocolate, very finely chopped (see Chocolate Notes)

12 to 16 ounces (340 to 455 grams) fresh raspberries, rinsed and patted dry

Sugar to taste

Sarah Bernhardt Chocolate Glaze (page 194) or Glace à l'Eau (page 195), cooled to the consistency of soft frosting

Ruffled chocolate fans (see page 196) (optional)

2 or 3 (unsprayed) roses (optional)

1 ounce (30 grams) white chocolate, melted, for piping the greeting

DIRECTIONS

• If using eau-de-vie, make a soaking syrup as follows: Combine the sugar and water in a small saucepan. Stir just to moisten all the sugar, then bring to a simmer, and simmer without stirring, about 2 minutes. Let cool, then add the eau-de-vie. If using Chambord or other sweet raspberry liqueur, use it straight—there is no need to make a syrup.

- To assemble the cake: In a medium bowl, beat the chilled crème fraîche with the vanilla until very thick but not stiff. Refrigerate until needed.

- Use a serrated knife to cut the génoise horizontally into 3 layers. Fit the top layer, cut side up, into the bottom of the cake pan. Brush it with up to 3 tablespoons of the framboise syrup or the Chambord. Set aside.

- In a small bowl, pour the boiling water over the chopped chocolate. Whisk until the chocolate is completely melted and smooth. Measure out ¾ cup of the crème fraîche. Immediately fold one-third of it into the chocolate mixture, then fold in the rest. Right away, before the mixture stiffens, spread all of the chocolate crème fraîche evenly over the moistened génoise.

- Moisten a second génoise layer very lightly with up to 2 tablespoons syrup and fit it moist side down into the pan. Press it in place. Moisten the top very lightly. Arrange a layer of berries over the génoise, leaving just a little space around each.

- Fold sugar to taste into the remaining crème fraîche and beat it a little to stiffen it slightly. Scoop the cream onto the berries. Spread and press it over and between them.

- Moisten the third chocolate génoise layer very lightly with up to 2 tablespoons syrup and fit it moist side down into the pan. Press it in place. Moisten the top of the génoise with the remaining syrup. Cover and refrigerate for several hours, or overnight.

- Release and remove the sides of the springform, or set the cheesecake pan on a canister or can of food and pull the sides of the pan down and off the cake. Set the cake on a tray or flat dish. Spread the top and sides with a very thin crumb coating of the glaze. Chill the cake for a few minutes to set the crumb coat.

- Reheat the remaining glaze to just 90°F. Place the chilled cake on a decorating turntable, a lazy Susan, or a rack set over a large tray. Pour all of the glaze over the top of the cake, allowing it to run down the sides. Use a metal icing spatula and as few strokes as necessary to make sure that the cake is completely covered. If there are bare spots left uncoated, use the spatula to scoop up excess glaze and touch it to those spots, but don't spread it (spreading glaze as it cools will cause it to look dull). If desired, press chocolate fans into the sides of the cake before the glaze is completely set; you can also glue the fans on later with warmed leftover glaze. Refrigerate the cake to set the glaze.

- When the glaze is set, decorate the top of the cake with 2 or 3 fresh roses and write "Happy Birthday" with melted white chocolate. Refrigerate until ready to serve.

CHOCOLATE NOTES

To use a lower- or higher-percentage chocolate, adjust the recipe as follows.

To use 54% to 58% chocolate: Use 5 ounces (140 grams) chocolate.

To use 70% to 72% chocolate: Increase the water to 3½ tablespoons, and dissolve 1 tablespoon (13 grams) sugar in it before adding the chocolate. Use 3½ ounces (100 grams) chocolate.

MOLTEN CHOCOLATE–RASPBERRY CAKES

Have you ever ordered one of these sexy little desserts in a restaurant only to find that the anticipated molten center has morphed into cake instead of flowing sauce? Because small desserts are more easily overbaked than large ones, and because baking times vary with different kinds of chocolate, I've concluded that the best and simplest insurance against disappointment (congealed sauce) is the buried-truffle method. During the short time in the oven, the truffle in each small cake melts to form a luscious sauce, while the cake gets fully baked. Although it sounds like a completely separate step, the truffles are actually created with a portion of the cake batter, so the whole process is quite efficient. / Serves 6

SPECIAL EQUIPMENT

Six 6-ounce custard cups or ramekins

INGREDIENTS

Sugar for the custard cups

8 ounces (225 grams) 54% to 62% chocolate, coarsely chopped (see Chocolate Notes)

6 tablespoons (85 grams) unsalted butter

¼ cup (55 grams) strained raspberry puree (from fresh or frozen unsweetened raspberries)

3 tablespoons plus 2 teaspoons (46 grams) sugar

2 tablespoons (12 grams) premium unsweetened cocoa powder (natural or Dutch-process)

2 large eggs, separated

1 large egg white

⅛ teaspoon cream of tartar

Fresh raspberries for garnish (optional)

Powdered sugar for dusting

DIRECTIONS

• Put a pie plate or cake pan in the freezer to chill. Liberally butter the insides of the custard cups, sprinkle with sugar, and tap out the excess.

• Melt the chocolate and butter in a medium heatproof bowl in a wide skillet of barely simmering water, stirring frequently until smooth. Remove the bowl from the skillet. Transfer 5 tablespoons of the chocolate mixture to a small bowl and set aside the rest. Add the raspberry puree and 2 teaspoons (8 grams) of the sugar to the 5 tablespoons chocolate and stir to blend. Scrape the raspberry mixture into a puddle in the chilled pie plate or pan and place in the freezer for 10 minutes or so to firm.

• When the raspberry-chocolate mixture is firm enough to hold a shape, use a teaspoon (or a tiny ice cream scoop) to form it into 6 truffles (they need not be perfectly round). Return the truffles to the freezer.

• Rewarm the remaining chocolate mixture in the skillet of water over low heat until warm to the touch. Remove from the heat and whisk in the cocoa and egg yolks.

• In a dry medium bowl, beat the egg whites and cream of tartar with an electric mixer until soft peaks form when the beaters are lifted. Gradually beat in the remaining 3 tablespoons (38 grams) sugar and continue beating until the whites are stiff and glossy but not dry. Fold about one-quarter of the egg whites into the batter. Scrape the remaining whites into the bowl and fold until blended. Using half of the batter, fill each cup about half-full. Press a truffle about halfway into the batter in the center of each cup. Top with the remaining batter and level the tops; make sure the truffles are completely covered by batter. Cover the cups with plastic wrap. Refrigerate for at least 3 hours or up to 3 days.

• Position a rack in the lower third of the oven and preheat the oven to 400°F.

• Twenty minutes before you want to serve the cakes, remove the plastic wrap and place the cups on a cookie sheet. Bake for 12 to 14 minutes, until the cakes are puffed and the truffles are melted (a toothpick inserted in the center of each cake should meet no resistance and the chocolate on the toothpick should feel warm rather than cool when you touch it to your lip). Let the cakes cool for about 3 minutes.

• Run a knife around the sides of each cup. Holding each cup with a pot holder, invert the cakes onto serving plates. Garnish with a few raspberries, if desired, and, using a fine-mesh strainer, sift a light dusting of powdered sugar over all. Serve immediately.

CHOCOLATE NOTES

I originally developed this dessert using 55% chocolate and loved the outcome. But 62% chocolate made it even better because the difference in texture between the slightly cakey outside and the gooey inside is more pronounced and exciting.

To use a higher-percentage chocolate, adjust the recipe as follows.

To use 64% to 66% chocolate:
Use 7½ ounces (215 grams) chocolate. Add 2 teaspoons water to the raspberry puree. Increase the sugar added to the raspberry-chocolate mixture to 1 tablespoon (13 grams). Reduce the cocoa to 1 tablespoon (6 grams).

To use 70% to 72% chocolate:
Use 7 ounces (200 grams) chocolate. Add 1 tablespoon water to the raspberry puree. Increase the sugar added to the raspberry-chocolate mixture to 1 tablespoon (13 grams). Omit the cocoa. Increase the sugar added to the egg whites to 4½ tablespoons (55 grams).

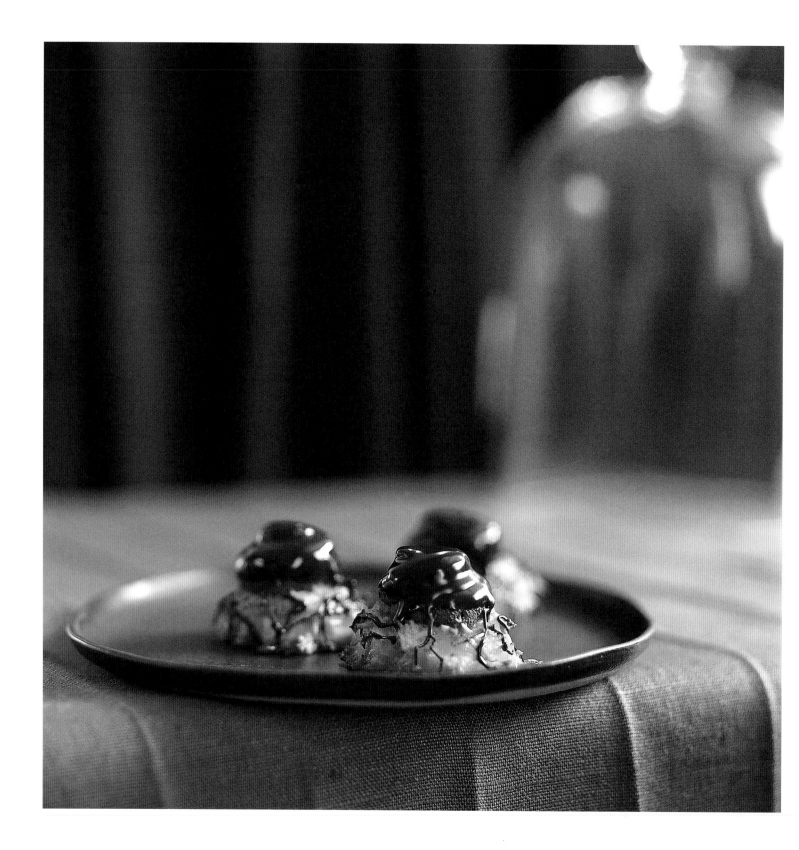

COCONUT SARAS

A Danish pastry chef created Sarah Bernhardt cookies to honor that divine late-nineteenth-century French actress. My version was a tall kiss of light whipped ganache atop a soft almond macaroon enveloped in bittersweet glaze, more an individual dessert than a cookie. Here I've returned them to a dainty size and reinvented them as chewy toasted coconut macaroons filled with soft light ganache and capped with a crisp coat of pure chocolate instead of the softer glaze. The new "Saras" were named for my friend Sara Slavin, who not only loves coconut but also has been the art director and prop stylist for every one of my (now eight) cookbooks. They are more divine than ever. / **Makes 20 to 24 pastries**

INGREDIENTS

4 large egg whites

3½ cups (255 grams) unsweetened dried flaked (not shredded) coconut, also called coconut chips, or 3 cups (9 ounces/ 255 grams) sweetened shredded coconut

¾ cup (150 grams) sugar

2 teaspoons pure vanilla extract

Generous ¼ teaspoon salt

½ recipe Whipped Chocolate Ganache Filling (page 189)

5 ounces (140 grams) 54% to 72% chocolate, coarsely chopped (see Chocolate Note)

SPECIAL EQUIPMENT

Cookie sheets

Pastry bag fitted with a plain tip with a 7/16- to ½-inch opening

Instant-read thermometer

DIRECTIONS

• To make the macaroons: Combine the egg whites, coconut, sugar, vanilla, and salt in a large stainless steel bowl. Set the bowl in a wide skillet of barely simmering water and stir, scraping the bottom to prevent burning, until the mixture is very hot to the touch and the egg whites have thickened slightly and turned from translucent to opaque, 6 to 7 minutes. Set the batter aside for 30 minutes to let the coconut absorb more of the goop.

• Position the racks in the upper and lower thirds of the oven, and preheat the oven to 350°F. Line two cookie sheets with parchment paper.

• If you used large flaked coconut, scoop 2 tablespoons of the mixture per cookie—or 1 tablespoon made with finer shredded coconut—about 2 inches apart onto the cookie sheets. Use your finger to make a hollow depression in the center of each cookie so it looks like a little nest. Bake for about 5 minutes, just until the coconut tips begins to color, rotating the pans from top to bottom and from front to back halfway through the baking time to ensure even baking. Lower the temperature to 325°F and bake for 10 to 15 minutes, again rotating the pans from top to bottom and front to back halfway through the baking time, until the cookies are a beautiful cream and gold with deeper brown edges. If the coconut tips are browning too fast, you can lower the heat to 300°F.

• Slide the cookies on the parchment onto cooling racks. Cool completely before removing them from the paper. (They can be stored in an airtight container at room temperature for 4 to 5 days, or frozen for up to 3 months.)

• To fill and dip the macaroons: Beat the chilled ganache just until the color lightens and the mixture becomes stiff enough to hold its shape—if you overbeat the ganache, it will have a granular texture. Scrape the ganache into the pastry bag. Pipe a 1-inch-high kiss-shaped mound (about 1 tablespoon of ganache) into each macaroon "nest." Refrigerate until well chilled, at least 1 hour.

• Place the chocolate in a medium heatproof bowl set in a wide skillet of barely simmering water. Stir until the chocolate is nearly melted, then remove from the heat and continue to stir until the chocolate is completely smooth. Wipe the moisture from the bottom of the bowl and transfer the chocolate to a very small bowl or cup. If necessary, let the chocolate cool to about 105°F. Hold a macaroon upside down and dip only the ganache kiss into the chocolate. Then turn the macaroon right side up, hold it over the bowl, and use a fork to drizzle a little chocolate around the edges. Set the macaroon on a tray. Repeat until all of the macaroons are dipped. Refrigerate to set the chocolate.

CHOCOLATE NOTE

For dipping, you can use the same chocolate you use in the ganache, or any other chocolate. You can use an even higher percentage chocolate than called for, but be sure you taste it first so you know what you are getting into.

CARMEN MERINGAY

Meringue is irresistible to me as a sculptural medium as well as a dessert component. Although I've gotten some big laughs (howls, actually) for attempting to make trompe l'oeil meringue asparagus, I always get raves for meringue shells. Named for the fun of it, Carmen Meringay is for show-offs: meringue is piped straight up the sheer walls of a vertical form, baked until dry and crisp, then removed from the form. Fill it with a double recipe of Bittersweet Semifreddo with Rose Cream and Sesame Crunch (page 132), or with layers of softened chocolate ice cream (you will need 2 to 2½ quarts) drizzled with chocolate sauce and interspersed with crushed praline (see page 203).

Put the filled shell into an airtight container and freeze until firm, or for up to a week before serving. If the ice cream is rock hard, refrigerate the filled shell for 10 to 15 minutes before finishing and serving. To serve, cover the filling with swirls of whipped cream and top with chocolate shavings (as shown in the photograph on page 185), crushed praline, or berries. Cut with a sharp knife dipped in hot water and wiped dry between slices.

For this stunt you want plain (not chocolate) meringue because it is stiff enough to hold a defined shape and light enough to cling to the sides of the form without sagging in the oven. The following instructions are for creating the form and piping the meringue. The filling is up to you. Use recipes from this book or other favorites. / Serves 12 to 14

INGREDIENTS

White Meringue (page 142)

DIRECTIONS

• Position a rack in the lower third of the oven and preheat the oven to 200°F. Cut a piece of parchment paper to cover a large baking sheet, then cut the paper crosswise in half. Set one piece aside.

• To make the form: Bend the corrugated cardboard into a cylinder 7 inches in diameter and secure the overlapping edges with tape. Stand the cardboard cylinder in the center of the parchment on the baking sheet. Push the cylinder into an oval shape or keep it round. Cut a

SPECIAL EQUIPMENT

Piece of flexible corrugated cardboard 25 to 30 inches long and 5 to 6 inches wide

Cellophane tape

Large pastry bag fitted with a ⅜-inch open star tip (Ateco #9824, #24, or #824)

piece of parchment big enough to wrap around and cover the cardboard cylinder completely. Secure the overlapping end of the parchment with tape but do not tape the parchment to the cardboard or the pan liner.

• Make the meringue and scrape it into the pastry bag. Starting at the bottom of the form, pipe a line of meringue up the outside of the form. Near the top, jerk the tip of the pastry bag upward to form a point. Starting at the bottom again, pipe a second line of meringue parallel to and right up against the first. Repeat until the form is covered with meringue. (If there are gaps in coverage or places where the piping barely touches, pipe some extra lines of meringue as necessary. Don't worry, this will look beautiful and reinforces the structure!)

• Slide the parchment with the form on it to one end of the baking sheet. Place the reserved parchment next to it. Pipe or spread the remaining meringue on the parchment to make a thin round or oval layer slightly smaller than the form.

• Bake for 2 hours. Turn off the oven and leave the meringue inside for at least another hour or overnight.

• Carefully detach the baked (and very fragile) meringue shell from the form as follows: First remove the corrugated cardboard by inserting a skewer or slim knife between it and the parchment attached to the meringue. Use the skewer to ease the cardboard toward the center, away from the meringue. Grasp the cardboard with your fingers and gather it together so you can remove it without nudging or bumping the meringue. Carefully, without bumping the meringue, reach in and grasp the end of the parchment. Gently peel the parchment off the meringue.

• Slide a metal spatula under the meringue shell and the layer to separate them from the parchment underneath. If necessary, trim the layer with a serrated knife so the meringue shell (lifted and set down carefully with two hands) fits completely over it. Store the shell and the bottom layer in an airtight container for up to several weeks, until needed.

Basic Wardrobe for Designing Desserts

Anyone who loves to create desserts with multiple elements must have a short list of reliable basic cake layers and cake sheets that can be split and sandwiched, layered, or rolled up around an endless menu of fillings, frostings, mousses, and creams. The recipes that follow are a few of my favorite chocolate basics, revised or reinvented to reflect my current preferences or to enable you to make them successfully with higher-percentage chocolates. Voilà, the best chocolate génoise I know (page 187), my favorite light whipped chocolate ganache filling (page 189), and more. You will also need some of these for other recipes in this book. All are equally valuable for countless other desserts, suggestions for which are given after each recipe. And additional basics, desserts unto themselves, can be found throughout the book:

Ice creams   (pages 50–61)

Albert's Mousse   (page 124)

Chocolate Marquise   (page 128)

White or Milk Chocolate Mousse   (page 134)

Chocolate Meringue   (page 141)

White Meringue   (page 142)

Nutty Chocolate Meringue   (page 142)

Cocoa Bean Cream   (page 251)

Bittersweet chocolate soufflé sheet   (page 159)

CHOCOLATE GÉNOISE

The bakery workhorse and primary building block of dozens of classic European layer cakes, chocolate génoise can be flavorless and dry as dust until it gets its designated drenching with liqueurs and syrups and/or slathering with buttercream. But it doesn't have to be. After years of making chocolate génoises, I like this one best. It is light but very flavorful, moist enough to snack on when it is naked, but still more splendid splashed and slathered, filled, and/or frosted. Before you begin, remember that when you make a génoise, all of the details matter. Yes, please sift the flour before measuring (unless you are measuring by weight, which is the best way to go anyway), and again and again and again with the cocoa afterward as instructed. Take no shortcuts. Use a stand mixer fitted with the whisk attachment if you have one.

/ **Makes one 8-inch round layer**

INGREDIENTS

4 tablespoons (55 grams) unsalted butter

1 teaspoon pure vanilla extract

⅓ cup plus 1 tablespoon (40 grams) sifted (before measuring) all-purpose flour

¼ cup plus 2 tablespoons (35 grams) premium unsweetened cocoa powder (natural or Dutch-process; see Chocolate Note)

4 large eggs

⅔ cup (135 grams) sugar

SPECIAL EQUIPMENT

8-inch round cake pan

Instant-read thermometer

DIRECTIONS

• Position a rack in the lower third of the oven and preheat the oven to 350°F. Line the bottom of the cake pan with parchment paper.

• To clarify the butter: In a very small saucepan, or in a narrow glass jar in the microwave, heat the butter, without stirring, until it is melted and very hot. The butter will separate into foam on top, clear yellow oil beneath, and water plus some milk solids on the bottom. Simply spoon off and discard the foam on the surface (tilt the pan if necessary). Transfer 3 tablespoons of the clear yellow butter (avoid the watery liquid on the bottom) to a medium heatproof bowl. Add the vanilla to the bowl and set aside.

continued

- Sift the flour and cocoa together three times; return to the sifter and set aside.

- In a large heatproof bowl, preferably the bowl of your electric mixer, use a whisk to combine the eggs and sugar thoroughly. Place the bowl in a wide skillet of barely simmering water. Whisking constantly, heat the eggs to lukewarm (about 105°F). Remove the bowl from the pan; leave the skillet on the stove but turn off the heat. With an electric mixer, beat the egg mixture at high speed until it has cooled, is tripled in volume, and resembles softly whipped cream. This may take as little as 3 to 5 minutes with a heavy-duty mixer or much longer with a less powerful mixer.

- Meanwhile, set the bowl of butter and vanilla in the skillet of hot water, with the burner off or on the lowest setting, so that the butter mixture stays hot.

- Sift about one-third of the flour and cocoa over the whipped eggs. Use your largest rubber spatula to fold in the mixture—quickly but gently—until combined. Fold in half the remaining flour and cocoa, then fold in the rest. Remove the hot butter mixture from the skillet. Scoop about 1 cup of the batter into the bowl and fold together with a small rubber spatula until completely combined. Use the large spatula to fold the butter mixture completely into the remaining batter. Turn the batter into the prepared pan and tilt to level.

- Bake until the cake begins to shrink slightly around the edges and the top springs back when pressed with your finger, 35 to 40 minutes. Cool the cake completely in the pan on a rack.

- To unmold, run a small knife or spatula around the inner edges of the pan to release the cake. Invert it onto a rack and remove the parchment liner. Turn the cake right side up, so that the "skin" on top of the cake does not stick to the rack. (The génoise can be wrapped and refrigerated for up to 2 days, or frozen for up to 3 months.)

CHOCOLATE NOTE

Some chocolate génoise cakes turn out a little drier with natural rather than Dutch-process cocoa, but this one is so light and relatively moist (as génoise goes) that the difference is negligible. You can use either with good results.

WHIPPED CHOCOLATE GANACHE FILLING

This is one of my all-time favorite fillings for cakes and roulades. It is light, creamy, and rich, but not at all intense, so it makes a brilliant contrast to stronger, more bittersweet flavors and a nice offset to the texture of cake or something crisp or chewy. I use this in the Tribute Cake (page 171) and in Coconut Saras (page 181). You can spread it over a bittersweet chocolate soufflé sheet (page 159) and make a rich and simple roulade. Don't be alarmed if the chilled ganache looks too soft to spread (I've had late-night phone calls about this): it will not stiffen until you whip it just before you use it. It is essential that you consult the Chocolate Notes if you plan to make this filling with higher-percentage chocolate, or you will lose the poetry of its light creamy texture. You can make this ganache, or any of the variations, up to four days in advance. / **Makes about 3½ cups**

INGREDIENTS

8 ounces (225 grams) 54% to 58% chocolate, chopped medium-fine (see Chocolate Notes)

2 cups heavy cream

DIRECTIONS

• To make the ganache: Place the chopped chocolate in a medium bowl. Heat the cream in a large heavy saucepan over medium-high heat until it comes to a gentle boil. Immediately pour the hot cream over the chocolate and stir until the chocolate is mostly melted. Let stand for 15 to 20 minutes to be sure all of the chocolate particles are completely melted.

• Stir the ganache until it looks perfectly smooth and free of unmelted speaks of chocolate. Let cool. Cover the bowl and refrigerate the ganache for at least 6 hours (I usually leave it over-night); it must be very cold or it will curdle when it is whipped. (The ganache can be prepared up to 4 days ahead.)

• When you are ready to use the ganache (and not before), whip it until it is stiff enough to hold a nice shape and seems spreadable, but don't overdo. Overwhipped ganache looks granular, so watch it carefully: I usually stop the mixer early and finish the whipping by hand. After whip-ping, the ganache will firm as it sits (and even more after it is chilled), so spread it immediately.

CHOCOLATE NOTES

Unlike most ganache, this one is whipped to a light, almost fluffy texture. High-percentage chocolates are superb here, but the ratio of chocolate to cream must be decreased, or the ganache will be too dense

To use a higher-percentage chocolate, adjust the recipe as follows. (At each level the flavor is less sweet but the texture is still light.)

To use 60% to 64% chocolate: Use 7 ounces (200 grams) chocolate and increase the cream to 2¼ cups.

To use 66% to 72% chocolate: Use 6 ounces (170 grams) chocolate, increase the cream to 2¼ cups, and add at least 4 teaspoons (17 grams), or up to 3 tablespoons (38 grams), sugar to the cream before heating it. Alter the technique slightly: pour half of the hot cream and sugar over the chocolate first and stir until smooth before adding the rest. (Without added sugar, the flavor of the ganache is a bit flat. The minimal 4 teaspoons sugar lifts and opens up the flavor—the way salt lifts the flavor of savory food—without adding perceptible sweetness. You can taste and adjust the sugar before chilling the ganache.)

If you accidentally overwhip, or if the ganache becomes too stiff to spread, warm your spatula by rinsing it under hot tap water and wiping it dry as necessary. (The warm spatula rescued me when I overwhipped ganache for three hundred during the Tribute Cake adventure—so don't worry.)

VARIATIONS

Whipped Gianduja Ganache Filling   Substitute 12 ounces (340 grams) gianduja (milk chocolate to which toasted hazelnut paste has been added [see Sources, page 317]) for the 8 ounces (225 grams) 54% to 58% chocolate.

Whipped Mocha Ganache Filling   Substitute 12 ounces (340 grams) milk chocolate for the 8 ounces (225 grams) 54% to 58% chocolate. Add 2 tablespoons (10 grams) regular roast (not espresso roast) coffee beans, coarsely crushed, to the cream and bring the cream to a simmer. Remove the pan from the stove, cover it, and allow to steep for 4 minutes. Pour the hot cream through a fine strainer onto the chocolate. Discard the coffee beans and proceed with the recipe.

Whipped Mexican Cinnamon Ganache Filling   Substitute 12 ounces (340 grams) milk chocolate for the 8 ounces (225 grams) 54% to 58% chocolate. Add a crushed 6-inch piece of Mexican cinnamon (*canela*) stick (see page 29) to the cream and bring to a simmer. Remove the pan from the stove, cover, and allow to steep for 5 minutes. Pour the hot cream through a fine strainer onto the chocolate. Discard the cinnamon and proceed with the recipe.

Whipped Mint-Infused Ganache Filling   Begin this ganache a day ahead. For the best flavor, strain and discard the mint after 12 hours, even if you are not ready to proceed with the recipe. If necessary, the mint-infused cream can wait in the refrigerator for up to a day before you make the ganache.

Combine the cream and 1 cup (30 grams) lightly packed coarsely chopped mint in a bowl, cover, and refrigerate overnight (10 to 12 hours). Strain the cream into a small saucepan, pressing gently on the leaves to extract all the cream. Discard the mint and proceed with the recipe.

Whipped Mint-Infused White Chocolate Ganache Filling This is excellent in desserts with ripe strawberries. Begin this ganache a day ahead.

Prepare the Mint-Infused Ganache as directed, using ½ cup (15 grams) coarsely chopped mint instead of 1 cup (30 grams) and substituting 12 ounces (340 grams) white chocolate for the 8 ounces (225 grams) 54% to 58% chocolate.

CHOCOLATE NOTES

To use a higher-percentage chocolate, adjust the recipe as follows.

To use 61% to 66% chocolate:
Increase the cream to 1¼ to 1½ cups. Pour only half of the cream over the chocolate and stir well before adding the rest.

To use 70% to 72% chocolate:
Reduce the chocolate to 7 ounces (200 grams) and increase the cream to 1 to 1¼ cups. Add about 1 tablespoon (13 grams) sugar to the cream before heating it. Pour only half of the cream over the chocolate and stir well before adding the rest.

You can adjust the sweetness of the ganache by adding more sugar after you make and taste it.

GANACHE GLAZE OR FROSTING

Pour it warm for a beautiful glaze, cool it and slather it like a frosting, or use it to fill the tartlets on page 229. Of the two amounts given for the cream, use the smaller quantity if making the glaze or filling and the larger if making frosting. This may seem counterintuitive, but spreading cool ganache makes it harder after it sets. / **Makes 1½ to 1¾ cups**

INGREDIENTS

8 ounces (225 grams) 54% to 60% chocolate, chopped into small pieces (see Chocolate Notes)

¾ to 1 cup heavy cream, plus extra as necessary

Pinch of salt (optional)

DIRECTIONS

• Place the chopped chocolate in a medium bowl. Bring the cream to a simmer and immediately pour it over the chocolate. Stir briskly until the chocolate is melted and smooth. If the glaze is too thick or looks curdled, stir in a little extra cream. Taste and consider adding the salt.

• To use as frosting—or for crumb coating a cake before glazing it—let cool, without stirring, to a soft frosting consistency. To use as glaze, reheat gently in a pan of hot water (or let cool if just made) to 90°F to 100°F (for optimal shine) before pouring. The consistency of the glaze or frosting can be adjusted at any time with more cream as necessary. (The glaze can be kept, covered and refrigerated, for up to a week; or freeze it in a sealed container for up to 6 months. Soften or defrost in a pan of hot water or in the microwave.)

BITTERSWEET CHOCOLATE GLAZE

For many years this was my "classic" rich butter glaze for chocolate tortes, which I now alternate with the Ganache Glaze (page 192) or Glace à l'Eau (page 195). This glaze sets firm but soft, with an even satiny appearance. Use it on any cake or torte that is kept and served at room temperature. For cakes that are chilled, use Sarah Bernhardt Chocolate Glaze (page 194) instead. / **Makes about 1 cup**

INGREDIENTS

6 ounces (170 grams) 54% to 72% chocolate, coarsely chopped (see Chocolate Note)

8 tablespoons (115 grams/1 stick) unsalted butter, cut into several pieces

1 tablespoon light corn syrup

Pinch of salt (optional)

DIRECTIONS

• Place the chocolate, butter, and corn syrup in a small heatproof bowl set in a wide skillet of barely simmering water. Stir frequently and gently (to prevent air bubbles) with a spatula or wooden spoon until the chocolate is almost completely melted. Remove the glaze from the water and set aside to finish melting, stirring once or twice until the glaze is perfectly smooth. Or, melt in a microwave on Medium (50%) power for about 2 minutes. Stir gently until completely smooth; do not whisk or beat. Taste and consider adding the salt. To use for crumb coating a cake before glazing it, let cool, without stirring, to a soft frosting consistency. To use as glaze, reheat gently in a pan of hot water (or let cool if just made) to 90°F (for optimal shine) before pouring. (The glaze can be kept, covered and refrigerated, for up to 2 weeks; or freeze it in a sealed container for up to 6 months. Soften or defrost in a pan of hot water or in the microwave.)

CHOCOLATE NOTE

I often make this glaze with a 70% chocolate. You can use an even higher percentage chocolate than called for, but be sure you taste it first so you know what you are getting into.

SARAH BERNHARDT CHOCOLATE GLAZE

I designed this thin bittersweet-chocolate-and-butter pouring glaze for my version of Sarah Bernhardt pastries, which were wildly popular at Cocolat. I use it on all kinds of cakes and desserts that require refrigeration because it does not harden to the point of cracking when chilled, and, if it is applied at the correct temperature, it stays beautiful even when cold. I use it on the Tribute Cake (page 171) and Julia's Cake (page 176), in place of the usual sweet fondant glaze on chocolate éclairs, and as a substitute for the pure chocolate coating on Coconut Saras (page 181).
/ **Makes 1²⁄₃ cups**

SPECIAL EQUIPMENT

Instant-read thermometer

INGREDIENTS

8 ounces (225 grams) 54% to 72% chocolate, cut into bits (see Chocolate Note)

12 tablespoons (170 grams/1½ sticks) unsalted butter, cut into several pieces

1 tablespoon light corn syrup

5 teaspoons water

Pinch of salt (optional)

DIRECTIONS

• Place the chocolate, butter, corn syrup, and water in a small heatproof bowl set in a wide skillet of barely simmering water and stir frequently until the chocolate is almost completely melted; do not overheat. Remove the glaze from the water bath and set aside to finish melting, stirring once or twice until perfectly smooth. Or, melt in a microwave on Medium (50%) power for about 2 minutes. Stir gently with a spatula or a wooden spoon until completely smooth; do not whisk or beat. Taste and consider adding the salt. To use for crumb coating a cake before glazing it, let cool, without stirring, to a soft frosting consistency. To use as glaze, reheat gently in a pan of hot water (or let cool if just made) to 88°F to 90°F (for optimal shine) before pouring. (The glaze can be kept, covered and refrigerated, for up to 2 weeks; or freeze it in a sealed container for up to 6 months. Soften or defrost in a pan of hot water or in the microwave.)

CHOCOLATE NOTE

You can use an even higher percentage chocolate than called for, but be sure you taste it first so you know what you are getting into.

GLACE À L'EAU

This intensely bittersweet glaze or frosting can be used as a substitute for Bittersweet Chocolate Glaze (page 193) or Sarah Bernhardt Chocolate Glaze (page 194). Glace à l'Eau, literally "water glaze," is simple to make and versatile. You can pour it like a glaze or cool it and spread it like frosting. / **Makes about 1¾ cups**

INGREDIENTS

8 ounces (225 grams) 54% to 62% chocolate, coarsely chopped (see Chocolate Note)

8 tablespoons (115 grams/1 stick) unsalted butter, cut into several pieces

½ cup water or strong coffee

Pinch of salt

SPECIAL EQUIPMENT

Instant-read thermometer

DIRECTIONS

• Combine all the ingredients in a small stainless steel bowl set in a wide skillet of barely simmering water; stir frequently until the chocolate and butter are almost completely melted. Remove from the heat and stir gently (to avoid creating air bubbles) until completely melted and smooth. To use as frosting—or for crumb coating a cake before glazing it—let cool without stirring to a soft frosting consistency. To use as glaze, reheat gently in a pan of hot water (or let cool if just made) to 90°F (for optimal shine) before pouring; if the glaze is too thick or looks curdled, adjust the consistency by stirring in a little water. (The glaze can be kept, covered, in the refrigerator for up to 2 weeks; freeze it in a sealed container for up to 6 months. Soften or defrost in a pan of hot water or the microwave before using.)

CHOCOLATE NOTE

This glaze is extremely bittersweet, even without using a high-percentage chocolate. You can use an even higher percentage chocolate than called for, but be sure you taste it first so you know what you are getting into. You can sweeten it with sugar if you find the flavor too intense and/or flat.

CHOCOLATE FANS AND RUFFLES

Chocolate fans and ruffles take lots of practice. If you can't make them obey at first (and it's inevitable you won't), the abstract shapes that you get in the meantime look terrific embedded in frosting or glued on with a little melted chocolate or leftover glaze. No one needs to know you were trying for fans and ruffles.

Ruffled fans with ragged or deckled edges are my favorite—perhaps even my signature—show-off trick with chocolate. Because they are made of pure chocolate with nothing added, they are as delicious as they are sensational to look at. Decorate an individual dessert or even a dish of ice cream or pudding with a single fan, or arrange lots of fans to resemble a giant flower with ruffled petals on a larger dessert.

The amount of chocolate is approximate, and you may not need every bit of it. The idea is to spread a relatively thin even coat of chocolate on the cookie sheets. As you get more skilled, you will spread the chocolate thinner and scrape the excess back into the bowl. Some chefs add a little flavorless cooking oil to the chocolate to make it less brittle, thus easy to cut after it's chilled on the finished dessert. If you would like to do that, add 1 tablespoon of oil to the chocolate when you melt it.

SPECIAL EQUIPMENT

Four unwarped, undented heavy-duty cookie sheets with smooth surfaces (do not use pans with special coatings or nonstick surfaces)

8-inch offset metal icing spatula

8-inch straight metal icing spatula with a flexible blade

Two extra cookie sheets or trays

INGREDIENTS

12 ounces (340 grams) dark, bittersweet, semisweet, milk, or white chocolate (no chocolate chips!), melted (see Chocolate Note)

1 to 2 ounces (30 to 55 grams) chocolate of a contrasting color, melted (optional)

DIRECTIONS

• Warm the back of one of the cookie sheets by holding it about 6 inches above a burner (gas or electric) and moving it back and forth in a slow circle until the bottom of the pan feels very warm all over (when you touch the underside rather than the inside) but not hot enough to burn your fingers. Turn the pan upside down on the counter and pour about one-quarter of the chocolate onto it. Spread it into a very thin, even layer with the offset spatula. Immediately, if desired, drizzle or streak the sheet randomly with a little of the contrasting chocolate. Refrigerate to harden the chocolate for at least 20 minutes, or up to several hours. Repeat to coat the remaining cookie sheets.

• Remove one chilled pan at a time from the refrigerator and let the chocolate soften until it is flexible when you try to scrape it from the pan. Line the two extra baking sheets with parchment or wax paper, for the finished shapes.

• *For fans (see illustration):* Place one short edge of the pan of chocolate up along the edge of the counter in front of you. Lean forward (wearing an apron!) against the counter to brace the pan and keep it from sliding forward as you work. If you are right-handed, start at the upper left-hand corner of the pan (if you are left-handed, reverse the directions as appropriate). Hold the straight spatula with two hands; use your left hand to hold the end of the blade with your third and fourth fingers against the back edge, and thumb and index fingers in front of the blade to gather the ruffle (yes, it is an awkward position!). Use your right hand to hold the blade near the handle, and press the blade firmly against the pan with that right thumb as you work. With the back edge raised only slightly off the pan, pull the front edge of the spatula firmly toward you, sliding it under the layer of chocolate. If all goes well (it probably won't at first), the chocolate will gather up against the thumb and index finger of your left hand and open into a fan near the handle of the spatula. With practice, you may be able to make 10 to 15 good-sized fans from each cookie sheet of chocolate. Remember, whatever shapes you do get will look dramatic arranged on a cake.

• *For easier shapes:* Brace the pan against the wall or the backsplash of your kitchen counter. Push the edge of a metal dough scraper or a putty knife away from you, at an angle against the chocolate, to make sheaves or curls or whatever ruffley shapes turn out.

• Either way, place the finished fans or shapes on one of the lined pans and refrigerate as soon as possible. If the finished shapes start to melt as you work, work with two pans at a time, rotating one in and one out of the refrigerator as needed to hold your finished work.

Tips: If the chocolate is too cold, it will crack and splinter when you try to slide the spatula—wait a few minutes to let soften at room temperature. If the chocolate is too warm, it will gum up or melt against the spatula—return it to the refrigerator for only a minute or so to firm up before trying again. The right temperature makes a big difference; so don't fight it. Sheets can be rechilled over and over again or allowed to soften longer at room temperature as necessary. If the temperature of the chocolate is perfect but you still can't get the shape you want, try altering the angle at which you are holding the spatula blade as you scrape; beginners usually tilt the blade up too much, when it should be almost but not quite flat against the pan. Once

CHOCOLATE NOTE

Any chocolate other than chocolate chips will work here, regardless of percentage.

you have a feel for the perfect chocolate temperature, you can remove more than one pan at a time from the refrigerator, or remove the pans at short intervals, depending on the warmth of the room and the speed at which you work.

VARIATION

Chocolate Ruffles   I normally just arrange ruffled chocolate fans together and call that a ruffle, but you can make an actual long ruffle using the fan technique by scraping the chocolate in longer pulls. Then, while the ruffle is still soft and flexible, arrange it directly on the dessert, perhaps in a spiral from the center.

DARK CHOCOLATE CURLS OR CIGARETTES

This is a simple way to make perfect chocolate curls or cigarettes! Use clarified butter for the best-tasting curls, shortening for the easiest-to-handle. Clarified butter softens the chocolate more than shortening does—hence less is needed. Clarified butter is used because the water in regular butter makes the chocolate less flexible and harder to curl. (See Chocolate Génoise, page 187, for instructions on clarifying butter.)

INGREDIENTS

5 ounces (140 grams) 54% to 60% chocolate (no chocolate chips!), finely chopped (see Chocolate Note)

1½ teaspoons clarified butter or 1 tablespoon vegetable shortening

SPECIAL EQUIPMENT

Miniloaf pan (6 by 3½ inches)

DIRECTIONS

• Line the loaf pan with plastic wrap, leaving an overhang along the long sides. Place the chocolate and clarified butter in a small stainless steel bowl in a pan of barely simmering water and stir constantly until melted and smooth.

• Scrape the chocolate into the plastic-wrap-lined loaf pan. Chill for at least 2 hours or until firm.

• Lift up the edges of the plastic wrap to remove the chocolate from the pan. Let stand for 10 to 15 minutes to soften slightly.

• Cut the chocolate lengthwise in half to form two long bars no wider than the cutting blade of your vegetable peeler. Scrape the chocolate firmly with the peeler for curls and cigarette shapes. If the curls splinter or crack, the chocolate is too cold; wait a few more minutes and try again. If the chocolate becomes too soft, return it briefly to the refrigerator to harden. Handle the chocolate curls with a toothpick to avoid fingerprints. Store in a tightly covered container in the refrigerator or freeze.

CHOCOLATE NOTE

It doesn't seem necessary to use more expensive higher-percentage chocolates for this decorative touch, but you could.

PIPING WITH MELTED CHOCOLATE

This is the easiest and most fun and elegant way to decorate birthday cakes or even cookies: with free-form curlicues, filigree, fancy borders, or birthday greetings. A little practice yields wondrous results.

Simply melt 1 ounce (30 grams) dark, semisweet, bittersweet, or milk chocolate, or even white chocolate (but not chocolate chips; see Chocolate Note). Make a small parchment or wax paper cone (see below). Prop the cone up in a small jar or bud vase and scrape the chocolate into the cone, filling it no more than halfway. Fold over and roll the top of the cone to seal, then snip off the tip. Press from the rolled-over paper at the top to pipe the chocolate.

Alternatively, you can scrape the chocolate into a small resealable bag, bunch the excess plastic in your fist to push the chocolate into one corner, snip off the corner, and squeeze out the chocolate to pipe.

Making a Parchment Piping Cone Cut an 8-by-12-inch piece of parchment paper or wax paper. Fold across opposite corners to form a right triangle. Hold the triangle on the counter with your left hand (if you are right-handed). Slide a sharp knife between the folds and cut along the fold into 2 right triangles (illustration 1).

Fold each triangle into a cone: Hold a triangle in your left hand with your thumb at the center of the hypotenuse, point D. Grasp point B with your other hand and roll it toward point C to form a cone (illustration 2).

Be certain that the tip of the cone remains completely closed. Continue to roll the cone toward point A, and fold the tip at point A over and into the open end of the cone to secure it (illustration 3).

The idea is to be able to fold the paper so that the cone does not come apart when you put it down. At first you may find this a bit awkward. Use some tape, if necessary, and master the finer points of cone making later. Right now you want to get on to the business of piping chocolate!

CHOCOLATE NOTE

Chocolate chips are not fluid enough when melted to flow beautifully from a piping cone.

CAREFREE CARAMEL (CARAMELIZED SUGAR)

Inspired by a technique in *Cook's Illustrated* magazine, this is my version of the easiest way to caramelize sugar. Because the sugar is kept below the surface of the water, there is no need for the usual precaution of washing down sugar crystals on the sides of the pan with a wet pastry brush to prevent crystallization.

Carefree Caramel is not a stand-alone recipe but the basis for the four recipes that follow: Caramel Shards, Spun Sugar, Praline, and Caramel-Glazed Nuts with Stems. Therefore, before you begin cooking the sugar, read the instructions and have the equipment at hand for making one of those. Once the caramel is ready, you will need to proceed immediately to the next step, lest the sugar burn.

INGREDIENTS

½ cup water

⅛ teaspoon cream of tartar

1 cup (200 grams) sugar

DIRECTIONS

• Have a white saucer and a skewer or small knife at the side of the stove to test the color of the syrup.

• Pour the water and cream of tartar into a 1-quart saucepan and set it over medium heat. Add the sugar, pouring it in a thin stream into the center of the pan to form a low mound. Don't stir, but if necessary, use your fingers to pat the sugar mound down until it is entirely moistened; any sugar at the edges of the pan will be safely below the water line. Cover the pan and cook for a few minutes (still without stirring), until when you lift the lid, the sugar has completely dissolved and the syrup looks clear. Uncover the pan and continue to cook, without stirring, until the syrup begins to color slightly. If the syrup seems to be coloring unevenly, swirl the pan gently, rather than stirring. To test the color, use the skewer or knife tip to drop a bead of syrup onto the white saucer from time to time. When a drop of syrup looks pale amber on the saucer, turn the heat to low and pay close attention. Continue to cook and test drops of syrup until it has darkened to a slightly reddish amber color. Immediately remove the pan from the heat.

continued

Caramel Shards   Have ready a foil- or parchment-lined baking sheet and a metal icing spatula. Make the caramel and immediately scrape it onto the baking sheet and tilt the pan to spread the caramel, or spread it even thinner with the spatula.

When it is cool enough to handle but still quite warm, break the caramel into shards, or coarsely chop. Store the warm pieces on parchment or foil in an airtight container (with silica gel if possible; see page 25) until needed. Sealing the caramel in an airtight container while it's still warm helps prevent it from becoming sticky.

Spun Sugar (photograph on page 129)   Spinning sugar is so easy that there is no reason to save it for the occasional showpiece dessert. Spun sugar turns a simple dish of ice cream or chocolate mousse into a celebration. You can make a reusable sugar-spinning tool from a wire whisk by snipping off the curved section of each wire (using a wire cutter) until the whisk resembles a bouquet of wire stems, or you can use a handful of skewers.

Have ready a pan of ice water, the altered whisk or a few wooden or metal skewers, and a sheet of foil or parchment or the dessert, ready to garnish.

Make the caramel. Set the saucepan in the ice water for a few seconds to stop further cooking.

Remove the pan from the ice water, and let the caramel cool and thicken for a minute or two. Dip the tips of the whisk or fanned skewers into the caramel and lift them 12 inches above the pan, watching how the caramel flows from the tips back into the pan. At first the caramel will form very fine threads as it flows off the whisk. As it cools, it will flow more slowly and form thicker golden threads: perfect spun sugar. Continue to dip and lift the whisk until this happens.

The drips and little globs of caramel that fall from the wires are extremely hot, but the threads are cool enough to touch. Grasp and pull the threads aside with your hand, coiling them into a pretty tangle directly on top of a dessert or onto the foil sheet. Continue to dip the whisk to make more spun sugar. After each dip, raise the whisk and wait until the heaviest flow of caramel subsides into threads before touching them. Pull the threads aside, out from under the whisk, so that any drops of caramel that fall cannot burn you. With your hands, shape the tangle of threads to form a nest, halo, or cloud. When the caramel becomes too thick, remelt it over the lowest heat, trying not to let it boil and scorch. Depending on the weather, spun sugar is short-lived. Serve desserts with spun sugar as soon as possible.

Do-Ahead Note: Although simple to make, spun sugar demands last-minute attention. I consider it performance art—guests love to watch—but the show is much easier to put on if the caramel is made ahead (in the form of shards) so it needs only remelting and spinning at the crucial moment. You can make an entire batch of caramel shards several days ahead and store them as described on page 202. At serving time, reserve a few shards for garnish, if desired, and crush the rest into a small saucepan or microwave-safe bowl. Over very low heat, or with 10-second bursts in the microwave, reheat the caramel until most of it is melted; it is not necessary for all of it to melt. Then spin the sugar and serve dessert!

Praline Have ready a foil- or parchment-lined baking sheet, a metal icing spatula, and about 1 cup (3½ to 4½ ounces/100 to 150 grams) coarsely chopped nuts, such as walnuts, pecans, or macadamias or toasted almonds or toasted skinned hazelnuts (see page 28). Make the caramel up to the point where the syrup looks light amber on the white plate. Add the nuts to the pan and turn them gently, using a clean dry wooden spoon or silicone spatula, just until they are completely coated with syrup. (Brisk stirring will cause the caramel to crystallize). Continue to cook, pushing the nuts around gently if the syrup is coloring unevenly, until a drop of syrup looks deep reddish amber on the white plate. Immediately scrape the mixture onto the lined sheet and spread it as thin as possible with the spatula.

When it is cool enough to handle but still quite warm, break the praline into shards, or coarsely chop. Store the warm pieces on parchment or foil in an airtight container or resealable plastic bag (with silica gel if possible; see page 25) until needed. Sealing the caramel in an airtight container while it's still warm helps prevent it from becoming sticky.

Caramel-Glazed Nuts with Stems Have ready a pan of ice water, cellophane tape, and a large bowl with flared sides. Impale 30 to 40 walnut or pecan halves, or whole hazelnuts, from the bottom on toothpicks. Make the caramel, and immediately set the saucepan in the ice water for a few seconds to stop the cooking and prevent the caramel from continuing to darken. Let the caramel cool to the consistency of honey. Remove the pan from the ice bath and hold it so that it is tilted at a 45-degree angle, making the caramel flow into a deep pool at one side. Dip the skewered nuts, one by one, into the hot caramel and keep each nut upside down, letting the caramel form a stem as it drips. Tape each toothpick to the rim of the bowl so that the nut dangles freely upside down. Trim the caramel stems with a pair of scissors. Store while still warm, or let cool and use immediately. To store, tape each toothpick to a sheet of foil, keeping the nuts slightly apart. Store in an airtight container (with silica gel, if possible; see page 25) until needed.

7

HOME BAKING

CAKES, PIES, AND COOKIES

About two years after I had stopped working for the new own-ers of Cocolat, my second book, *Chocolate and the Art of Low-Fat Desserts,* was already a year old. I was teaching a lot, but I had not written a new book proposal, or anything but an occa-sional article. Professionally, I was dragging my feet. Mostly, I was being a mom. (Regenerating, I can say from this distance.)

Lucy was entering the first grade, already a reader and passion-ate writer of her own little books, and an artist. I daydreamed briefly about collaborating with her on an illustrated cookbook. But she was saved when I concluded that her young psyche might not survive being art-directed by her mother. Then my agent told me that *Joy of Cooking,* originally published in 1931, was being revised for the first time in twenty-five years, and its editor wanted me to help with two important chapters.

By the mid-1990s, the state of cooking and food in this country had become so diverse and so driven by specialized expertise and passion that there was no single supercook who could pos-sibly revise all the recipes and text in every chapter of America's culinary bible. So the editor enlisted a team to rewrite the book on a chapter-by-chapter basis.

Work on the cake chapter alone was the equivalent of writing an entire book. I turned in over three hundred manuscript pages, including perhaps twice as many recipes as there was room to include in the new book. I didn't mind. Working on the new *Joy* turned out to be an unexpected midlife and career transition. I brought everything I had to the project and emerged from it with even more.

I came to the revision's American kitchen table with a wealth of knowledge and experience in the use of chocolate, mostly in European-style cakes, desserts, and chocolate truffles. What I didn't feel that I knew as much about, except for cheesecakes, was American cake making. I dove into the subject with a pas-sion, learning as fast as I could by testing recipes and by study-ing the work of the colleagues and cookbook authors I trusted the most. My nearly obsessive tendency to experiment stood me in good stead. I felt it was essential to test and taste every single recipe before deciding to recommend that it be dropped, kept as is, or revised. In doing so, I saw, more clearly than ever before, how details make a difference, how even the smallest changes in techniques and measurements affect results.

The old *Joy* did not necessarily need all new dessert and cake recipes, but even some of the keepers required tuning up to get bigger, brighter flavors. When I finally ventured into the actual revisions, I instinctively began to use what I had learned about fat and flavor while working on low-fat recipes. I saw at once that the dessert recipes weren't flavorful enough for con-temporary palates either, so I began judiciously decreasing sugar and fat, not for dietary purposes, but simply to create heightened flavors.

Quite apart from the enormous education I acquired during this period, the greatest gift from the experience was inadver-tent. Because I physically could not make and taste every rec-ipe, I recruited people to help: home bakers and professionals. Some were already friends or acquaintances, others were not. All were women. They turned up separately every other day or so bringing cake. Visits were brief and businesslike, yet wonderfully comfortable. Sipping coffee and taking notes, I discovered a new way of working, centered (in every respect) in my home kitchen.

As if by magic, we re-created a slice of life straight from the old *Joy of Cooking:* the casual dropping-in of women friends to share coffee for a moment, an interruption of the daily routine of keeping house and raising children. It was a thoroughly pleasant throwback to a time when women did not work outside the home as much as they do today, but still constantly shared information and experience with one another. It is now the way I order my professional life.

The recipes were a revelation as well. For years, I had been knee-deep in chocolate and European desserts. I was now tasting and testing the American baker's repertoire, including classic butter cakes, pound cakes, American sponge cakes (with leavening!), chiffon cakes, and angel cakes. Muffins, scones, and corn breads came under scrutiny when I turned to the quick bread chapter, infusing it with some low-fat alternatives as well. To help with quick breads, I hired Maya Klein, who had been planning to become a professor of economics but was starting a family instead, and whose real passion (aside from husband and babies) was cooking.

Working on biscuits was her introduction to my obsession with testing and comparing. We tested plain biscuits with four different amounts of baking powder, each baked at three different temperatures. We tried different amounts of fat and sugar too.

We have continued to taste and test and say "what if " to each other through each successive book.

In addition to improving my baking techniques and finding a new way to work, the project also shifted my focus in an unexpected but quite natural direction: I began paying more attention to simpler recipes for home cooks while, at the same time, digging even deeper into the technical aspects of chocolate and cocoa. I seemed to be going in two opposite directions. But that duality was reconciled when I remembered a particularly valuable hallmark of the old and new *Joy of Cooking:* Options and variations were offered to the cook in the recipes themselves, and even more variations were suggested in separate sections titled "Ideas for . . ." I loved that way of empowering the cook with choices and knowledge from experiments, testing, and experience. Years later, the Chocolate Notes for nearly every recipe in this book have become a way to accommodate the differences among chocolates and offer the cook a wealth of informed choices.

Testing and experimenting, the combined legacy of my upbringing, self-taught bakery experience, and stint with the *Joy* have all helped me temper technical knowledge with hands-on experience. Research and reading alone could not have yielded the richness of detail and nuance that infuse the Chocolate Notes and the Dessert Maker's Guide to High-Percentage Chocolates (see page 302)—brand-new resources for the curious and chocolate-loving cook.

CHOCOLATE CHEESECAKE

The tart taste of cream cheese, sour cream, and dark chocolate really appeals to me, so you'll find this cheesecake less sweet and far more chocolatey than most commercial and restaurant offerings. I developed the original version for Cocolat years ago, when I had fewer chocolate choices to work with. I used to intensify the flavor by adding a little cocoa powder, still a good technique when you need it. The recipe got "lost" and then turned up again when I was working on the cheesecake section of the new *Joy*. A good recipe doesn't die, it just gets better. Now I make the cake with a fruity 70% chocolate (but see the Chocolate Notes for other chocolate options), skip the cocoa powder, and make my own wafers for the crust. I've still never tasted a chocolate cheesecake that I like better. / Serves 14 to 16

SPECIAL EQUIPMENT

9-inch springform pan or cheesecake pan with a removable bottom

INGREDIENTS

FOR THE CRUST

1½ cups (190 grams) chocolate wafer crumbs, homemade (page 233) or store-bought

5 tablespoons (70 grams) unsalted butter, melted

¼ cup (50 grams) sugar

1½ teaspoons instant espresso powder

FOR THE CHEESECAKE

⅓ cup boiling water

6½ ounces (185 grams) 70% chocolate, finely chopped (see Chocolate Notes)

1 pound (455 grams) cream cheese, at room temperature

¾ cup (150 grams) sugar

1 teaspoon pure vanilla extract

3 large eggs, at room temperature

One 16-ounce (455-gram) container sour cream

DIRECTIONS

• To make the crust: Position a rack in the lower third of the oven and preheat the oven to 350°F. Grease the cake pan.

• Use a fork to blend together all the crust ingredients in a medium bowl. Press evenly over the bottom and about halfway up the sides of the pan. Prick the bottom of the crust with the fork. Bake for 10 minutes. Let cool on a rack before filling (leave the oven on).

• To prepare the cheesecake: In a small bowl, pour the boiling water over the chocolate and stir until the chocolate is completely melted and smooth. Set aside.

• In a large bowl, beat the softened cream cheese with an electric mixer just until smooth, about 30 seconds at high speed (or use a heavy-duty stand mixer and beat on medium speed with the flat beater attachment). Scrape the bowl and beaters well. Turn the mixer back on medium to low speed and gradually add the sugar. Continue to beat until smooth and creamy, then add the vanilla. Add the eggs one at a time, beating just until each is incorporated and scraping the bowl and beaters before adding the next one. Add the sour cream and beat just until incorporated. Pour in the warm chocolate mixture and beat on low speed just until well blended. Pour the batter into the crust and place the pan on a cookie sheet.

• Bake for 35 to 40 minutes, or until the cake has puffed and looks set about 1½ inches in from the sides of the pan but still jiggles in the center when the pan is tapped. Remove the cake from the oven. Slide the tip of a thin paring knife carefully around the top edge of the cake to detach it from the pan, but do not remove the pan sides. Place the pan on a rack and cover the pan and rack with a large inverted bowl or pot so that the cake cools slowly to room temperature.

• Cover the cooled cake and chill for at least 5 hours, preferably 24, before serving. The flavors are even more intense after 48 hours.

CHOCOLATE NOTES

To use lower-percentage chocolates, adjust the recipe as follows.

To use 54% to 62%: Use 8 ounces (225 grams) chocolate. Increase the sugar to ⅔ cup (135 grams) and add 1 tablespoon (6 grams) premium unsweetened natural or Dutch-process cocoa powder with the sour cream.

To use 64% to 66% chocolate: Use 7 ounces (200 grams) chocolate.

*MARBLE CHEESECAKE

Updated and improved, this is one of the best cheesecakes I make, even though a slice has only about two hundred calories and less than eight grams of fat. What it does have is plenty of cheese flavor and a satisfying swirl of rich dark chocolate without the excessive sweetness of commercial cheesecake. I used to teach this recipe alongside luxuriously rich and decadent desserts. It was only from the ingredients list, never from the taste or texture, that students realized that this cake has a fraction of the fat of a traditional cheesecake.

Avoid nonfat cream cheeses and spreads because they taste artificial. I like the flavor of Neufchâtel cream cheese and low-fat cottage cheese or quark, the excellent creamy type of yogurt cheese now available at cheese shops and also at the best supermarkets. I have also added simple steps to make the texture richer and *less wet* (the bane of some low-fat home-made cheesecakes). Thus the cottage cheese or quark is drained and the cake pan is lined with absorbent coffee filters. It's still a simple recipe, but, as always, the details make a difference!

Instead of one 8-inch cake, you can make two 6-inch cheesecakes from this recipe. Bake 5 to 10 minutes less.

For best flavor and texture, make this one day before serving. / Serves 10 to 12

INGREDIENTS

One 16-ounce (455-gram) container low-fat (2%) quark or small-curd cottage cheese

3 tablespoons (18 grams) premium unsweetened cocoa powder (natural or Dutch-process)

¼ teaspoon instant espresso powder (such as Medaglia d'Oro) or a generous ¼ teaspoon instant coffee powder

1 cup plus 1 tablespoon (213 grams) sugar

3 tablespoons water

1½ teaspoons strained fresh lemon juice (if using cottage cheese)

One 8-ounce (225 grams) package Neufchâtel cream cheese (Kraft in the box also is good—don't buy the kind in the tub)

3 cold large eggs

¾ teaspoon ground vanilla beans, or 1 tablespoon pure vanilla extract

¼ teaspoon salt

¼ cup (30 grams) graham cracker crumbs or chocolate wafer crumbs, homemade (page 233) or store-bought

SPECIAL EQUIPMENT

Four round coffee filters at least 8 inches in diameter (iron or weight them if necessary to flatten them), or several cone-shaped filters

8-inch round cake pan (not a springform), at least 2 inches deep

8-inch cardboard cake circle (optional)

continued

DIRECTIONS

• Line a strainer with several layers of folded paper towels topped with one of the coffee filters. Scrape the quark or cottage cheese on top and set the strainer over a bowl. Cover and refrigerate for at least 30 minutes to drain. (Don't worry if the cheese does not exude much liquid; some brands do, some don't.)

• Position a rack in the lower third of the oven and preheat the oven to 350°F. Lightly grease the sides of the cake pan and line the bottom with coffee filters: lay the round ones on top of one another, or arrange cone-shaped filters in an overlapping pattern to cover the bottom of the pan. Put a kettle of water on to boil.

• In a small bowl, whisk the cocoa, coffee powder, 1 tablespoon (13 grams) of the sugar, and the 3 tablespoons water until smooth. Set aside.

• Place the drained cheese (if using cottage cheese, add the lemon juice now) in a food processor and process for 2½ to 3 minutes, until silky-smooth, scraping the sides and bottom of the bowl once or twice as necessary. Leave the cheese in the processor.

• Soften the Neufchâtel cheese in the microwave on High (100%) power for about 30 seconds. Or warm it gently in the top of a double boiler. Stir until smooth and soft, like thick mayonnaise. Scrape into the processor. Add the eggs, the remaining 1 cup (200 grams) sugar, the vanilla, and salt. Pulse only until all the ingredients are incorporated and the mixture is perfectly smooth. Do not overprocess or the batter will become too thin.

• Stir 1 cup of the batter into the cocoa mixture. Pour all of the plain batter into the prepared pan (on top of the coffee filters). To prevent the chocolate batter from sinking into the vanilla batter, pour or spoon it gently—in several puddles—over the top, making sure it doesn't cover all of the vanilla batter. Draw a knife or teaspoon through the puddles to marble the batters without really mixing them together. (The cake tastes best and most chocolatey with separate pockets of vanilla and chocolate rather than a blend.) If necessary, jiggle the pan gently to level the batter.

• Place the cake pan in a baking pan at least 1 inch larger all around than the cake pan, pull out the oven rack, and set the pans on the rack. Carefully pour boiling water around the cake pan to a depth of about 1 inch. Slide the oven rack in gently and bake until the cheesecake has puffed and risen slightly around the edges and is just beginning to shrink from the edges of the pan, 40 to 45 minutes. Remove the cheesecake from the water bath and cool on a rack. When completely cool, cover and chill for at least 12 hours, or for up to 2 days, before serving.

• To serve, run a thin knife blade around the side of the pan to release the cake. Cover the pan with tightly stretched plastic wrap. Place a flat dish upside down over the plastic. Invert the pan and dish and rap the pan gently until the cheesecake is released from the pan. Remove the pan and peel the coffee filters from the bottom of the cake. Place a cake circle or serving plate on the cake and carefully invert again so that the cake is right side up. Remove the plastic wrap. Press the crumbs around the sides of the cake. Cut with a sharp thin knife dipped in hot water and wiped dry between cuts.

TIGER CAKE

A chocolate marble cake made with extra virgin olive oil and a pinch of white pepper? Stay with me. The flavors are subtle and delicious, the cake is moist with a close-to-pound-cake texture, it's not too sweet, and the stripes are beautiful. The pepper does its work sotto voce, accentuating the olive oil flavor and somehow adding an elusive almond flavor with just a little heat. Too esoteric? The five-year-old boy who named the cake (for the stripes, of course) says it's his favorite, but grown-ups like it too. It's a little sneaky in that it seems plain at first, then you notice you've eaten the whole piece and have started slicing seconds.

This cake is even better on the second day. Toasting brings out more flavor too; try a slice for breakfast. Finally, the cake is easy to make and seems to be self-marbling: The liquid layers of batter sink and mingle in the oven of their own accord, with gorgeous results. / Serves 12

INGREDIENTS

½ cup (45 grams) premium unsweetened natural cocoa powder (not alkalized or Dutch-process) (see Chocolate Note)

2½ cups (500 grams) sugar

⅓ cup water

3 cups (385 grams) all-purpose flour

2 teaspoons baking powder

¼ teaspoon salt

1 cup flavorful extra virgin olive oil

1 teaspoon pure vanilla extract

½ teaspoon finely ground white pepper

5 cold large eggs

1 cup cold milk

SPECIAL EQUIPMENT

10- to 12-cup tube or Bundt pan or two 6-cup loaf pans

DIRECTIONS

• Position a rack in the lower third of the oven and preheat the oven to 350°F. Grease and flour the cake pan or line the loaf pans with parchment.

• In a small bowl, whisk the cocoa, ½ cup (100 grams) of the sugar, and the water together until well blended. Set aside.

• Mix the flour, baking powder, and salt thoroughly and sift together onto a piece of wax paper. Set aside.

• In a large mixer bowl using the whisk attachment, or with a handheld mixer that has two beaters, beat the remaining 2 cups (400 grams) sugar, the oil, vanilla, and pepper until well

CHOCOLATE NOTE

Natural cocoa powder is a *must* here. Dutch-process (alkalized) cocoa adds an unpleasant taste because it reacts with the leavening and the olive oil in the cake.

blended. Add the eggs one at a time, beating well after each addition. Continue to beat at medium speed in the stand mixer, or high speed with the handheld mixer, until the mixture is thick and pale, 3 to 5 minutes. Stop the mixer and add one-third of the flour mixture. Beat on low speed just until blended. Stop the mixer and add half of the milk. Beat just until it is blended. Repeat with another third of the flour, the remaining milk, and then the remaining flour.

• Pour 3 cups of the batter into another bowl and stir in the cocoa mixture. Pour one-third of the plain batter into the prepared tube pan (or divide it between the loaves) and top with one-third of the chocolate batter. Repeat with the remaining batters. Don't worry about marbling the batters—that happens beautifully during the baking.

• Bake until a cake tester comes out clean, about 1 hour and 10 minutes for either the tube pan or loaf pans. Cool the cake in the pan(s) on a rack for about 15 minutes. Slide a skewer around the tube pan or slide a thin knife around the sides of the loaf pans to release the cake(s). Invert the pan(s) and invert again, setting the cake right side up on a rack to cool completely.

*A LIGHT CHOCOLATE POUND CAKE

Although this simple and delicious chocolate pound cake has very little fat, it still has the velvet texture and flavor of a real butter cake—because it is one! Beating the butter with the flour tenderizes the cake. Coating the flour particles with fat waterproofs them, which prevents the cake-toughening gluten that normally forms when the liquid is beaten into the batter. / Serves 12

INGREDIENTS

1 cup plus 2 tablespoons (225 grams) sugar

1 cup (130 grams) all-purpose flour

½ cup (50 grams) premium unsweetened natural (not Dutch-process) cocoa powder (see Chocolate Note)

⅜ teaspoon baking soda

¼ teaspoon salt

4 tablespoons (55 grams) unsalted butter, softened

1 cold large egg

2 cold large egg whites

1 teaspoon instant espresso powder (such as Medaglia d'Oro), or 1¼ teaspoons instant coffee powder or crystals

1 teaspoon pure vanilla extract

½ cup cold low-fat (1%) milk

Powdered sugar for dusting (optional)

SPECIAL EQUIPMENT

6-cup fluted tube pan

DIRECTIONS

• Position a rack in the lower third of the oven and preheat the oven to 350°F. Spray the tube pan with vegetable oil spray.

• In a large bowl, whisk together the sugar, flour, cocoa, baking soda, and salt. Add the butter, egg, and egg whites. Set a timer for 2 minutes, and begin beating with an electric mixer on medium speed. When the dry ingredients are moistened but not wet, increase the speed to high and beat until the 2 minutes are up.

• Combine the espresso powder, vanilla, and cold milk and add to the batter. Beat at high speed for exactly 2 more minutes. Scrape the batter into the pan and spread it evenly. Bake just until a wooden toothpick inserted in the center of the cake comes out clean, 35 to 40 minutes. Do not overbake. Cool in the pan on a wire rack for 10 minutes before unmolding onto the rack to cool completely. Serve dusted with powdered sugar, if desired.

CHOCOLATE NOTE

You must use natural cocoa here: Dutch-process (alkalized) cocoa will interact badly with the baking soda.

RASPBERRY-LACED CHOCOLATE CAKE

Substituting fresh raspberry puree for the buttermilk in my favorite chocolate loaf cake—on a whim, really—led to this soft-textured, moist little gem. Be sure that the raspberry puree, butter, and eggs are all at room temperature before beginning. / Serves 10

SPECIAL EQUIPMENT

6-cup decorative tube pan, such as a Turk's Head or Kugelhopf pan

Skewer, toothpick, or artist's brush if making cupcakes

INGREDIENTS

1 cup (130 grams) all-purpose flour

½ cup (50 grams) premium unsweetened Dutch-process (alkalized) cocoa powder (see Chocolate Note)

¼ teaspoon baking powder

¼ teaspoon baking soda

½ teaspoon salt

½ cup seedless raspberry puree (from frozen unsweetened raspberries or from ¾ pint fresh raspberries)

3 tablespoons brandy or rum

1 teaspoon pure vanilla extract

10 tablespoons (140 grams/1¼ sticks) unsalted butter, softened

1⅓ cups (265 grams) sugar

3 large eggs

Powdered sugar for dusting (optional)

DIRECTIONS

• Position a rack in the lower third of the oven and preheat the oven to 350°F. Spray the tube pan with vegetable oil spray.

• Whisk together the flour, cocoa, baking powder, baking soda, and salt in a bowl, then sift onto a sheet of wax paper. Set aside.

• Combine the raspberry puree, brandy, and vanilla in a small bowl; set aside.

• In a large mixer bowl, with an electric mixer using the paddle attachment, or with a handheld mixer that has two beaters, beat the butter on medium speed for a few seconds, until creamy. Add the sugar in a steady stream and continue to beat (on high speed with a handheld mixer or medium speed with a heavy-duty mixer) until light and fluffy, 4 to 5 minutes.

• Break the eggs into a cup or a small bowl and whisk to combine the whites and yolks. Take a full 2½ to 3 minutes to dribble the eggs gradually into the butter mixture, beating constantly.

• Stop the mixer and add one-third of the flour mixture. Beat on low speed only until no flour is visible. Stop the mixer and add half of the raspberry mixture. Beat only until absorbed. Repeat with half of the remaining flour, all of the remaining raspberry mixture, and, finally, the remaining flour. Scrape the bowl as necessary and beat on low speed only enough to incorporate the ingredients after each addition.

• Scrape the batter into the pan and spread it evenly. Bake until the cake starts to shrink away from the sides of the pan and a toothpick inserted in the center comes out dry, 40 to 45 minutes. Let the cake cool in the pan on a rack for 10 minutes, then invert onto a rack and let cool completely. (The cake can be wrapped well and kept at room temperature for 4 to 5 days, or it can be frozen for up to 3 months.)

• Using a fine-mesh strainer, sift powdered sugar over the cake just before serving, if desired.

VARIATION

Raspberry-Laced Chocolate Cupcakes with Marbled Glaze (photograph on page 147)   In a muffin tin with fluted paper liners, or greased cups, bake the batter, about 20 minutes. When the cupcakes are completely cool, make Bittersweet Chocolate Glaze (page 193) or Ganache Glaze (page 192). Melt 1 ounce (30 grams) milk chocolate and 1 ounce (30 grams) white chocolate in two small bowls. Dip one cupcake top (or bottom) into the glaze. Turn the cupcake glaze side up. Dip the tip of your finger or a rubber spatula into the melted chocolates and drizzle a little of each on the glaze. Swirl a skewer, toothpick, or tiny artist's brush through the wet glaze to marble the chocolates. Repeat with the remaining cupcakes. Let the glaze set at room temperature.

CHOCOLATE NOTE

Dutch-process cocoa is a must here; natural cocoa will not work with this combination of leavenings.

CHOCOLATE FOR THANKSGIVING

Although chocolate was always my family's favorite flavor, it was never prominent on our Thanksgiving table. My mother's apple pie was the undisputed centerpiece of the holiday. Pumpkin and mince pies used to flank it, usually brought by family members or guests; they were essentially shills. My father would make elaborate noises over those other pies, offering them first and with great enthusiasm, encouraging generous portions, all the while winking at us kids. The unspoken message was that there would be more apple pie left over for us if the guests filled up on the mince and pumpkin.

My family shared a deep sense of connection to that apple pie. We told stories about it, joked about it, and argued passionately about every change in its fifty-year evolution. It grew up and old with some; the grandchildren never tasted it with two crusts instead of one, or without a few cranberries, or whatever else my mother, never content with the status quo, decided to do to it "this time." Although I fought or at least rolled my eyes at some of her changes during those years (puh-lease, not whole wheat flour!), the pie was always delicious. The recipe details were obviously not sacrosanct, but my mother always held to one ritual: she produced enough extra pies to allow pie eating for breakfast, lunch, and dinner several days running during the holiday marathon. Even in my childhood, we were allowed to eat pie instead of breakfast on those few magical days. Ultimately the pie lost both crusts and became an apple crisp with crunchy

oatmeal and walnut topping and bits of dried apricots inside, but that is another story. . . .

I never wanted to see the apple pie take second place, but there came a time when I wanted to put a chocolate dessert on the Thanksgiving table alongside it, if only to fulfill the role of the long forgotten mince. What would be appropriate?

Was there a chocolate dessert befitting the mood and the flavors associated with the season, its crisp crackling air and brilliant sunlight, and the ritual nuts and apples and pumpkins of the greatest American food holiday of them all? (If you are waiting to hear about the turkey, I'll have to admit that my family of food lovers and epicureans includes vegetarians and other fish-loving folk, such that turkey went the way of the second piecrust long ago, and was replaced with a magnificent whole wild salmon, barbecued to breathtaking perfection by my father.) Thanksgiving never seemed like a day for my chocolate tortes or anything fancy, foreign, or Frenchified. No one, not even my family, watched football while eating leftover chocolate mousse.

I needed a thoroughly American dessert with some chocolate in it. It had to be rich and voluptuous without being too dressy for our Thanksgiving table. Chocolate pecan pie had possibilities, but the task was delicate. I could not let the chocolate ruin the pie, or vice versa: balance was key. The worst possible outcome would be a dessert that insulted the pecan pie lovers *and* disappointed chocolate lovers at the same time.

In fits and starts over a period of a dozen years, I worked on a recipe for chocolate pecan pie. This one, originally published in my book *Chocolate Holidays,* now with a new and flakier crust, is the best to date. It is the essence of pecan pie with a rich undertone of chocolate and spirits. And the information in the Chocolate Notes allows you to use different types of chocolate without destroying the delicate balance of flavors in this pie. I thank Steven Schmidt again for teaching me—so many years ago—that filling a hot prebaked crust with a warm filling results in a piecrust that is never soggy. Happy Thanksgiving!

OVERLEAF: Making Chocolate Pecan Pie (page 222).

CHOCOLATE PECAN PIE

A little yogurt makes a flaky piecrust extra tender *and* makes the butter taste extra good! Bleached all-purpose flour is not as tasty as unbleached, but it makes a more tender piecrust. If using unbleached flour, add the extra tablespoon of butter for tenderness. / **Serves 8 to 10**

SPECIAL EQUIPMENT

9-inch glass pie pan

INGREDIENTS

FOR THE CRUST

1⅓ cups (175 grams) all-purpose flour

½ teaspoon salt

8 tablespoons (115 grams/1 stick) unsalted butter, or 9 tablespoons (130 grams) if using unbleached flour

¼ cup plain yogurt

1 tablespoon ice water, plus more if necessary

FOR THE FILLING

2 cups (7 ounces/200 grams) pecan halves

2 ounces (55 grams) 54% to 64% chocolate, coarsely chopped (see Chocolate Notes)

¼ cup light corn syrup

1 tablespoon (14 grams) unsalted butter, melted

1 cup (170 grams) lightly packed dark brown sugar

¼ teaspoon salt

1 tablespoon rum, bourbon, or brandy

1 teaspoon pure vanilla extract

3 large eggs

DIRECTIONS

• To make the crust: Thoroughly mix the flour and salt in a large bowl. Cut the butter into chunks and add it to the bowl. Using two knives or a pastry blender, cut the butter into successively smaller pieces, scraping the bottom of the bowl and tossing the pieces to coat and separate them with flour as you work, until the largest pieces of butter are the size of peas and the rest bread-crumb size. (Do not let the butter melt or form a paste.) Mix the yogurt with the 1 tablespoon ice water and drizzle it over the flour mixture, tossing with a rubber spatula or a fork, folding and pressing the dough to distribute the moisture. If necessary, drizzle up to 1 more tablespoon water, until the dough is just moist enough to hold together when pressed. Dump the dough onto a sheet of plastic wrap and compress it into a flat disk, pressing in any loose pieces. Wrap in the plastic wrap and refrigerate for at least 1 hour, or for up to 3 days.

- Remove the dough from the refrigerator and let it stand until it is pliable enough to roll without severe cracking. On a lightly floured surface, roll the dough into a 14-inch circle about ⅛ inch thick, rotating and dusting the surface with flour to keep it from sticking. Brush the excess flour from the rolled-out circle, fold the circle into quarters, and transfer it to the pie pan. Unfold, easing the pastry into the pan without stretching it. Trim the overhang to about 1 inch. Turn the excess dough under and flute or crimp the edge. Refrigerate for at least 45 minutes before baking. (Reserve a few dough scraps for later patching if necessary.)

- Toast the nuts while the dough is chilling: Position a rack in the lower third of the oven and preheat the oven to 350°F. Spread the nuts on a baking sheet and bake for 6 to 9 minutes, until fragrant and lightly colored. Set aside.

- Increase the oven temperature to 400°F and let preheat.

- Press a 12-inch square of foil, shiny side down, against the bottom and up the sides of the crust. Tent the edges of the foil over (not touching) the edges of the crust, like an awning, to prevent overbrowning. Prick the bottom of the crust all over with a fork, piercing right through the foil. Fill the foil-lined crust with dried beans or pie weights.

- Bake the crust for 20 minutes. Remove the foil liner and weights. Bake for 10 to 12 minutes more, until the bottom of the crust is golden brown.

- While the crust is baking, make the filling: Combine the chocolate, corn syrup, and butter in the top of a double boiler over barely simmering water. Stir until the chocolate is completely melted and the mixture is smooth. Stir in the brown sugar, salt, rum, and vanilla. Add the eggs and stir until the mixture is well blended and hot to the touch. Set the double boiler aside, stirring the filling from time to time.

- When the crust is baked, remove it from the oven. (Leave the oven on.) If necessary, press bits of reserved dough into any holes or cracks in the crust. Pour the pecans into the crust and the hot filling over the nuts.

- Bake until the filling is puffed and cracked at the edges and brown in patches but still jiggles in the center when nudged, 10 to 12 minutes. A knife inserted in the pie will emerge very gooey. If the edges of the crust are browning too fast before the pie is done, cover with a 12-inch square of foil with a 7-inch circle cut out from its center. Cool the pie on a rack. Serve warm or at room temperature.

CHOCOLATE NOTES

To use a higher-percentage chocolate, adjust the recipe as follows.

To use 66% to 72% chocolate: Use 1½ ounces (45 grams) chocolate.

To use unsweetened (or 99%) chocolate: Use 1 ounce (30 grams) chocolate.

WARM MOCHA TART

Two weeks of nonstop shortbread testing produced an unorthodox surprise: perfect short-bread made with melted butter. That shortbread became an exquisitely crunchy and flavorful base for lemon bars, a crust for cheesecake, and, ultimately, my favorite sweet tart crust. I even bake brownie batter on top of it. This remarkable crust barely shrinks in the pan, so there is no need to weight or even prick it before baking. To ensure that the bottom remains crunchy, bake the crust fully, to a deep golden brown, before pouring in the filling.

At the same time I was playing with the new tart crust, I was experimenting with different cocoas, tasting and comparing natural and Dutch-process in all kinds of recipes. Voilà, rich warm cocoa custard in the simplest crust. / Serves 8 to 10

SPECIAL EQUIPMENT

9½-inch fluted tart pan with a removable bottom

INGREDIENTS

FOR THE CRUST

7 tablespoons (100 grams) unsalted butter, melted

¼ cup (50 grams) sugar

⅛ teaspoon salt

¾ teaspoon pure vanilla extract

1 cup (130 grams) all-purpose flour

FOR THE FILLING

3 tablespoons (45 grams) unsalted butter, cut into chunks

½ cup (100 grams) sugar

¼ cup (25 grams) premium unsweetened cocoa powder (natural or Dutch-process) (see Chocolate Note)

1 cup heavy cream

1¼ teaspoons instant espresso powder (such as Medaglia d'Oro), or 1½ teaspoons instant coffee powder or crystals

½ teaspoon pure vanilla extract

1 large egg, lightly beaten

DIRECTIONS

• Position a rack in the lower third of the oven and preheat the oven to 350°F.

• To make the tart crust: Mix the butter, sugar, salt, and vanilla in a medium bowl. Add the flour and mix just until well blended. Don't worry if the dough seems too soft. Press all of the dough very thinly and evenly into the bottom and up the sides of the tart pan.

continued

- Bake for 20 to 25 minutes, or until the crust is a deep golden brown.

- Meanwhile, make the filling: Place the butter, sugar, cocoa powder, and cream in a medium saucepan and cook over medium heat, stirring, until the mixture is blended and smooth and begins to simmer around the edges. Remove from the heat and stir in the espresso powder and vanilla.

- Just before the crust is ready, whisk the egg thoroughly into the hot chocolate mixture.

- Pour the filling into the hot crust and turn off the oven. Leave the tart in the oven until it quivers like tender Jell-O in the center when the pan is nudged, 10 to 12 minutes. Cool on a rack.

- Serve the tart warm or at room temperature.

VARIATION

Espresso Walnut Tart The same tart in a walnut cookie crust produces a subtler but still delicious effect. You could also make it with toasted skinned hazelnuts—then I would omit the espresso powder.

Reduce the butter to 6 tablespoons (85 grams) and add 2 teaspoons brandy and 1 teaspoon instant espresso powder (or a heaping teaspoon instant coffee powder or crystals) with the sugar, salt, and vanilla. In a food processor, pulverize $\frac{1}{3}$ cup (35 grams) walnut pieces with $\frac{3}{4}$ cup (105 grams) flour until fine. Substitute this mixture for the flour. Proceed as directed.

CHOCOLATE NOTE

Either natural or Dutch-process cocoa works well here. The former has a livelier, more complex, fruity flavor, while the latter has a cozy old-fashioned flavor reminiscent of chocolate pudding. You choose.

BITTERSWEET TARTLETS WITH HAZELNUTS, ORANGE, AND ANISE

PHOTOGRAPH ON PAGE 271

Here the filling is made with chocolate rather than cocoa, so you can try any of your favorite brands. These tartlets, garnished with aromatic ingredients, were inspired by a bout of mendiant making (see page 297). Restraint is the key to making the spice and chocolate a sublime experience. Mysterious understatement is better than a blow upside the head. Sensitivity to spices is highly variable from one person to the next; what is splendidly subtle to one may not be enough for others. If your gathering is informal and friendly, pass some crushed anise separately at the table. Let those who love it, or who find your treatment too elusive, add a pinch to their own portion. It creates a nice conversation topic, and fragrant fingertips, in any case.

For the less adventuresome but totally committed chocolate lovers, these tartlets are fabulous served on their own, without their exotic toppings, or sprinkled instead with handfuls of cocoa nibs. / **Makes 10 or 12 tartlets**

INGREDIENTS

FOR THE CRUST

7 tablespoons (100 grams) unsalted butter, melted

3 tablespoons (38 grams) sugar

¾ teaspoon pure vanilla extract

⅛ teaspoon salt

1 cup (130 grams) all-purpose flour

FOR THE FILLING

1 recipe Ganache Glaze (page 192), made with the lesser amount of cream

3 tablespoons (20 grams) chopped, toasted, and skinned hazelnuts (see page 28)

1 ounce (30 grams) candied orange peel, slivered or chopped

½ teaspoon anise seeds, slightly crushed in a mortar

A pinch of flaky sea salt (optional)

SPECIAL EQUIPMENT

Ten 3½-inch (measured across the top) or twelve 3-inch fluted tartlet pans (about ⅝ inch deep)

DIRECTIONS

• Position a rack in the lower third of the oven and preheat the oven to 350°F.

• To make the crust: Combine the melted butter, sugar, vanilla, and salt in a medium bowl. Mix in the flour just until blended. Don't worry if the dough seems too soft. Divide the dough into

10 or 12 equal pieces. Press one piece very thinly and evenly across the bottom and up the sides of each pan. This takes patience—the amount of dough is just right. To help shape crusts evenly, lay a piece of plastic wrap over each one and press a small, flat-bottom straight-sided measuring (or similar) cup into the bottom and against the sides of each one.

• Place the pans on a cookie sheet. Bake for 15 to 20 minutes, until the crusts are a deep golden brown. Check after about 10 minutes. If the bottoms or sides of the crusts are puffed out of shape, press the bottom and sides gently with a small, flat-bottomed, straight-sided measuring (or similar) cup. Continue to bake until done.

• Cool the crusts on a rack.

• When the crusts are completely cool, unmold them as follows: Invert one pan in your hand and squeeze the pan gently on two opposite sides to release the crust. Set the crust right side up on the pan—they are fragile; handle with care. Repeat to unmold the remaining crusts.

• Make the ganache as directed, adding a pinch or two of salt to taste. Let cool to between 90°F and 100° F. Fill the tart crusts with ganache. Let cool at room temperature until set, at least 2 hours.

• Just before serving, scatter the chopped hazelnuts and slivers of candied orange peel over the tarts, then sprinkle with the crushed anise. If desired, top each tart with a few grains of slightly crushed salt flakes. (The tarts are best on the day they are made.)

VARIATIONS

Ancho Chile and Cherry Tartlets   Substitute walnuts or pecans for the hazelnuts, a few dried sweet cherries for the orange peel, and ground dried ancho (if you have a choice) powder or a commercial chili powder for the anise seeds.

CHOCOLATE NOTES

To use a higher-percentage chocolate, adjust the recipe as follows.

To use 62% to 64% chocolate: Use 7 ounces (200 grams) chocolate.

To use 66% to 72% chocolate: Use 5½ ounces (155 grams) chocolate, and increase the sugar to ⅓ cup (65 grams).

MELTING CHOCOLATE COOKIE TARTLETS

These rustic-looking craggy-topped tartlets with a crunchy crust and chewy-yet-soft-centered chocolate filling were the inspiration of one of my students. Alicia Hitchcock makes thousands of tartlets by filling my melted butter shortbread crust with my melting chocolate meringue cookie batter. Here's "our" recipe. / *Makes 10 or 12 tartlets*

INGREDIENTS

FOR THE CRUST

7 tablespoons (100 grams) unsalted butter, melted

3 tablespoons (38 grams) sugar

¾ teaspoon pure vanilla extract

⅛ teaspoon salt

1 cup (130 grams) all-purpose flour

FOR THE FILLING

6 ounces (170 grams) 54% to 62% chocolate, coarsely chopped (see Chocolate Notes)

2 large egg whites, at room temperature

⅛ teaspoon cream of tartar

½ teaspoon pure vanilla extract

¼ cup (50 grams) sugar

¾ cup (75 grams) chopped pecans or walnuts

SPECIAL EQUIPMENT

Ten 3½-inch (measured across the top) or twelve 3-inch fluted tartlet pans (about ⅝ inch deep)

DIRECTIONS

• Position a rack in the lower third of the oven and preheat the oven to 350°F.

• To make the crust: Mix the butter, sugar, vanilla, and salt in a medium bowl. Add the flour and mix just until well blended. Don't worry if the dough seems too soft. Divide the dough into 10 or 12 equal pieces. Press one piece of dough very thinly and evenly across the bottom and up the sides of each tartlet pan. This takes some patience—there is just enough dough. To help shape crusts evenly, lay a piece of plastic wrap over each one and press a small, flat-bottom straight-sided measuring (or similar) cup into the bottom and against the sides of each one.

• Place the pans on a cookie sheet. Bake for 15 to 20 minutes, until a deep golden brown. Check after about 10 minutes. If the bottoms or sides of the crusts are puffed out of shape, press the bottom and sides gently with a small, flat-bottomed, straight-sided measuring (or similar) cup.

CHOCOLATE NOTES

To use a higher-percentage chocolate, adjust the recipe as follows.

To use 64% to 66% chocolate: Use 5 ounces (140 grams) chocolate.

To use 70% to 72% chocolate: Use 4½ ounces (130 grams) chocolate, and increase the sugar to ⅓ cup (65 grams).

continued

• While the crusts are baking, make the filling: Melt the chocolate in a medium heatproof bowl set in a wide skillet of barely simmering water, or in the microwave on Medium (50%) power for 3½ to 4 minutes, stirring frequently until the chocolate is almost completely melted. Remove from the heat and stir until completely melted. Set aside.

• In a large bowl, beat the egg whites with the cream of tartar and vanilla until soft peaks form when you lift the beaters. Gradually add the sugar and continue to beat until the egg whites are stiff but not dry. Pour the nuts and all of the warm chocolate over the egg whites and fold with a rubber spatula until the color of the batter is uniform.

• As soon as the tartlet crusts are ready, divide the filling equally among them. Make sure that batter touches the crust all around the edges. Return to the oven and bake until the filling is dry or slightly cracked on top, about 10 minutes. Cool on a rack.

• To unmold, use the point of a paring knife to loosen one edge of the crust from the pan, then tip the tarts into your hand. Serve warm or at room temperature.

Variations Fold into the filling 2 ounces (55 grams) crystallized ginger, finely chopped; 4 ounces (115 grams) moist prunes, chopped into ¼-inch pieces; or 4 ounces (115 grams) candied chestnuts, chopped.

Substitute toasted pine nuts for the pecans.

*REAL CHOCOLATE WAFERS

PHOTOGRAPH ON PAGE 267

Plain, crisp, and not too sweet or too rich, these are good served with the creamy crustless Marble Cheesecake (page 211). They also make the best cookie crumbs for the sides of the cake. / **Makes 40 to 45 cookies**

INGREDIENTS

1 cup (130 grams) all-purpose flour

½ cup plus 1 tablespoon (55 grams) premium unsweetened cocoa powder (natural or Dutch-process) (see Chocolate Note)

¼ teaspoon baking soda

¼ teaspoon salt

6 tablespoons (85 grams) unsalted butter, slightly softened

½ cup (85 grams) lightly packed brown sugar

½ cup plus 2 tablespoons (125 grams) granulated sugar

1 teaspoon pure vanilla extract

3 tablespoons low-fat (1%) milk or water

DIRECTIONS

• In a medium bowl, whisk together the flour, cocoa, baking soda, and salt. Set aside.

• In another medium bowl, beat the butter with an electric mixer until creamy. Add the sugars and vanilla. Beat on high speed for about 1 minute. Beat in the milk. On low speed, beat in the flour mixture just until incorporated. Gather the dough together with your hands and form it into a neat 9- to 10-inch log. Wrap it in wax paper, folding or twisting the ends of the paper without pinching or flattening the log. Chill for at least 45 minutes, or until needed. (The dough can be refrigerated for up to 3 days, or double-wrapped and frozen for up to 3 months.)

• Place the oven racks in the upper and lower thirds of the oven and preheat the oven to 350°F. Line two baking sheets with parchment paper.

• Use a sharp knife to slice rounds of chilled dough a scant ¼ inch thick. Place them 1 inch apart on baking sheets. Bake for 10 to 12 minutes, rotating the baking sheets from top to bottom and front to back about halfway through. The cookies will puff and crackle on top, then settle down slightly when done. Set the pans, or just the liners, on wire racks to cool completely.

• Store in an airtight container for up to 2 weeks, or freeze for up to 2 months.

CHOCOLATE NOTE

My preference here is for natural cocoa, which has the liveliest and most complex flavor, but use Dutch-process if you prefer it.

*SAUCEPAN FUDGE DROPS

These easy super-chocolatey cookies have crunchy edges and chewy, fudgy centers. They taste much richer than they are. / **Makes about 32 cookies**

INGREDIENTS

1 cup (130 grams) all-purpose flour

¼ teaspoon baking soda

⅛ teaspoon salt

5 tablespoons (70 grams) unsalted butter

½ cup plus 1 tablespoon (55 grams) premium unsweetened cocoa powder (natural or Dutch-process) (see Chocolate Note)

⅔ cup (130 grams) granulated sugar

⅓ cup (60 grams) packed light brown sugar

⅓ cup low-fat or nonfat yogurt

1 teaspoon pure vanilla extract

2 to 3 teaspoons powdered sugar for dusting

DIRECTIONS

• Whisk the flour, baking soda, and salt together thoroughly. Set aside.

• In a medium saucepan, heat the butter until it is melted and sizzling. Off the heat, stir in the cocoa until blended and smooth. Stir in the sugars until blended; the mixture will be stiff and sandy. Mix in the yogurt and vanilla. Add the flour mixture all at once and fold and stir just until it is entirely moistened and incorporated into the cocoa mixture—do not stir more than necessary. Let the batter rest for 15 to 30 minutes.

• Meanwhile, arrange the racks in the upper and lower thirds of the oven and preheat the oven to 350°F. Line two cookie sheets with parchment paper.

• Drop tablespoons of the dough 1½ inches apart onto the lined cookie sheets. Use a fine strainer to sift powdered sugar over the tops.

• Bake until the cookies look dry and cracked on top but still feel a little soft when pressed, 9 to 11 minutes. Rotate the sheets from top to bottom and front to back about halfway through the baking. Slide the cookies, on the paper, off the sheets and onto racks to cool; or set the pans on the racks and let cool.

• The cookies will keep for 2 to 3 days in an airtight container, although they soften and lose their crunchy exterior.

CHOCOLATE NOTE

My preference here is for natural cocoa, which has the liveliest and most complex flavor, but use Dutch-process if you prefer it.

BITTERSWEET DECADENCE COOKIES

Ultra-chocolatey and richer than sin, slightly crunchy on the outside with a divinely soft center, these are not delicate or subtle, but the jolt of bittersweet is irresistible. I reorganized and revised the original recipe from one in a newspaper—to make the cookies more chocolatey and intense—by reducing the sugar and butter. Now I've revised it again so that I can make it with higher-percentage chocolates without compromising that perfect contrast of textures. For the best cookies of all, chop your own chocolate for the chunks, or use a premium brand of chocolate chunks rather than ordinary chocolate chips. You can choose a chocolate for the chunks that contrasts in sweetness with the chocolate in the cookie batter. / **Makes 36 cookies**

INGREDIENTS

¼ cup (30 grams) all-purpose flour

¼ teaspoon baking powder

⅛ teaspoon salt

8 ounces (225 grams) 54% to 60% chocolate, coarsely chopped (see Chocolate Notes)

2 tablespoons (30 grams) unsalted butter

2 large eggs

½ cup (100 grams) sugar

1 teaspoon pure vanilla extract

2 cups (200 grams) walnuts or pecans, broken or chopped into large pieces

6 ounces (170 grams) 54% to 72% chocolate, chopped into chunks, or store-bought chocolate chunks (see Chocolate Notes)

DIRECTIONS

• Position the racks in the upper and lower thirds of the oven and preheat the oven to 350°F. Line two cookie sheets (see Note) with parchment paper.

• In a small bowl, mix the flour, baking powder, and salt together thoroughly; set aside.

• Place the 8 ounces (225 grams) of chocolate and the butter in a large stainless steel bowl in a wide skillet of barely simmering water and stir frequently just until melted and smooth. Remove the chocolate from the skillet and set it aside. Leave the heat on under the skillet.

• In a large heatproof bowl, whisk the eggs, sugar, and vanilla together thoroughly. Set the bowl in the skillet and stir until the mixture is lukewarm to the touch. Stir the egg mixture into the warm (not hot) chocolate. Stir in the flour mixture, then the nuts and chocolate chunks.

continued

CHOCOLATE NOTES

To use higher-percentage chocolate to make cookies that are increasingly bittersweet, without sacrificing the texture or the pretty gloss on the surface of the cookies, adjust the recipe as follows.

To use 61% to 64% chocolate: Use 7 ounces (200 grams) chocolate. Increase the sugar to ½ cup plus 1 tablespoon (110 grams).

To use 66% chocolate: Use 6½ ounces (185 grams) chocolate. Increase the butter to 3 tablespoons (45 grams) and the sugar to ½ cup plus 2 tablespoons (125 grams).

To use 70% to 72% chocolate: Use 5½ ounces (155 grams) chocolate. Increase the butter to 3 tablespoons (45 grams) and the sugar to ¾ cup (150 grams).

For the chunks, use any chocolate you like, the same as or different from the batter. No alterations are necessary.

• Drop slightly rounded tablespoons of batter 1½ inches apart onto the lined cookie sheets. Bake until the surface of the cookies looks dry and set but the center is still gooey, 12 to 14 minutes. Slide the cookies, still on the parchment, onto racks, or set the pans on the racks. Let cool completely. Store in a tightly sealed container.

Note: I am fussy about cookie sheets. These cookies will have the best flavor and texture if they are baked on sheets lined with parchment paper, which insulates them just enough but still allows the cookies to be a little crusty on the outside and soft within. Cushioned pans and silicone liners make the texture of the cookies too uniform for my taste. Pans with dark surfaces (even if they are nonstick) tend to scorch rich chocolate cookie bottoms before the centers are cooked.

TRULY CREAMY EGG CREAM

An egg cream is an exquisitely refreshing drink made with a little milk or cream, chocolate syrup, and a generous spritz of seltzer. It is not very sweet and not very rich, nor does it contain eggs. A California girl raised in non-Jewish suburbs, I didn't taste my first egg cream until I was in college at Berkeley. The effect was Proustian just the same. The egg cream tasted exactly like the cold fizzy liquid sipped from countless childhood chocolate ice cream sodas, when just enough of the ice cream had melted and mingled with the chocolate syrup and soda water. In my soda days, there was never enough of that thirst-quenching counterpoint to the sweet rich ice cream in the tall glass. Years later, the humble egg cream was, and still is, a fitting riposte. There's plenty of bubbly liquid, it's remarkably low in calories and fat, and it's wonderfully satisfying, especially when made with your own syrup.

Bottled seltzer water is fine, but if you love egg creams, you'll want to buy a siphon to turn ordinary (or filtered) water into seltzer. (Soda siphons are available from cookware stores or mail-order catalogs; see Sources, page 317.) Egg creams are made to order, one glass at a time. This "recipe" is flexible, and you will quickly fine-tune the variables (fizzy, creamy, chocolatey) to your own taste.

INGREDIENTS

Milk, half-and-half, or cream

Cocoa Syrup (page 244)

Cold seltzer water (bottled or from a siphon)

DIRECTIONS

• Fill a 12-ounce glass one-quarter to one-half full of milk or whichever cream you are using. (I use the lesser amount of half-and-half to get maximum fizz with enough creaminess for my taste.) Now there are two ways to go: either stir 2 to 3 tablespoons of cocoa syrup into the milk before filling the glass with seltzer, or add the seltzer to the milk first and then add the cocoa syrup. Stir briskly. If syrup is added before seltzer, the foam on the egg cream will be cocoa-colored. If syrup is added after seltzer, the foam will stay white! Delicious either way.

CREAM SCONES WITH CHOCOLATE CHUNKS

Like plain bread and chocolate, there is something at once elemental and sumptuous about these tender, not too sweet scones made entirely with cream, instead of butter, and laced with chunks of the best (your favorite) dark chocolate. / *Makes 12 scones*

INGREDIENTS

2 cups (255 grams) all-purpose flour

¼ cup (50 grams) sugar, plus additional sugar for sprinkling

2½ teaspoons (10 grams) baking powder

½ teaspoon salt

3 to 4 ounces (85 to 115 grams) 54% to 70% chocolate, coarsely chopped (see Chocolate Note)

1¼ cups heavy cream

1 tablespoon milk or cream for brushing the tops

DIRECTIONS

• Line a baking sheet with a double layer of parchment paper.

• In a large bowl, whisk the flour, sugar, baking powder, and salt together thoroughly. Stir in the chopped chocolate. Make a well in the center and pour the cream into it. Use a rubber spatula to push the dry ingredients from the sides of the bowl into the well, cutting and turning the mixture just until the dry ingredients are almost entirely moistened and the dough looks rough and shaggy. Gather the dough into a lump and knead it gently against the sides of the bowl five or more times, pressing in the loose pieces, until the dough just holds together (it should not be smooth) and the sides of the bowl are fairly clean.

• On a lightly floured board, pat the dough into an 8½-inch round about ¾ inch thick. Cut into 12 wedges. Place them at least 1 inch apart on the lined baking sheet. Let them rest at room temperature for about 45 minutes.

• Position a rack in the center of the oven and preheat the oven to 425°F.

• Brush the tops of the scones with milk or cream and sprinkle lightly with sugar. Bake until the tops are golden brown, 12 to 15 minutes. Let cool on a rack, then serve warm or at room temperature.

CHOCOLATE NOTE

You can use an even higher percentage chocolate than called for, but be sure you taste it first so you know what you are getting into.

LESSONS FROM A CHOCOLATE SAUCE

At my house, it is important to have a really good chocolate sauce recipe available in case of emergency. Even if your house doesn't have emergencies of this nature, you can still use the recipe opposite. Good chocolate sauce and a little good vanilla ice cream make a dessert more delicious and satisfying than 90 percent of those you could order in even a top-flight restaurant. Good chocolate sauce and an assortment of ripe fruits and chunks of cake will get you chocolate fondue. And when things look bleak, good chocolate sauce and a spoon will make you smile.

The recipe that follows immediately is one I have used forever. It is flexible and contains some interesting lessons about flavor, perhaps about life.

There is a simple secret to good chocolate sauce: you need good chocolate. Don't buy the individually wrapped squares of chocolate at the supermarket. Buy chocolate you love to eat, because the sauce is mostly chocolate and you are going to eat it. A recipe like this shows off all of the qualities, good or bad, of the chocolate you use. The many options and imprecise measurements in this recipe may suggest either that I can't make up my mind or that I don't think the details really matter. Neither is true. I know what I like, and every detail is important.

But what do you like? Depending on the choices you make, you can have a sauce that is rich and creamy or intensely bittersweet, or anything in between. You can have a thin sauce that mingles pleasantly with the melted ice cream in the bottom of the bowl, or one that thickens like fudge and makes you groan a little with pleasure. You can make the sauce with a gentle 55% chocolate or a powerful 70%—it all depends on your tastes.

Once you've selected your chocolate, you are ready to consider the milk versus cream question. Milk is the more convenient choice if you don't usually keep cream in the refrigerator (and that's what I used when I first made this sauce). So you might make the sauce with milk, all the while thinking that cream would be better if only you felt like going to the store. But you might be wrong. Richer is not always better. Milk allows the taste of the chocolate to come through more—but that also means it does less to hide flavor flaws. Chocolate sauce made with milk has the most intense bittersweet chocolate flavor. So, if you are using a harsh or mediocre-tasting chocolate, don't make your sauce with milk! If your milk-based sauce is delicious but a tad too tart or austere, stir in bits of the optional butter to round out the flavor. Way over at the other end of the taste spectrum, chocolate sauce made with heavy cream—although still bittersweet—is positively voluptuous and creamy. It is also decidedly milder, less chocolatey, and less bittersweet. Half-and-half or a combination of milk and cream lands you somewhere between. If you've read my story about the nectarine (see page 45), you will rightly guess that I have also made this sauce with water! A versatile sauce indeed.

ALICE'S CHOCOLATE SAUCE

This extremely accommodating recipe can be made with any dark chocolate. The range given for the milk or cream and the recipe instructions will guide you to adjust the liquid upward as needed for higher-percentage chocolate. / Makes 1¾ cups

INGREDIENTS

10 ounces (285 grams) 54% to 70% chocolate, finely chopped (see Chocolate Notes)

½ to 1 cup milk, half-and-half, heavy cream, or any combination

2 tablespoons (30 grams) unsalted butter (if using milk instead of cream, but optional)

½ teaspoon pure vanilla extract (optional)

Pinch of salt, or more to taste

DIRECTIONS

• Put the chocolate and ½ cup of the milk or cream in a large heatproof bowl set in a wide skillet of barely simmering water and stir frequently until the chocolate is melted and smooth. If the sauce is too thick or looks curdled, add more milk. Or add more liquid if the sauce hardens more than you want it to when you spoon a little "test" over ice or a tiny scoop of ice cream! If you have used milk (or even water), taste the sauce and, if you like, tone down the flavor intensity by adding some or all of the butter, bit by bit. Remove the sauce from the water and stir in the vanilla, if using, and salt.

• Use the warm sauce immediately, or set it aside and rewarm it briefly in a pan of hot water when you need it. (The sauce keeps in a closed container for several days in the refrigerator, and it can be frozen for up to 3 months.)

CHOCOLATE NOTES

You can use an even higher percentage chocolate than called for, but be sure you taste it first so you know what you are getting into.

If you go overboard by using a chocolate that is too intense or bitter, stir in extra sugar and perhaps some cream until you love it.

BITTERSWEET HOT FUDGE SAUCE

Here's a more traditional hot fudge sauce, but updated (with less butter and sugar) so you can really taste the flavors in the chocolate. This is a pretty adult sauce, breathtaking over vanilla ice cream, but the children of my acquaintance don't seem to turn it down!
/ **Makes about 2 cups**

SPECIAL EQUIPMENT

Instant-read thermometer

INGREDIENTS

10 ounces (285 grams) 66% to 70% chocolate, finely chopped (see Chocolate Notes)

¾ cup heavy cream

¼ cup plus 2 tablespoons (75 grams) sugar

3 tablespoons light corn syrup

2 tablespoons water

CHOCOLATE NOTES

To use a lower-percentage chocolate, adjust the recipe as follows.

To use 61% to 64% chocolate:
Use 12 ounces (340 grams) chocolate. Reduce the sugar to ¼ cup (50 grams) and the corn syrup to 1 tablespoon.

To use 54% to 60% chocolate:
Use 14 ounces (400 grams) chocolate. Reduce the sugar to 2 tablespoons (25 grams) and the corn syrup to 1 tablespoon.

DIRECTIONS

• This sauce is foolproof so long as you heat it slowly. Combine all of the ingredients in the top of a double boiler over (and touching) barely simmering water. Stir frequently until all the chocolate has melted. Then stir occasionally until the sauce is thick and glossy and is between 160° and 165°F (the exact temperature is not critical so long as you are close), 15 to 20 minutes (going slowly is the key here). Remove from the heat.

• Serve the sauce immediately or set it aside until needed. It can be kept, in a covered container, refrigerated for at least a week, or frozen for 3 months. Reheat in a double boiler or microwave on Medium (50%) power, using short bursts and stirring frequently. Do not simmer or boil.

ALICE'S COCOA FUDGE SAUCE

I created this recipe for the original Scharffen Berger natural cocoa powder, which was especially fruity and aromatic, but any good-quality cocoa powder that you love can be used. Cooled to spreading consistency, this sauce makes a great cake frosting or filling for butter cookies or graham crackers. / **Makes 1½ cups**

INGREDIENTS

½ cup (50 grams) premium unsweetened cocoa powder (natural or Dutch-process) (see Chocolate Note)

½ cup (100 grams) sugar

½ cup heavy cream

3 tablespoons (45 grams) unsalted butter, cut into bits

½ teaspoon pure vanilla extract (optional)

Pinch of salt (optional)

DIRECTIONS

• Place the cocoa and sugar in a small heavy saucepan. Stir in just enough of the cream to make a smooth, thick paste, then stir in the rest of the cream and add the butter pieces. Stir over low heat until the butter is melted and the sauce is smooth and hot but not simmering. Taste and add the vanilla and salt, if desired.

• Spoon the warm sauce over ice cream. Or, for frosting, cool until spreadable. (The sauce keeps in a covered container in the refrigerator for 1 week, or it can be frozen for up to 3 months.) To reheat (and thaw), put the sauce in a heatproof bowl set in a wide skillet of barely simmering water, and stir occasionally until the sauce is the desired consistency. Or microwave on Medium (50%) power, using short bursts and stirring frequently. Do not allow the sauce to simmer or boil.

CHOCOLATE NOTE

Cocoas vary. You can taste and adjust the flavor with extra sugar if it is too harsh or bitter, or tone down the intensity with a little extra butter or cream.

COCOA SYRUP

This flavorful bittersweet syrup tastes better than store-bought. It's far less rich than cream- or butter-based chocolate sauces, takes just minutes to make, and keeps well. Serve it over ice cream or keep it on hand (in a squeeze bottle) to produce a Truly Creamy Egg Cream (page 237) at a moment's notice. / **Makes 1¾ cups**

INGREDIENTS

¾ cup (70 grams) premium unsweetened cocoa powder (natural or Dutch-process)

1 cup (200 grams) sugar

Pinch of salt

1 cup boiling water

1 teaspoon pure vanilla extract (optional)

DIRECTIONS

• Mix the cocoa powder, sugar, and salt in a small saucepan. Stir in enough boiling water to form a smooth paste; stir in the remaining water. Heat the mixture over low heat, stirring constantly, just until it starts to bubble at the edges. Remove from the heat, stir in the vanilla, if using, and let cool. Scrape into a squeeze bottle or jar and store in the refrigerator for up to 3 weeks.

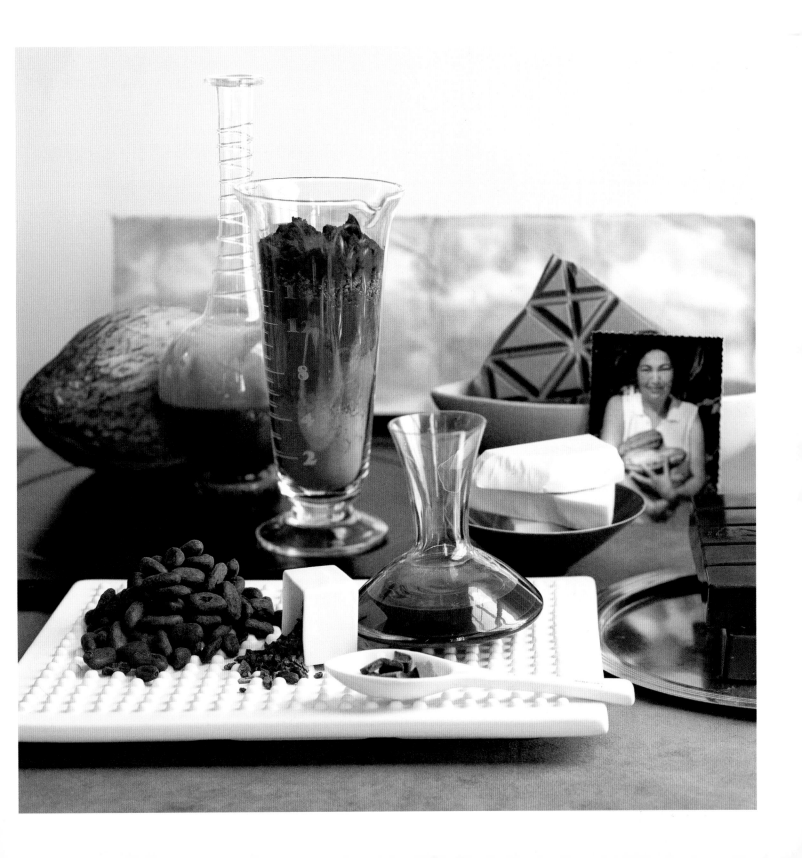

THE SWEET AND THE SAVORY
PLAYING WITH NIBS AND DINING ON CHOCOLATE

WHAT I LEARNED FROM THE BEANS

Making footprints where there are none (or very few) is more fun than almost anything I can think of. Imagine enjoying orange juice yet never having tasted an orange. Or imagine being intimately familiar with peanut butter without ever having eaten peanuts. Although chocolate reigns supreme in the dessert pantheon, most home cooks and chocolate lovers are still unfamiliar with cocoa beans, the purest, most elemental form of chocolate.

When *Bittersweet* was published in 2003, cocoa beans had just become available to chefs and to home cooks in the form of cocoa nibs. Nibs are cocoa beans on the brink of becoming chocolate. They are tiny nuggets of roasted (usually), shelled, and cracked beans, not yet crushed or ground to homogeneity, not yet transformed into chocolate liquor or further processed into the smoother and more refined forms of sweetened chocolate we are used to. Cocoa beans are about the size and shape of kidney beans. Nibs, which are broken rather than uniformly chopped pieces, resemble pecan shells shattered by a nutcracker, and they vary in size from bits that are less than ⅛ inch to shards sometimes ½ inch long. These are often jagged on one side and smooth and curved on the other. In one handful of nibs, you will see shades of mahogany and charcoal brown, slatey grays, and hints of mauve.

Chocolatiers had begun to incorporate nibs into fine chocolate and some pretty sophisticated chocolate bars; but only a few American pastry chefs had started to explore their uses. I had been playing with them for several years. From my first handful, I was excited about working with a very high quality but less processed form of a familiar ingredient. I saw it as a chance to work with "primitive" chocolate, a chance to rethink, redefine, and reinvent chocolate desserts, and savory dishes too (see Chocolate for Dinner, page 274).

When you smell and taste cocoa nibs for the first time, you know at once they must be some form of chocolate. Yet nibs are most intriguing for the ways in which they are different from the chocolate we know. They are dry and crunchy, even crunchier and noisier than toasted nuts. They are unsweetened and austere to a palate that expects "chocolate."

Nibs taste bitter at first. As an analogy, remember your first cup of espresso. Then remember how you got used to it, perhaps learned to love it. If your nibs are a blend of different cocoa beans, each little piece will taste different from its brothers. When you taste them one at a time, you are tasting just some of the hundreds of individual flavors that go into making the taste we think of as chocolate. Nibs range from winy or fruity and tart to earthy or nutlike. They can be tannic or astringent or taste like tea or cherries or peanuts . . . the list of comparison flavors is endless.

Although nibs can be mixed into batters or doughs like chocolate chips, they do not behave at all like chocolate chips. Chocolate chips are sweet and smooth and crowd-pleasing; arguably, they improve anything from tough and doughy cookies to mediocre cakes and muffins. Cocoa nibs are much less accommodating. They don't automatically improve anything, and, at their worst, they are bitter and gritty. At their best, however, they are divinely crunchy, filled with nuance. Nibs are stubborn and complex. When used in contrast to something creamy and smooth, they can be perfection, or just a mouthful of soggy grit—it all depends. They must be coaxed and cajoled. I learned from experience that they have a definite affinity for certain flavors and textures, including nuts, raisins, blackberries, many spices, brown sugar, and cream. They seem to have an equal antipathy for egg yolks, yeast, baking soda, fresh mint, and certain moist cakes and breads.

Early on, I realized that what I wanted to do with nibs was emphasize their subtle, unique characteristics rather than transform them into a crude form of chocolate by grinding and sweetening them in the course of preparing a recipe. I wanted to work with the nutty, bitter, earthy, less familiar flavors and, where possible, the extraordinary crunch. To do this, I decided to think of the nibs as nuts instead of as chocolate. What would I do with a new kind of chocolate-flavored nut?

I started with simple butter cookies. At first I was unimpressed by the flavor. I shrugged and figured I would have to start over again. But two days after I had baked them, the same cookies had become extraordinarily tender, melt-in-your-mouth delicacies with an undertone of indescribable flavor: like chocolate but not like chocolate, like nuts but like no nut I had ever tasted. They were subtle but rich, and I loved them. I concluded that cookies, especially crunchy ones with plenty of butter, are a perfect medium for nibs—butter cookies improve with age anyway. So as the flavor of the nibs is imbuing the cookie, all the other flavors, as well as the cookie's texture, are also improving. And because the nibs retain their crunch—they are so much crunchier than the cookie or any of the nuts that might be in the cookie—they make the cookie seem even more tender and delicate by contrast.

Success with dry, crunchy butter cookies led to the assumption that shortbread, Mexican wedding cakes, and biscotti would also be nib friendly. But I discovered that nibs get overroasted, bitter, and very unpleasant if they are baked for too long. My shortbread recipe bakes for at least 1 hour, Mexican wedding cakes take 25 to 30 minutes, and biscotti are twice-baked. I decided to stick with cookies with shorter baking times.

Even before I'd discovered that the long baking time required for crisp meringues might be a problem if I added nibs, I'd tasted a few nibs with a bite of plain crisp meringue and learned two things. First, the contrast between sweet and bitter was too extreme: the meringues tasted horribly sweet and the nibs terribly bitter. Second, the meringue dissolved much faster than the nibs, leaving a mouthful of bitter, naked nibs. Nibs seemed to work better in a medium that lasts longer in your mouth and has flavors that linger, or enough fat (such as in ice cream), to coat your palate, while you finish chewing the nibs. With hindsight, I should have tried loading lots of nibs into the meringue (changing the balance of sweet and bitter) and baking it in small shapes for less time. This was brought to my attention much later, when I tasted fantastic nibby meringues from Tartine, San Francisco's now famous bakery! I did find nibs to be successful in a not too sweet, soft, nutty meringue, inspired by marjolaine layers, with which I make a simple roulade filled with blackberry preserves and whipped cream.

Meanwhile, fat also affects the contrast between sweet and bitter: Nibs taste fine in traditional chocolate chip cookie dough, which is plenty sweet, with both brown and white sugars, and also very rich in butter. But a nibby chocolate chip cookie really sings when walnuts and currants are added. The walnuts and currants accentuate the natural fruit and nut flavors in the nibs and bring all of the flavors together. Nibs are also delicious with coffee and thus very successful in a very rich, gooey, bittersweet chocolate cookie with freshly ground coffee beans. Here the nibs add chocolate intensity to an already over-the-top chocolate experience, much the same way they add excitement to a chocolate bar.

Next, I tried infusing nibs in liquids. I found them to be good in coffee—just put them in the filter or the press pot with the ground coffee—but too weird in tea. They were OK in hot milk—but not before bed unless you want to stay awake. Nibs in cream turned out to be a revelation. I heated a handful in heavy cream and let it all steep, then strained the nibs out and chilled the cream. I whipped the cold infused cream with just a whisper of sugar. The result was a sort of light, whipped albino chocolate ganache, positively exquisite, and like nothing I had ever tasted. If you've ever fantasized about white chocolate that is not sweet, that has a true chocolate flavor and a fresh creamy taste, your dreams have come true.

Cocoa Bean Cream (page 251) is just the palest shade of creamy tan, so innocent that its rich flavor will take you by surprise. I use it to top hot bittersweet chocolate soufflés, or *café filtre* or hot chocolate, or as a cake filling. The possibilities are endless. My favorite bartender helped me create a Nibby Alexander: Armagnac and sweetened nib-infused cream served in a martini glass with a dusting of cocoa powder and a twist of candied orange peel. This luxurious dessert drink capped a sumptuous evening called "For the Love of Science and Chocolate," to benefit the Berkeley Lawrence Hall of Science.

Nib-infused cream also became the base for a sensational Double Cocoa Nib Ice Cream (page 56) and divine panna cotta and then a simple cornstarch pudding, which turned out to be lovely comfort food. At first I wasn't sure about the pudding. My daughter and I were taking turns dipping spoons into it, pausing to think a moment after each little taste, trying to decide whether it was really good or just very novel. Finally, observing that the dish was empty and we had begun a second, she said, "Mom, I think we like this."

While cream turned out to be a perfect medium for nibs, adding eggs often muddied and distorted their flavor. Thus panna cotta was delicious but crème caramel was awful; cornstarch pudding was good but cup custard was terrible; and so forth. Cocoa bean ice cream with a custard base wasn't nearly as good as one with a base of pure cream.

Then I dreamed of nibby bread. In my mind, I could taste a gutsy whole-grain bread laced with nibs, or a rustic natural sourdough, or a suave brioche. But so far every cocoa bean bread has disappointed. I experimented with scones, soda bread, and banana bread. The nibs tended to absorb moisture and take on the unpleasant texture of damp nuts, and the flavors were bitter and astringent. They also seemed to react badly with the baking soda in soda bread, and the banana bread I had high hopes for somehow didn't work. The usually appealing bitter flavors in some grains brought out the worst in the nibs, and I suspect they had a bad reaction with the yeast as well. I decided to satisfy my desire for bread with cocoa beans by sprinkling nibs directly on my bread and butter, or even on a warm corn tortilla, sometimes with a little sugar, maybe even a little cinnamon. But I continue to experiment with nibs because, well, you just never know.

Postscript: In the years since my first adventures with cocoa nibs, chefs have created, published, and found fans for nibby breads, including banana bread, scones, cakes, pancakes, and the other types of desserts that didn't work for me. I may not agree, but I am thrilled to see cocoa nibs on more chefs' radars!

COCOA BEAN CREAM

This is one of the first things that I made with cocoa nibs. It is the stuff of dreams. Don't miss it.

/ **Makes about 2 cups**

INGREDIENTS

1 cup heavy cream

2 rounded tablespoons (20 grams) roasted
cocoa nibs

Sugar to taste

DIRECTIONS

• Bring the cream and nibs to a boil in a small saucepan. Remove from the heat, cover, and let
stand for 20 minutes.

• Strain the cream into a bowl, pressing on the solids to extract all the liquid. Discard the nibs.
Chill the cream for at least 6 hours; it must be thoroughly cold in order to whip properly.

• When ready to use, whip the cream, adding sugar to taste as the cream thickens.

CANDIED COCOA NIBS

A thin coating of melted sugar adds extra crunch, a sheen, and a little welcome sweetness to cocoa nibs. Once you have these pretty morsels on hand, you will sprinkle them on salads, add them to a cheese tray with some dried fruit, use them as a crunchy topping on ice cream, and toss them into trail mix or over your breakfast cereal. And that's just for starters.

Candied nibs are easy to make but the process requires attention. Some chefs cook the nibs and sugar together; but by the time the sugar is melted, the nibs are usually scorched. Here the sugar is cooked before the nibs are folded in. A bit of butter goes in at the end (so that the nib clusters will break apart easily later) and then the whole business is scraped out onto parchment paper. The entire procedure takes little more than 5 minutes! / **Makes about ¾ cup**

INGREDIENTS

½ teaspoon butter

2 tablespoons water

A pinch of cream of tartar

¼ cup (50 grams) sugar

½ cup (55 grams) cacao nibs
(I prefer roasted rather than raw nibs
but the choice is yours)

DIRECTIONS

• Line a baking sheet with parchment paper. Position the butter, a silicone spatula, and the prepared pan close to the stove.

• Add the water and cream of tartar to a small (1- to 1½-quart) saucepan with a lid. Pour the sugar into the center of the pan (so it does not touch the sides) and swirl or shake the pan gently to wet all of the sugar, without stirring. Cover the pan and heat to a boil over medium-high heat. Continue to cook, covered, for about 2½ minutes to dissolve the sugar into syrup. Uncover the pan and continue to cook, without stirring, until the syrup begins to color very slightly—usually you will see just a bit of golden color near the edges of the pan.

• Add the nibs and lower the heat to medium-low. Use the silicone spatula to fold the nibs and syrup together gently but purposefully, scraping the syrup from the bottom and sides of the pan over the nibs repeatedly, just until all of the nibs are coated and shiny. (Brisk stirring can cause the syrup to recrystallize; this is not the end of the world, but the results will not be as shiny or as crunchy as otherwise.)

• Turn the heat to low. Immediately add the butter and stir just until it is melted and mixed in. Immediately scrape the nibs onto the prepared pan and spread them out as much as possible—you may need a little knife to scrape the nibs from the spatula or to help spread them out on the parchment. Don't worry about clumps or thick places; when the nibs are cool they will break apart into lacy clusters or small bits, depending on what you want. When cool, move to a sealed container or zipper-lock bag. Nibs keep for months in an airtight container.

COCOA NIB PANNA COTTA

This dreamy, delicately set dessert is flavored with an infusion of roasted cocoa beans. The taste is exotic, the texture positively sensual. But you must measure the gelatin like a miser . . . or risk turning an exquisite confection into a dish of Jell-O. / Serves 6

SPECIAL EQUIPMENT

Instant-read thermometer

6 wide martini glasses
(or six 6-ounce ramekins)

INGREDIENTS

½ cup (60 grams) roasted cocoa nibs

3¼ cups heavy cream

2¾ teaspoons unflavored gelatin

1 cup cold whole milk

¼ cup plus 2 tablespoons (75 grams) sugar

Pinch of salt

Fresh blackberries or blackberry puree, well sugared

DIRECTIONS

• Bring the nibs and cream to a boil in a medium saucepan over medium-high heat. Remove from the heat, cover, and let steep for 20 minutes.

• Meanwhile, sprinkle the gelatin over the cold milk in a small bowl and set aside to let the gelatin soften.

• Strain the cream, pressing lightly on the nibs to extract all the liquid. Discard the nibs. Return the cream to the saucepan, add the sugar, and bring to a simmer. Pour into a heatproof bowl. Gradually stir in the milk, then the salt. Set the bowl in a larger bowl of ice cubes and water and stir frequently until the mixture thickens and registers 50°F on an instant-read thermometer.

• Divide evenly among the martini glasses (or ramekins). Cover with plastic wrap and chill overnight.

• Serve the panna cotta in their glasses or ramekins. Or, wrap each ramekin in a hot wrung-out wet towel and unmold onto dessert plates. Accompany with well-sugared berries or berry puree.

NIBBY PUDDING

Oooh—this pudding is creamy, smooth, and comforting. It's also quite sensual. The earthy but delicate flavor of roasted cocoa beans infused in light cream is quietly exciting. / **Serves 6**

SPECIAL EQUIPMENT

Six 4- to 6-ounce ramekins or custard cups

INGREDIENTS

3 cups half-and-half

¼ cup plus 2 tablespoons (45 grams) roasted cocoa nibs

½ cup (100 grams) sugar

3 tablespoons plus 2 teaspoons (30 grams) cornstarch

Scant ¼ teaspoon salt

DIRECTIONS

• In a small saucepan, bring the half-and-half and nibs to a gentle boil over medium heat. Remove from the heat, cover, and let steep for 20 minutes.

• Strain the half-and-half into a bowl, pressing on the nibs to extract most of the liquid. Discard the nibs.

• In a medium heavy saucepan, mix the sugar, cornstarch, and salt with about ⅓ cup of the infused half-and-half to form a smooth paste. Stir in the remaining half-and-half. Place over medium heat and stir constantly with a heatproof rubber spatula or wooden spoon until the mixture begins to thicken. Reduce the heat to low and continue stirring until the pudding begins to simmer. Simmer, stirring, for 1 more minute.

• Remove from the heat and pour into the ramekins or custard cups. Serve warm, cool, or chilled.

NIBBY PECAN COOKIES

PHOTOGRAPH ON PAGE 267

The dough for these looks like a beautiful piece of granite flecked with bits of russet and burnt umber. The cookies are exquisitely tender and crunchy. The flavor of the cocoa beans develops and infuses the cookies over time, so I strongly recommend that you make the dough a day before baking and bake the cookies at least twenty-four hours before you serve them—longer is even better. / **Makes about forty-eight 2-inch cookies**

INGREDIENTS

1 cup (3½ ounces/100 grams) pecan halves

14 tablespoons (200 grams) unsalted butter, softened

¾ cup (150 grams) sugar

¼ teaspoon salt (slightly rounded if you like)

1 tablespoon plus 1 teaspoon bourbon (optional)

1½ teaspoons pure vanilla extract

⅓ cup (40 grams) roasted cocoa nibs

2 cups (255 grams) all-purpose flour

DIRECTIONS

• Preheat the oven to 325°F.

• Spread the pecans on a cookie sheet. Toast them in the oven for 7 to 8 minutes, or until fragrant and lightly colored. Let cool, then chop.

• Combine the butter, sugar, salt, bourbon, if using, and vanilla in a medium bowl and, using a large spoon or an electric mixer on high speed, beat until smooth and creamy but not fluffy (about 1 minute with a mixer). Stir or beat in the pecans and cocoa nibs. Turn off the mixer, if you are using one, and add all the flour at once. Beat on low speed to prevent the flour from flying out, just until the flour is fully incorporated. Or stir in the flour until incorporated. If necessary, finish mixing with your hands.

• *For slice-and-bake cookies:* Form the dough into a 12-inch log about 2 inches thick.

• *For rolled and cut cookies:* Divide it in half and form into two flat patties. Wrap the dough and refrigerate for at least 2 hours, preferably overnight. (The dough can be frozen for up to 3 months.)

continued

• Position the racks in the upper and lower thirds of the oven and preheat the oven to 350°F. Line two cookie sheets with parchment paper.

• *To slice and bake cookies:* Use a sharp knife to cut the cold dough log into ¼-inch-thick slices. Place the cookies at least 1½ inches apart on the lined cookie sheets.

• *To roll and cut cookies:* Remove one patty from the refrigerator and let it sit at room temperature until supple enough to roll but still quite firm—it will continue to soften as you work. Roll the dough out between two pieces of wax paper or between heavy plastic sheets (from a heavy-duty plastic bag) to a thickness of ¼ inch. Turn the dough over once or twice while you are rolling it out to check for deep wrinkles; if necessary, peel off and smooth the paper or plastic over the dough before continuing to roll it. Peel off the top sheet of paper or plastic and place it in front of you. Invert the dough onto the paper and peel off the second sheet. Cut out cookies as close together as possible to minimize scraps, dipping the edges of cookie cutters in flour as necessary to prevent sticking. Use the point of a paring knife to lift and remove scraps as you transfer cookies, using a narrow metal spatula, to ungreased cookie sheets, placing the cookies at least 1½ inches apart. (If the dough gets too soft at any time while you are working, slide a cookie sheet underneath the paper or plastic and refrigerate the dough for a few minutes until it firms up again.) Repeat with the second piece of dough. Press all of the dough scraps together gently (don't overwork them with too much kneading), reroll, and cut out more cookies.

• Bake for 12 to 14 minutes, or until the cookies are light golden brown at the edges, rotating the cookie sheets from top to bottom and front to back halfway through the baking. Set the cookie sheets or just the liners on racks. Let cool completely. For best flavor and texture, store the cookies in an airtight container for at least 24 hours before serving. (They can be stored airtight for at least 1 month.)

Nibby Cocoa Cookies   If you omit the nuts, increase the nibs, and add cocoa, you get these tender, crunchy cookies with even more complex but subtle chocolate flavors.

Omit the pecans and bourbon. Decrease the vanilla to 1 teaspoon. Whisk ¼ cup (25 grams) premium unsweetened cocoa powder (natural or Dutch-process) into the flour before adding it to the dough. Increase the nibs to ½ cup (60 grams). Bake the cookies for 10 to 12 minutes, or until they have puffed slightly and fallen, and feel firm to the touch.

Substitutions   I like this recipe with walnuts or with toasted skinned hazelnuts (page 28) instead of pecans, or substitute ¼ teaspoon ground vanilla beans, which you can do yourself or buy (see page 30), for 1 teaspoon of the vanilla extract. I also like to use sea salt that is slightly coarser than table salt—then I often use a tad more than ¼ teaspoon, as this adds a little extra flavor excitement.

NIBBY ESPRESSO COOKIES

This is an intense and sophisticated chocolate experience, best enjoyed in the form of tiny cookies—and probably not appreciated by children. I love them. / **Makes sixty 1¾-inch cookies**

INGREDIENTS

⅓ cup (45 grams) all-purpose flour

¼ teaspoon baking powder

¼ teaspoon salt

5 tablespoons (70 grams) unsalted butter

6 ounces (170 grams) unsweetened 99% to 100% chocolate (preferably the very highest quality), coarsely chopped

2 large eggs, at room temperature

1⅓ cups (265 grams) sugar

1½ teaspoons finely ground coffee beans (freshly ground)

1 teaspoon pure vanilla extract

½ cup (60 grams) roasted cocoa nibs

DIRECTIONS

• Combine the flour, baking powder, and salt in a small bowl and mix together thoroughly with a whisk. Set aside.

• Place the butter and chocolate in a medium stainless steel bowl in a wide skillet of barely simmering water and stir occasionally until melted and smooth. Remove from the heat and set aside.

• In a large bowl, using an electric mixer, beat the eggs, sugar, coffee beans, and vanilla until pale and thick, about 5 minutes. Stir in the chocolate mixture. Stir in the flour mixture and, finally, the nibs. Cover the dough and refrigerate until firm, about 1 hour, or up to 4 days.

• Position the racks in the upper and lower thirds of the oven and preheat the oven to 350°F. Line two cookie sheets with parchment paper.

• Drop rounded teaspoonfuls of batter 1½ inches apart on the lined cookie sheets. Bake, rotating the sheets from top to bottom and front to back halfway through the baking time to ensure even baking, until the cookies are puffed and dry on the surface but still soft and gooey within, 7 to 9 minutes. Set the cookie sheets or just the liners onto racks. Let cool completely. (The cookies can be stored, airtight, at room temperature for 2 days or frozen for longer storage.)

NIBBY NUT AND RAISIN COOKIES

PHOTOGRAPH ON PAGE 267

These cookies are especially delicious if you chill the dough overnight before baking. And, for the best cookies of all—that is, ones that are brown and crunchy at the edges and chewy in the centers—eschew parchment paper, silicone-coated pan liners, and/or cushioned pans, and simply bake on unlined, ungreased baking sheets. / *Makes about 60 cookies*

INGREDIENTS

2¼ cups (285 grams) all-purpose flour

1 teaspoon baking soda

½ pound (225 grams/2 sticks) unsalted butter, melted and still warm

¾ cup (150 grams) granulated sugar

¾ cup (130 grams) lightly packed brown sugar

¾ teaspoon salt

2 large eggs

1 teaspoon pure vanilla extract

⅔ cup (80 grams) roasted cocoa nibs

1 cup (105 grams) finely chopped walnuts

1 cup (140 grams) dried currants or raisins

DIRECTIONS

• Whisk the flour and baking soda together thoroughly. Set aside.

• In a large bowl, combine the melted butter, sugars, and salt. Stir in the eggs and vanilla. Stir in the flour mixture just until all of the dry ingredients are moistened, then stir in the nibs, nuts, and currants. If possible, cover and chill the dough for at least 2 hours, preferably overnight.

• Position the oven racks in the upper and lower thirds of the oven and preheat the oven to 375°F. Remove the dough from the refrigerator to soften.

• Scoop up level tablespoonfuls of dough and place them 2 inches apart on ungreased cookie sheets. Bake, rotating the cookie sheets from top to bottom and front to back about halfway through the baking time, for 8 to 10 minutes, or until the cookies are golden brown at the edges and no longer look wet on top.

• Use a metal pancake turner to transfer the cookies to a wire rack and let cool completely. (The cookies keep, in a tightly sealed container, for several days.)

ALMOND STICKS WITH COCOA NIBS

Crunchy, subtle, and not too sweet, these cookies look like extra-thin miniature biscotti and have the intriguing nutty flavor of roasted cocoa nibs. / *Makes about thirty-two 6-inch sticks*

INGREDIENTS

¾ cup (110 grams) whole blanched almonds

1 cup plus 2 tablespoons (145 grams) all-purpose flour

⅔ cup (135 grams) sugar

¼ teaspoon salt

6 tablespoons (85 grams) unsalted butter, cut into chunks

2 tablespoons water, plus more if necessary

1 teaspoon pure vanilla extract

⅛ teaspoon pure almond extract

¼ cup (30 grams) roasted cocoa nibs

DIRECTIONS

• Combine the almonds, flour, sugar, and salt in a food processor and pulse until the almonds are reduced to a fine meal. Add the butter and pulse until the mixture turns into crumbs. Combine the 2 tablespoons water, vanilla, and almond extract, drizzle them into the processor bowl, and pulse until the dough looks damp. Add the cocoa nibs and pulse until evenly dispersed.

• The dough will not form a smooth cohesive mass—it will be crumbly, but it should stick together when you press it (pulse in another teaspoon or two of water if necessary). Turn it out onto a large sheet of foil and form it into a 6-by-9-inch rectangle a scant ½ inch thick. Fold the foil over the dough and press firmly with your hands to compress it, then wrap it airtight. Slide a cookie sheet under the package and refrigerate for at least 2 hours, or overnight.

• Position the racks in the upper and lower thirds of the oven and preheat the oven to 350°F. Line two cookie sheets with parchment paper.

• Use a long sharp knife to trim one short edge of the dough rectangle to even it. Then cut a slice a scant ⅜ inch wide and use the knife to transfer the delicate slice to the cookie sheet. Repeat with the rest of the dough, transferring each slice as it is cut and placing them at least 1 inch apart.

• Bake, rotating the cookie sheets from top to bottom and front to back halfway through the baking time, for 12 to 14 minutes, or until the cookies are golden at the edges. Set the cookie sheets or liners on racks to cool. (The cookies can be stored, airtight, for several days.)

OPPOSITE: Almond Sticks with Cocoa Nibs and Rich Hot Chocolate (page 162).

COCOA BEAN TASSIES

I applied my own sleight of hand to a long remembered delicacy called pecan tassies from Margaret Fox's *Café Beaujolais Cookbook*. Even Margaret approves of these miniature tartlets filled with a sweet gooey sauce offset with cracked cocoa beans. / **Makes 24 small pastries**

SPECIAL EQUIPMENT

Two 12-cup miniature muffin pans

INGREDIENTS

FOR THE PASTRY

12 tablespoons (170 grams/1½ sticks) unsalted butter, melted

¼ cup plus 2 tablespoons (75 grams) sugar

1 teaspoon pure vanilla extract

Scant ¼ teaspoon salt

1½ cups (190 grams) all-purpose flour

FOR THE FILLING

1 large egg white

¾ cup (130 grams) lightly packed light brown or golden brown sugar

1 tablespoon (14 grams) unsalted butter, melted

1 cup (115 grams) roasted cocoa nibs, chopped into small bits

1 teaspoon pure vanilla extract

Generous pinch of salt

DIRECTIONS

• Position a rack in the lower third of the oven and preheat the oven to 400°F.

• To make the pastry: Combine the melted butter, sugar, vanilla, and salt in a medium bowl. Add the flour and mix just until incorporated.

• Divide the dough in half and press each half into a flattened 4-inch square. Cut each square into 12 equal pieces and shape each piece into a ball. Place one dough ball in each muffin cup and press it evenly over the bottom and all the way up the sides of the cup, forming a neat rim.

• To make the filling: In a medium bowl, beat the egg white until foamy. Stir in the brown sugar, melted butter, cocoa nibs, vanilla, and salt. Divide the filling evenly among the tartlet shells.

• Bake the tassies for 10 minutes, then reduce the oven temperature to 250°F and bake for 20 minutes more, or until the pastry is well browned on the edges and underneath (lift one out with the point of a knife to check). Let cool in the pans on a rack. (Stored in an airtight container, these remain delicious for about 3 days, with the chocolate flavor intensifying from day to day.)

CURRANT AND NIB RUGELACH

PHOTOGRAPH ON PAGE 267

Rugelach at its best is a wondrously flaky yet unbelievably foolproof little horn of pastry pretending to be a cookie. There are various fillings, of which I have always loved the classic—cinnamon, nuts, and raisins—best. So, when it turned out that nibs are also good with raisins (or currants), I had to make room for a new favorite. / *Makes 48 cookies*

INGREDIENTS

FOR THE PASTRY

2½ cups (320 grams) all-purpose flour

2 tablespoons (25 grams) sugar

¼ teaspoon salt

½ pound (225 grams/2 sticks) cold unsalted butter

One 8-ounce (225-gram) package cream cheese, chilled

FOR THE FILLING

2 tablespoons (25 grams) granulated sugar

½ cup (85 grams) lightly packed light brown or golden brown sugar

1 teaspoon ground cinnamon

½ cup (60 grams) cocoa nibs, finely chopped into small bits

½ cup (70 grams) dried currants

DIRECTIONS

• *To make the pastry in a stand mixer:* Combine the flour, sugar, and salt in the bowl of an electric mixer. Using the paddle attachment, mix briefly to distribute the ingredients. Cut each stick of butter into 8 pieces, and add them to the bowl. Mix on low speed until most of the mixture resembles very coarse bread crumbs, with a few larger pieces of butter the size of hazelnuts. Cut the cream cheese into 1-inch cubes and add them to the bowl. Mix on medium-low speed for 30 to 60 seconds, just until the mixture is damp and shaggy-looking and holds together when pressed with your fingers.

• *To make the pastry in a food processor:* Combine the flour, sugar, and salt in a food processor and pulse a few times to mix. Cut the butter into ¾-inch cubes and add to the flour mixture. Pulse until the butter pieces range in size from coarse bread crumbs to hazelnuts. Cut the cream cheese into 1-inch cubes and add to the mixture. Pulse just until the dough looks damp and shaggy and holds together when pressed with your fingers.

• Scrape the dough onto a work surface and knead it two or three times to incorporate any loose pieces. There should be large streaks of cream cheese. Divide the dough into

4 pieces. Press each piece into a flat patty about 4 inches in diameter, wrap in plastic wrap, and refrigerate until firm, about 4 hours.

• Position the racks in the upper and lower thirds of the oven and preheat the oven to 350°F. Line two cookie sheets with parchment or wax paper or aluminum foil.

• To make the filling: Mix the sugars, cinnamon, nibs, and currants together in a medium bowl.

• Remove one piece of dough from the refrigerator; if necessary, let it stand until pliable enough to roll, but not too soft. Roll it out between two pieces of wax paper into a 12-inch circle a scant ⅛ inch thick. Peel off the top sheet of wax paper, and place the paper on the counter or a cutting board. Flip the dough onto the paper and peel off the second sheet. Sprinkle a quarter of the filling over the dough. Gently roll over the filling with a rolling pin to press it into the dough. Cut the dough into 12 equal wedges like a pie. Starting at the wide end of one wedge, roll it up and place it, with the dough point underneath to prevent it from unrolling, on one of the cookie sheets. Repeat with the remaining wedges, placing them 1½ inches apart.

• Repeat with the remaining dough and filling. (If at any time the dough becomes too soft to roll, return it to the refrigerator to firm up.)

• Bake, rotating the sheets from top to bottom and front to back halfway through the baking time, for about 25 minutes, or until light golden brown at the edges. Set the cookie sheets or just the liners on racks to cool completely. (The rugelach are best on the day they are baked, but they can be stored, airtight, for about 5 days.)

OPPOSITE, CLOCKWISE FROM TOP: Nibby Nut and Raisin Cookies (page 261); Nibby Pecan Cookies (page 257); Currant and Nib Rugelach (page 265); Bittersweet Decadence Cookie (page 235); Real Chocolate Wafers (page 233); Nibby Hazelnut Cookies (page 259).

COCOA BEAN ALMOND ROULADE

A simple filling of blackberry or black raspberry preserves and fresh whipped cream in a soft meringue studded with toasted nuts and lots of toasted cocoa beans makes a light and sophisticated dessert with intriguing flavors and textures. Or dress it up with a cloak of chocolate ganache glaze. Don't miss the variation with Cocoa Bean Cream. / Serves 10 to 12

SPECIAL EQUIPMENT

11-by-17-inch or 12-by-17-inch jelly-roll pan or half sheet pan

INGREDIENTS

FOR THE ROULADE

1½ cups (7½ ounces/215 grams) unblanched whole almonds

1½ tablespoons (12 grams) all-purpose flour

¾ cup (150 grams) sugar

¼ cup plus 2 tablespoons (45 grams) roasted cocoa nibs

6 large egg whites (about ¾ cup), at room temperature

½ teaspoon cream of tartar

Powdered sugar for dusting

FOR THE FILLING

Scant ½ cup blackberry or black raspberry fruit spread or jam

1 cup heavy cream

½ teaspoon pure vanilla extract

Ganache Glaze (page 192; optional)

DIRECTIONS

• Position a rack in the center of the oven and preheat the oven to 325°F. Line the baking pan with parchment paper.

• Spread the almonds on a cookie sheet. Toast them in the oven for 7 to 8 minutes, or until fragrant and lightly colored. Let cool completely.

• Combine the toasted almonds, flour, and ½ cup (100 grams) of the sugar in a food processor and pulse to a medium-fine texture. Add the nibs and pulse to a fine meal. Set aside.

• In a clean, dry mixer bowl or other large bowl, combine the egg whites with the cream of tartar and beat with an electric mixer at medium speed until soft peaks form when the beaters are lifted. Increase the speed and gradually add the remaining ¼ cup (100 grams) sugar, then beat until the meringue forms stiff but not dry peaks. Pour the nut mixture over the meringue, and fold it in with a large rubber spatula just until evenly dispersed. Spread the batter evenly in the lined pan.

• Bake for 25 to 30 minutes, or until the cake is golden brown and springy to the touch. Let cool completely in the pan on a rack. (The cake can be prepared up to 2 days ahead; cover the pan tightly with foil or plastic wrap and store at room temperature.)

• To assemble the cake: Using a fine-mesh strainer, shake a very light dusting of powdered sugar over the cake. Run a small knife around the edges of the cake to release it from the pan. Cover with a sheet of foil. Holding the foil and pan edges together at both ends, invert the pan onto the counter. Remove the pan and peel off the parchment liner.

• Spread a very thin layer of fruit spread evenly over the cake. In a large bowl, whip the cream with the vanilla until it holds a good shape without being stiff (it will stiffen further when you spread it). Spread the cream over the jam. Starting at one short edge, roll the cake up like a jelly roll. Wrap the roll in the foil and refrigerate until ready to serve. (The roulade can be refrigerated for up to 24 hours.)

• To serve, unwrap the roulade and transfer to a serving platter. Sift additional powdered sugar over the top, if desired, or frost with the ganache glaze, pouring it or spreading it over the roll.

VARIATION

Cocoa Bean Cream Almond Roulade   Substitute Cocoa Bean Cream (page 251) for the heavy cream and omit the vanilla extract.

OVERLEAF, FROM LEFT TO RIGHT: Cocoa Bean Almond Roulade; Bittersweet Deception (page 130); Bittersweet Tartlets with Ancho Chile and Cherry (page 230), with Hazelnuts, Orange, and Anise (page 229), and with cocoa nibs.

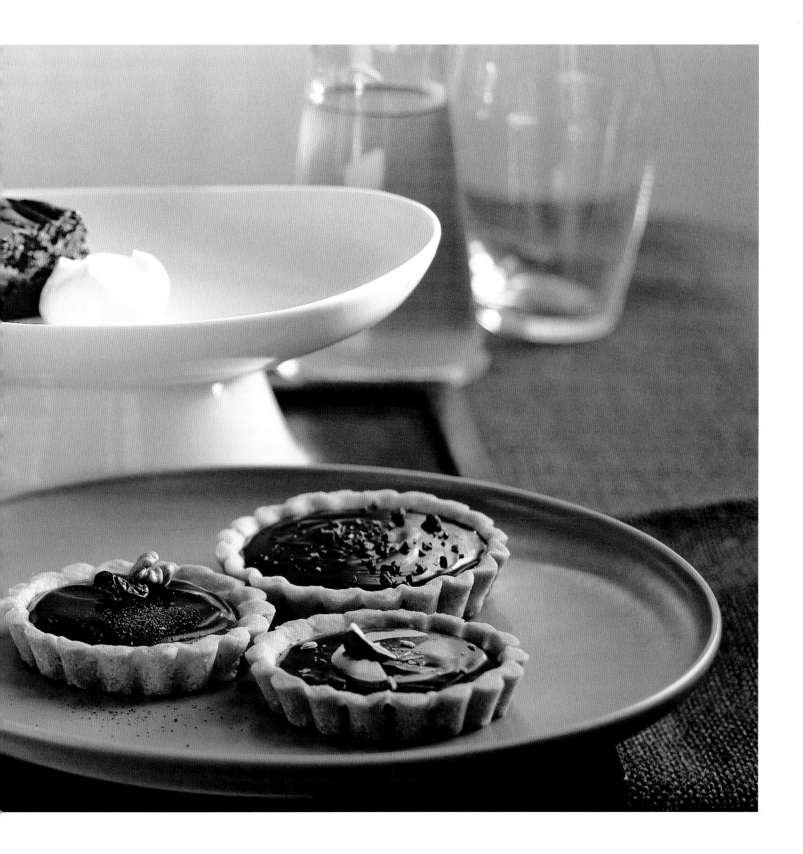

BUCKWHEAT COCOA CREPES WITH HONEY

After eating a bowl of hot leftover kasha with warm milk and crushed cocoa nibs for breakfast one morning, I thought nibs might add a little shading and depth to the toasty, earthy flavor of traditional Breton buckwheat crepes. But the nibs turned soggy in the crepes, so I turned to cocoa powder and was rewarded with these flavorful wraps, which are delicious with honey. Add a little vanilla ice cream or crème fraîche and make them into a dressy dessert, sprinkled with nibs or Candied Cocoa Nibs, of course. / *Makes about 14 crepes*

INGREDIENTS

FOR THE CREPES

½ cup (65 grams) buckwheat flour

½ cup plus 2 tablespoons (80 grams) all-purpose flour

¼ cup (20 grams) premium unsweetened natural cocoa powder (see Chocolate Note)

1 cup milk

¾ cup water, plus more if necessary

3 large eggs

3 tablespoons vegetable oil

½ teaspoon salt

Vegetable oil for cooking the crepes

½ to ⅔ cup honey for drizzling

Vanilla ice cream, crème fraîche, or sour cream (optional)

3 to 4 tablespoons (25 to 30 grams) roasted cocoa nibs or Candied Cocoa Nibs (page 252), lightly crushed

DIRECTIONS

• To make the crepe batter: Combine all the ingredients in a blender or food processor and blend until perfectly smooth. Transfer to a bowl, cover, and refrigerate for at least 1 hour, or up to 1 day.

• When it is ready to cook, the batter should be the consistency of buttermilk. If it is too thick, stir in 1 to 2 tablespoons water. Lay a sheet of wax paper on the counter, or oil a baking sheet.

• Heat an 8-inch crepe pan or frying pan over medium heat. Film the pan with about 1 teaspoon vegetable oil. Stir the batter, pour a scant ⅓ cup into the crepe pan, and immediately swirl and tilt the pan to cover the bottom evenly. Cook for about 1 minute, until the surface looks set, then loosen the crepe at one edge. Peek to see if the crepe is golden brown underneath. Turn it over and cook for another 30 seconds, then flip the crepe out of the pan onto the wax paper or baking sheet.

• Repeat with the remaining batter, oiling the pan as necessary. Stack the cooked crepes, separating them with wax paper. If serving immediately, keep the crepes warm in a 250°F oven; or let cool, wrap, and refrigerate for up to 2 days (or freeze for up to 1 month).

• To reheat stored crepes, warm each one in a hot lightly buttered pan for about 30 seconds, on one side only.

• To serve, drizzle each hot crepe with about 2 teaspoons honey and roll up or fold into quarters. If you like, gild the lily with vanilla ice cream (or crème fraîche or sour cream). Sprinkle with the nibs and serve, two per person.

CHOCOLATE NOTE

I like the flavor of these crepes best with natural cocoa powder, but there is no reason you can't make them with Dutch-process cocoa if you prefer it.

CHOCOLATE FOR DINNER

Playing with cocoa nibs encouraged me to rethink my prior assumptions about chocolate. Because they were new to me, I had approached the nibs with a little of the Buddhist "beginner's mind": open curiosity and conscious rejection of preconceived notions. When I began paying the same careful attention to the flavors in chocolate, rather than limiting my expectations to dessert or candy, I went quite naturally to savory dishes, just as had European cooks who tasted chocolate for the first time several hundred years ago.

It would be less hard to imagine the ways in which we might be using chocolate had the king of Spain not sweetened this exotic new food with almost equally exotic sugar. When he put those two stimulants together, he unleashed a force of nature. Sweetened chocolate is so compelling that we've ignored savory chocolate dishes, with the exception of a few surviving icons such as mole poblano. I have been guilty of thinking it simply academic, weird, or gimmicky to put chocolate with meat or vegetables. With chicken livers? I would once have dismissed that as a blatant bid for attention.

But playing with chocolate in savory dishes changed my attitude from dismissive to curious and excited. It was like learning what to do with nibs in desserts, or my two-day marathon with capuaçu, the cousin of chocolate, or creating low-fat desserts without other people's rules. Experiments that began with an open mind, then drew on the sum of my knowledge and experience, became a challenge for my palate and imagination.

And because I was playing with an open mind, I was led directly to, yes, chicken livers and chocolate even before I found a historical precedent for the combination! In the same way, I was drawn to try chocolate with various types of olives and olive oil, cheeses, fresh and cured meats, and certain vegetables such as squash, eggplant, and green beans. I was mostly following my own palate, rather than reading or doing research, but I was not surprised later to see that other chefs had landed on similar shores, both before and after me. I realized that for years I had cherished Giuliano Bugialli's pasta recipe for meat sauce with savory chocolate without exploring the topic further!

What I learned from playing with chocolate in savory dishes is that these are more likely to be subtle and sophisticated than weird or contrived. Chocolate adds a luxurious texture to sauces, for example, in coq au vin, mushrooms in wine sauce, meat sauces for pasta, and mole (of course). And cocoa nibs, the most primitive chocolate ingredient, add intriguing earthy flavors and an appealing crunch to myriad savory dishes. There is a much larger world of chocolate—in terms of both form and function—than we have known. These recipes are just a beginning.

CRUNCHY BABY GREENS

PHOTOGRAPH ON PAGE 290

A recipe that's not a recipe at all. Salad was the first savory dish that came to mind when I tasted roasted cocoa nibs. I put it on the menu, followed by pasta with Giuliano's Sweet and Savory Meat Sauce with Chocolate (page 287), when sixty members of the American Institute of Food and Wine came to lunch at a little industrial garage space that was the first Scharffen Berger Chocolate Maker factory in South San Francisco. Even in that crowd, I'm not sure anyone had tasted cocoa nibs, and absolutely no one had tasted them in a salad. Before too long, salads with cocoa nibs started showing up, first on local restaurant menus, then everywhere.

Like toasted hazelnuts or walnuts, cocoa beans add a fine crunch and rich earthy flavor to a perfect minimalist salad. From here you can go on to add intrigue: perhaps with a handful of dried currants, shaved fennel, Niçoise olives, or paper-thin rings of sweet red onion. Or serve the salad with a hot round of goat cheese, accompanied by toasted baguette slices brushed with olive oil.

INGREDIENTS

Mixed baby greens, such as mesclun or spring salad mix, rinsed and spun or patted dry

Your best extra virgin olive oil

Good red wine vinegar

Sea salt

Freshly ground black pepper

Roasted cocoa nibs or Candied Cocoa Nibs (page 252)

DIRECTIONS

• Toss the greens with just enough oil to coat, and splash judiciously with vinegar. Then toss again. Season with salt and pepper to taste. Sprinkle with nibs and serve.

CHEESE-STUFFED FIGS DIPPED IN CHOCOLATE

Here ripe figs are stuffed with a secret creamy filling and coated with crisp dark chocolate and crunchy toasted nuts. Add them to an after-dinner cheese tray or serve them for dessert with an oloroso sherry or aged tawny port. Everyday cream cheese is delicious and obvious, but the more interesting and decadent cheeses really shine here. / *Makes 20 dipped figs*

INGREDIENTS

20 ripe figs

¼ cup (60 grams) soft creamy cheese such as ordinary cream cheese, fresh ricotta, mascarpone, or even a triple-cream cheese such as Mt. Tam or Brillat-Savarin

5 ounces (140 grams) dark chocolate (any percentage), chopped

⅓ cup (45 grams) chopped toasted almonds or walnuts

• Rinse the figs and wipe them dry. Cut a short gash in one side of a fig near the bottom. Stuff with about ½ teaspoon of cheese, then smooth over the cheese so the fig remains shapely. Stuff the remaining figs and chill them for at least 30 minutes.

• Put the chocolate in a small stainless steel bowl set in a wide skillet of almost simmering water; stir frequently until most of the chocolate is melted. Remove the bowl from the water and stir until the chocolate is completely melted. Line a baking sheet with wax paper. Make sure the figs are dry. Dip a fig into the chocolate and let the excess chocolate drip into the bowl. Sprinkle the dipped fig with toasted nuts and set on the lined sheet. Dip the remaining figs. Refrigerate the figs until serving.

CHOCOLATE NOTE

I usually choose a 62% or 70% chocolate for these.

CHOPPED EGGPLANT WITH COCOA NIBS

Guessing that the flavors of eggplant and cocoa beans might be sympathetic, I adapted a popular Middle Eastern appetizer. The nibs add a nutty, almost meaty dimension to the dish. Delicious. / **Makes about 4 cups**

INGREDIENTS

2 large eggplants

Salt

Olive oil

1 medium yellow onion, coarsely chopped

¼ cup (18 grams) chopped Italian parsley

¼ cup (30 grams) cocoa nibs, finely chopped into small bits

⅓ cup (35 grams) chopped walnuts, optional

Freshly ground black pepper

DIRECTIONS

• Wash the eggplants and trim off the stem ends. Cut the eggplants into ⅓-inch-thick slices. Sprinkle salt liberally over both sides of each slice and stand the slices on their edges in a colander on a deep plate or in the sink. Allow the juices to drain for at least 30 minutes.

• Preheat the oven to 450°F. Grease two baking sheets with olive oil.

• Rinse the eggplant slices briefly to remove excess salt, then blot dry with paper towels. Brush both sides of each slice with olive oil and arrange them in one layer on the baking sheets. (If they don't fit, cut some in half and arrange them like a jigsaw puzzle.) Bake, turning once, until browned and very soft, about 10 minutes per side.

• While the eggplant is baking, film a large frying pan with olive oil, add the onion, and cook slowly, over medium-low heat, until it is deep golden brown. Sprinkle the onion with a little salt and set aside.

• When the eggplant is done, transfer it to a cutting board and coarsely chop with a large sharp knife, taking care not to leave any long pieces of skin. Transfer to a bowl. Add the onion, mashing and stirring with a fork. Mix in the parsley, chopped nibs, and walnuts, if using. Taste and adjust the salt, and add a little freshly ground pepper to taste.

CHOCOLATE-OLIVE OIL CROSTINI

These crostini are too simple for words! They make an irresistible appetizer or snack, and they're not bad for breakfast either. Scharffen Berger 62% Cacao Semisweet Chocolate is a particularly fine partner with fruity extra virgin olive oil, crunchy bread, and flaky sea salt here, but any dark chocolate you like will work well.

Nothing else is needed, but you can invent endless variations too. For instance, sprinkle the crostini with pinches of smoked hot paprika, espelette pepper, or chili powder. Or sprinkle on fresh or dried herbs such as rosemary or thyme. Just keep tasting and inventing. / **Makes 25 to 30 pieces**

INGREDIENTS

1 sweet (not sourdough) baguette

Extra virgin olive oil

3 to 4 ounces (85 to 115 grams) 62% chocolate

Flaky sea salt

OPTIONAL EMBELLISHMENTS

Espelette pepper

Smoked hot or sweet paprika

Dried or fresh herbs

DIRECTIONS

• Preheat the oven to 350°F with a rack in the center of the oven.

• Slice the baguette on a slight diagonal into pieces about ½ inch thick, and place the slices on a cookie sheet. Toast for about 15 minutes or until the slices are light golden at the edges and perfectly crisp and crunchy. Brush the tops liberally with olive oil. Melt the chocolate and drizzle over the slices. Season with tiny pinches of salt and any of the optional flavors you like.

• Serve alone or with cocktails.

NIBBY PESTO

The flavors of extra virgin olive oil (and olives too) blend seamlessly with the flavor of roasted cacao nibs and bring out the nutty savory qualities of both. You can make simple crostini with this versatile condiment, as described below, or smear it on a thin round of baked pizza dough for a dramatic pizzetta. Other options include using it as a sandwich condiment, dipping crudités into it, tossing it with pasta or steamed green beans, drizzling it on chunks of roasted winter squash, or garnishing a soup with it. Toss it with spaghetti or buckwheat noodles, or use it as a base for salad dressing. / **Makes about ⅔ cup**

INGREDIENTS

⅓ cup (40 grams) roasted cacao nibs

⅓ cup extra virgin olive oil

12 to 15 Niçoise olives, rinsed, patted dry, and pitted

Fresh basil leaves (optional)

Salt

Espelette pepper, chili powder, or hot paprika (optional)

DIRECTIONS

• In a mini processor or mortar, grind the nibs with about half of the olive oil. Add the olives and a few basil leaves, if using, until the mixture resembles a gritty paste. Mix in the remaining oil. Season with salt and, if using, espelette pepper to taste.

VARIATIONS

Nibby Pesto Crostini   Grill or toast slices of French bread until crisp and golden. Spread the toasts with Nibby Pesto. Serve warm if possible.

Crostini variations   Top Nibby Pesto Crostini with a little thin sliced prosciutto, a shaving of aged Parmesan or Asiago cheese, torn basil, parsley, and/or toasted pine nuts.

CHOPPED CHICKEN LIVERS WITH SHERRY-COCOA PAN SAUCE

Don't be shocked at the idea of liver and chocolate. It's a natural if you just stop thinking of chocolate as being only for dessert. In *A True History of Chocolate,* Michael and Sophie Coe cite an eighteenth-century cookbook by the priest Felici Libera that includes a recipe for sliced liver dipped in chocolate and fried. Instead, I've sautéed chicken livers and finished them with a velvety little pan sauce thickened with cocoa. If you don't want *chopped* liver, serve the dish hot, directly from the sauté pan, over egg noodles or strips of fried polenta. / **Makes 1⅓ cups**

INGREDIENTS

¼ cup (35 grams) raisins

¼ cup dry amontillado or other medium-dry sherry

Olive oil

½ cup (70 grams) diced yellow onion

Salt

10 ounces (285 grams) chicken livers, rinsed, trimmed, and cut into quarters

Freshly ground black pepper

2 teaspoons premium unsweetened natural cocoa powder

2 tablespoons water

Coarsely chopped Italian parsley for garnish (optional)

DIRECTIONS

• Coarsely chop the raisins and put them in a cup with the sherry. Set aside.

• Film the bottom of a medium nonstick frying pan with olive oil. Add the onion and cook slowly, over medium-low heat, allowing it to turn soft and translucent and then brown. Sprinkle with a pinch or two of salt. Scrape into a bowl and reserve.

• Add a little more oil to the pan and sauté the chicken livers gently until brown on the outside but still red within. Sprinkle with salt and pepper. Pour the sherry and raisins over the livers. Add the cocoa and water and stir to blend. Cook, stirring, until the liquid is reduced and thickened and the livers are barely pink inside. Scrape the mixture into the bowl with the onion and let cool slightly.

• On a cutting board with a large knife or in a mezzaluna, chop the livers to a coarse paste. Taste and adjust the salt and pepper. Sprinkle with chopped parsley, if desired. Serve warm or chilled on crackers or warm pita bread.

ROASTED SQUASH SOUP WITH COCOA BEAN CREAM

PHOTOGRAPH ON PAGE 290

A perfectly simple and delicious fall soup with the added delight of drizzled cream infused with crushed cocoa beans. You can garnish the soup with Nibby Pesto (page 279) instead of the infused cream. / Serves 4 to 6

INGREDIENTS

One 2½- to 3-pound (1.1- to 1.4-kilogram) butternut squash

1 medium yellow onion, cut into eighths

2 tablespoons olive oil

½ teaspoon salt, plus more if necessary

4 cups chicken stock, vegetable broth, or water

1 tablespoon chopped fresh sage leaves or 1 teaspoon crushed dried sage

Freshly ground white pepper

Whole or ground nutmeg

3 tablespoons (23 grams) roasted cocoa nibs

½ cup heavy cream

DIRECTIONS

• Preheat the oven to 450°F. Line a baking sheet with aluminum foil.

• Half and seed the squash and cut it into slices about 1 inch thick. Put the squash and onion on the baking sheet, drizzle with the olive oil, and sprinkle with the salt. With your hands, toss to coat the squash and onion with the oil. Roast for about 45 minutes, turning the pieces once, until the squash is quite tender and golden brown.

• Transfer the onion to a blender or food processor. As soon as you can handle the squash, scoop the flesh from the skin and add it to the blender along with any juices left on the foil. Add about 1 cup of the stock and puree until smooth. Transfer to a medium saucepan and add the remaining stock and the sage. Cover and bring to a simmer over medium heat. Correct the salt and season with pepper and a little freshly grated or ground nutmeg to taste.

• Meanwhile, just before serving, use a rolling pin to crush the cocoa nibs lightly between sheets of parchment paper, or crush them in a mortar. Combine the nibs and cream in a small saucepan, bring to a simmer, and simmer for 1 or 2 minutes to infuse the nibs' flavor into the cream. Ladle the soup into bowls and spoon a drizzle of cream and cocoa nibs over each bowl.

NIBBY ASPARAGUS WITH PROSCIUTTO

Elegant finger food or a plated first course, this dish is at its most aromatic and delicious when served hot or warm. / *Serves 4 to 6*

INGREDIENTS

1 to 1½ pounds (455 to 680 grams) asparagus

2 tablespoons fruity extra virgin olive oil

2 tablespoons (15 grams) roasted cocoa nibs, lightly crushed with a rolling pin

2 to 3 thin slices prosciutto, trimmed of excess fat and sliced into long slender shreds

DIRECTIONS

• Bring a large pot of salted water to a boil. Snap the woody ends from the asparagus, rinse, and peel the stems (if you like). Cook the asparagus in boiling water just until barely tender and still bright green, 3 to 5 minutes.

• Meanwhile, in a very small saucepan, warm the oil and crushed cocoa nibs over the lowest heat for 2 to 3 minutes to infuse the oil with the nibs' flavor; do not simmer.

• When the asparagus is ready, drain and spread out on layers of paper towels; let stand for a minute to evaporate the excess moisture. Transfer the asparagus to a platter and toss with the crushed nibs, warm oil, and prosciutto shreds. Serve hot or warm.

VARIATION

Nibby Green Beans   This simple and superb dish celebrates fresh green beans instead of asparagus and calls for balsamic vinegar and sea salt instead of salty prosciutto. A first course unto itself, or a splendid vegetable dish. We often end up eating the warm beans with our fingers before we even get to the table.

Substitute green beans, rinsed and ends trimmed, for the asparagus. Omit the prosciutto. Toss the beans with the warm olive oil and nibs, then toss again with 2 to 3 teaspoons balsamic vinegar and a sprinkling of fleur de sel or coarsely ground sea salt, to taste.

WILD MUSHROOM RAGOUT

I had a little Rioja and a bag of wild mushrooms in the fridge, and I was about to go out of town. Thinking about fall flavors and woodsy mushrooms reminded me of the unopened bottle of quatre épices (nutmeg, pepper, clove, and cardamom) I'd brought home from France and put in the spice drawer.

Guilt over the mushrooms that would otherwise spoil, nostalgia for a French autumn, and the opportunity to open the spices resulted in a princely ragout that I have "translated" so that you needn't own a bottle of quatre épices. This robust savory dish tastes big and rich enough that you might believe it contains meat or game, although it has none. The sauce is dark and velvety with a depth that suggests hours of long, slow simmering when, in fact, it is fairly quick to make. *Bon appétit.* / **Makes 4 small main-course servings, or 4 to 6 appetizer servings, served with polenta or noodles**

INGREDIENTS

1 pound (455 grams) mixed wild (and cultivated) mushrooms, such as portobellos, chanterelles, shiitake, cèpes, and cremini

2 to 3 tablespoons olive oil

2 garlic cloves, finely minced

⅔ cup dry red wine (I have used Rioja, merlot, and Châteauneuf-du-Pape)

A scant ⅛ teaspoon each of ground nutmeg, ground cardamom, and white pepper

Pinch or two of ground cloves

¼ teaspoon salt

¼ cup water

1 tablespoon (5 grams) finely chopped unsweetened chocolate or 2½ teaspoons premium unsweetened natural cocoa powder

DIRECTIONS

• Keeping the different mushrooms separate, rinse briefly and dry them, then slice ¼ inch thick; discard the stems if they seem tough. Heat a large skillet over medium-high heat and add about 1 teaspoon of the olive oil. Add one type of mushroom and sauté, stirring frequently until browned, 2 to 3 minutes. Scrape them into a bowl and set aside. Repeat with each mushroom type, adding more oil as necessary and scraping them into the same bowl. If you are not using a nonstick pan, between batches you may dissolve the browned bits from the pan with a little water, then scrape the juices into the bowl.

continued

• Remove the pan from the heat to cool slightly, then set over medium-low heat. Add 1 more tablespoon of the olive oil and the garlic; sauté until soft but not browned. Return the mushrooms and any accumulated juices to the pan, add the wine, spices, and salt, and simmer for 2 to 3 minutes to evaporate the alcohol in the wine.

• Add the water, cover, and simmer for 6 to 10 minutes to cook the mushrooms and release their juices into the sauce. Uncover and cook until the sauce is reduced and slightly syrupy. Stir in the chocolate until it melts and smoothes the sauce. Taste and correct the seasonings, if necessary. Serve over fried or soft polenta or egg noodles.

GIULIANO'S SWEET AND SAVORY MEAT SAUCE WITH CHOCOLATE

This recipe from Giuliano Bugialli, which appeared in his *Classic Techniques of Italian Cooking*, was, many years ago, my first taste of chocolate in a memorable savory dish. The finishing flavor combination of sweet raisins, "sour" vinegar, pine nuts, and chocolate is called *dolce-forte* in Italian, as it is both sweet and strong—or sour. Although the dish is said to be Florentine, the pine nuts and raisins suggest a sixteenth-century Sicilian provenance and the culinary influence of Spanish Jews escaping the Inquisition. Please don't imagine hot fudge sauce over pasta: the chocolate adds an earthy depth and complexity, richness, and a voluptuous texture that is completely in harmony with the meaty flavor of the sauce.

I have taken small liberties: Giuliano uses ½ cup olive oil instead of my 3 to 4 tablespoons, and he originally called for chocolate chips instead of bittersweet or semisweet chocolate. And he serves the sauce over homemade tagliatelle made with cocoa powder. The optional cocoa nibs are my addition. / Serves 6

INGREDIENTS

1 medium red onion

3 celery stalks

2 medium carrots

1 medium garlic clove

10 sprigs Italian parsley, leaves only

4 ounces (115 grams) pancetta, or 2 ounces (55 grams) boiled ham plus 2 ounces (55 grams) salt pork

3 to 4 tablespoons olive oil

1 pound (455 grams) lean ground beef

1¼ cups dry red wine

1 cup drained canned Italian tomatoes, or ¾ cup tomato puree

Salt and freshly ground black pepper to taste

½ cup red wine vinegar

¼ cup (35 grams) raisins

2 tablespoons (15 grams) pine nuts

¾ ounce (25 grams) 55% to 62% chocolate, finely chopped (see Chocolate Note)

1 tablespoon (13 grams) sugar

1 pound (455 grams) dried or fresh tagliatelle or other egg pasta

Cocoa nibs, crushed with a rolling pin or coarsely chopped into bits, to pass at the table (optional)

CHOCOLATE NOTE

To use higher-percentage chocolate, start with a little less chocolate than called for. Taste and adjust to get the balance of savory and sweet: the sauce should not taste blatantly chocolatey. If you want to use unsweetened chocolate, start with ¼ to ⅓ ounce (7 to 10 grams) and go from there.

continued

DIRECTIONS

• Finely chop the onion, celery, carrots, garlic, and parsley. Dice the pancetta. In a large sauté pan, heat the olive oil. Add the chopped vegetables, parsley, and pancetta, and sauté slowly over low heat for about 15 minutes, until the vegetables are translucent and beginning to brown. Add the ground meat and stir it into the sautéed ingredients with a fork or wooden spoon. When the meat is no longer pink, add the wine and simmer to evaporate it, about 5 minutes.

• Meanwhile, unless using puree, pass the tomatoes through a food mill.

• When the wine has evaporated, add the tomato puree to the pan. Season lightly with salt and pepper, and simmer slowly for about 25 minutes.

• Meanwhile, prepare the *dolce-forte:* Combine the wine vinegar, raisins, pine nuts, chocolate, and sugar in a small bowl; set aside.

• Bring a large pot of salted water to a boil.

• When the sauce is ready, stir in the *dolce-forte* and simmer 5 minutes longer. Correct the seasoning with salt and pepper, and add additional vinegar, sugar, or chocolate if necessary.

• Cook the pasta just until al dente. Reserve some of the cooking water, then drain the pasta. Pour a little sauce into the bottom of a serving dish and top with the pasta and the remaining sauce. Toss the pasta and sauce together, moistening it with a little of the reserved pasta water if necessary. If you like, pass a bowl of cocoa nibs at the table to sprinkle over the pasta.

A LITTLE SAUCE FOR PASTA

PHOTOGRAPH ON PAGE 290

Another pasta sauce using chocolate as a savory flavor—but this time it's nibs. In the time that it takes to boil the water and cook the pasta, you can prepare this simple sauce, which is really no more than a harmonious assortment of flavorful ingredients and textures warmed in garlicky olive oil. As always with this genre of sauce, exact amounts are subject to your mood and taste, and their availability. In other words, if you like the sauce, eventually you will make it with handfuls of ingredients and without a recipe in front of you. Cocoa nibs, of course, are not authentic to the Mediterranean cuisine evoked by the other flavors in this dish, but tomatoes are not indigenous to Italy either! While the idea of it may push the envelope, the actual flavor of unsweetened chocolate readily complements the sweet caramelized carrots, robust olives, garlic, and parsley, and that nibby crunch is so appealing. / *Serves 6*

INGREDIENTS

1 pound (455 grams) dried pasta

Flavorful extra virgin olive oil

1 cup (145 grams) diced carrots

8 garlic cloves, chopped

¼ cup (30 grams) roasted cocoa nibs

2 ounces (55 grams) thinly sliced prosciutto, cut into small dice

½ cup (2 ounces/55 grams) pine nuts

⅓ to ½ cup (45 to 65 grams) chopped pitted Niçoise olives

Salt and freshly ground black pepper

1 cup (70 grams) coarsely chopped Italian parsley

DIRECTIONS

• Bring a large pot of water with a handful of salt to a boil. Add the pasta and cook just until al dente.

• While the pasta is cooking, film a large skillet with a little olive oil and heat over medium-high heat. When the oil is hot, cook the carrots until slightly browned and tender, about 5 minutes. Scrape the carrots into a bowl, return the skillet to the heat, and add a little more olive oil. Cook the garlic slowly until soft and beginning to brown. Turn off the heat and stir in the nibs, prosciutto, pine nuts, olives, and carrots. Sprinkle with salt, if necessary, and a few grinds of fresh pepper. Set the skillet aside.

continued

• When the pasta is ready, scoop out and reserve a cup of the cooking water; drain the pasta. Rewarm the contents of the skillet over medium heat, add the drained pasta and the parsley, and stir for a minute or two to combine everything and blend the flavors; add a little of the reserved pasta water as necessary to moisten the mixture. Taste and correct the salt and pepper, drizzle with a little olive oil, and serve immediately.

FROM LEFT TO RIGHT: Roasted Squash Soup with Cocoa Bean Cream (page 281); Crunchy Baby Greens (page 275); A Little Sauce for Pasta (page 289) with fettuccine.

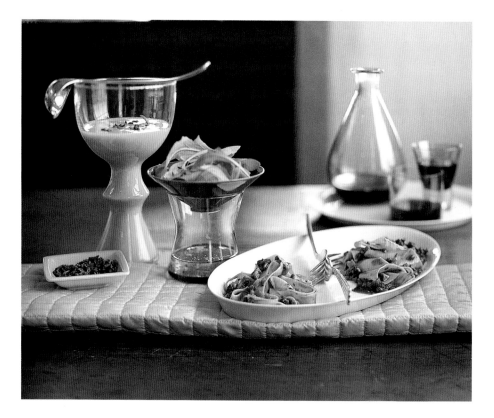

COQ (OR LAPIN) AU VIN

Coq au vin is normally enriched and flavored with smoky bacon, which I have omitted here, since I do not like smoky flavors with chocolate. Chocolate adds its own rich meaty flavor and nuance to this superb dish. It also thickens the sauce without additional flour and deepens the color.

Even a purely classic coq au vin (i.e., sans chocolate) is improved by taking care to remove excess fat along the way. This defines and brightens the flavors and makes the dish at the same time both more elegant and less rich. I stretch the "work" pleasantly over four days. I usually marinate for two days and cook on day three, remembering to sip the leftover wine as I sauté, simmer, and skim. On the fourth day, there's nothing left to do but remove and discard the solidified fat and reheat the whole business with a little chocolate while boiling some noodles.

If you like rabbit, the substitution is easy and excellent. However, since the rabbit has no protective skin, the browning step must be done over gentler heat to avoid toughening the flesh.

/ Serves 8

INGREDIENTS

1½ bottles drinkable red wine (such as merlot, zinfandel, or Rioja)

2 large yellow onions, thinly sliced

2 large carrots, sliced

8 garlic cloves, chopped

4 sprigs Italian parsley, plus chopped parsley for garnish

4 sprigs thyme, or ½ teaspoon dried thyme

2 bay leaves

2 large chickens (each 3½ to 4 pounds/ 1.6 to 1.8 kilos), or 3 rabbits (each 2½ to 3 pounds/1.1 to 1.3 kilos), each cut into 8 serving pieces

1 teaspoon salt, plus more to taste

¼ cup (30 grams) all-purpose flour

About ¼ cup olive oil

1 pound (455 grams) small button mushrooms, rinsed and patted dry, stems removed and reserved

½ cup cognac or other brandy

3 cups chicken stock

1½ pounds (685 grams) pearl onions (about 4½ cups), blanched briefly in boiling water for easier peeling

½ ounce (15 grams) unsweetened chocolate, finely chopped, or 1½ tablespoons (9 grams) premium unsweetened natural cocoa powder

Freshly ground black pepper

continued

DIRECTIONS

• At least 1 day, or up to 3 days, before you plan to serve, marinate the chicken: In a medium nonreactive saucepan, combine the wine, onions, carrots, garlic, parsley sprigs, thyme, and bay leaves. To evaporate the alcohol, bring to a simmer and cook until the marinade no longer smells harsh or tastes of alcohol, 3 to 5 minutes. (You can hasten the evaporation by carefully igniting the surface of the simmering wine with a long match or wooden skewer; if you can't get it to ignite, it's OK to give up.) Remove from the heat and let cool completely.

• Divide the chicken pieces between two large zipper-lock freezer bags. Add half the cooled marinade (with its vegetables and herbs) to each. Press to expel the air and seal the bags. Place the bags in a large bowl (in case of leakage) and refrigerate for 24 to 48 hours, turning them from time to time.

• One day before serving, if possible, remove the chicken pieces from the marinade and set aside. Strain the marinade into a large saucepan, and reserve the vegetables. Bring the marinade to a simmer over low heat. Let barely simmer for about 5 minutes, to allow the proteins to rise and coagulate on the surface. Set a large strainer lined with a paper towel over a bowl. Without stirring or disturbing the marinade more than necessary, ladle it gently into the strainer. Discard the coagulated scum in the towel and reserve the strained liquid.

• Dry the chicken pieces with paper towels. Sprinkle with the salt and dust with flour. Heat 2 tablespoons of the oil in a large skillet over high heat. When the oil is very hot but not smoking, brown the chicken pieces a few at a time, transferring them to a bowl as they brown. Then brown the reserved vegetables and the mushroom stems in the oil remaining in the skillet.

• Pour the brandy over the vegetables and scrape up the brown crusty bits from the bottom of the pan. When the brandy has nearly evaporated, scrape the mixture into a large heavy pot or Dutch oven (set the skillet aside). Add the strained marinade, chicken stock, and chicken pieces. Cover and simmer until the chicken is tender, 1 to 1½ hours.

• While the chicken is cooking, add a little more oil to the skillet. Sauté the onions until golden brown and tender. Scrape them into a bowl. Sauté the mushroom caps and add them to the onions. Set aside.

• When the chicken is tender, scrape off any marinated vegetables from the pieces and transfer the chicken to the bowl with the mushrooms and onions. Strain the sauce into a bowl, pressing lightly on the solids to extract as much liquid as possible, then discard the vegetables. Skim as much fat from the sauce as you can. Return the sauce to the pot and simmer until it is reduced to 4 cups. If you are serving the chicken within a short time, skip the next paragraph.

• If you are working ahead, cover and refrigerate the chicken. Pour the sauce into a separate container, cover, and refrigerate for as long as overnight. When ready to continue the recipe, remove and discard the congealed fat from the top of the sauce, and reheat the sauce in the Dutch oven.

• To serve, combine the chocolate or cocoa and a couple of spoonfuls of the heated sauce in a cup and stir until the chocolate is melted and smooth. Scrape the chocolate mixture into the pot. Add the chicken, onions, and mushrooms and heat through (this takes longer, of course, if the chicken was refrigerated; I sometimes warm it slightly in the microwave before adding it to the sauce). Taste and correct the salt, and add a few grinds of pepper to taste. Serve with egg noodles and a generous handful of chopped parsley.

MOLE COLORADITO

This recipe is author Nancy Zaslavsky's marvelous mole, finished, of course, with chocolate. After tasting it in San Miguel de Allende, I reproduced it at home in Berkeley to make sure that it wasn't just the margaritas and Mexican mountain air that made it taste so good. It wasn't.

The recipe here is for the sauce. For the chicken, you have several options. Nancy serves a quarter of a small chicken in a pool of sauce on each plate, drizzled with a little sauce and a generous sprinkling of sesame seeds. Or, for a crowd, poach lots of half chicken breasts (bone in and skin left on) in water or light stock with a few herbs until almost cooked through. When the chicken is cool enough to handle, pull the skin off and discard. Remove the meat from the bones, tearing the meat into big shreds. Put the shreds in a big pot with the mole. By the time the mole is reheated, the chicken will be cooked through but still marvelously moist and juicy. Any way you serve it, have lots of hot corn tortillas on hand for sopping, mopping, or wrapping.

Ancho and guajillo chiles (or the suggested alternatives) are available in Mexican markets and some supermarkets. Nancy uses Mexican chocolate, naturally. I abandon authenticity in that department and use the best bittersweet 70% that I can find. / **Makes about 1 quart, or enough for 8 servings**

INGREDIENTS

8 dried ancho chiles or dried mulato chiles

8 dried guajillo chiles or dried New Mexico chiles

½ cup (70 grams) raisins

1 large unpeeled white onion, quartered

8 unpeeled garlic cloves

2-inch cinnamon stick (*canela* or true Ceylon cinnamon, if possible; see page 29)

½ cup (70 grams) unblanched whole almonds

½ teaspoon dried thyme

1 teaspoon dried oregano, preferably Mexican

1 teaspoon salt (Nancy uses kosher)

Freshly ground black pepper

3 ripe plum tomatoes

2 tablespoons vegetable oil

One 2-ounce (55-gram) tablet Mexican chocolate, broken up, or 1½ ounces (45 grams) 54% to 72% chocolate, chopped (see Chocolate Note)

About 3 cups hot chicken stock

Sugar to taste (optional)

Toasted sesame seeds for garnish

DIRECTIONS

• To make the chile paste, split the chiles open down the side and remove the seeds and stems. On a hot griddle or in a hot cast-iron skillet, toast the chiles on both sides, flattening them with a spatula, until their skins blister and change color. Put the chiles in a bowl, add the raisins, and cover with hot water. Let soak for 30 minutes.

• Drain the chiles and raisins, then puree them in a blender, adding a little water as necessary (no more than ½ cup). Strain the puree through a medium sieve into a bowl.

• Reheat the griddle or the skillet and toast the onion quarters and garlic cloves, turning them from time to time, until they have just a few blackened spots. Put the onions in a clean blender. Peel the garlic and add to the blender. Toast the cinnamon briefly on the hot griddle, until fragrant, and add to the blender.

• Toast the almonds in a small skillet over medium heat until fragrant and the insides are golden brown. Add the almonds to the onion and garlic in the blender, then add the thyme, oregano, salt, and about 6 grinds of pepper. Puree, adding water as necessary. Strain into the chiles.

• Place the tomatoes on the hot griddle and turn them from time to time, just until they have a few blackened spots—they should not be completely soft or falling apart. Peel the tomatoes, puree in the blender, and strain.

• Heat the oil in a wide deep pot until hot. Add the chile mixture (watch out, it will splatter) and cook, stirring, for a few minutes to further toast the ingredients and concentrate the flavors. Add the chocolate, lower the heat, and simmer for 15 minutes, or until thickened. Taste and adjust the seasonings (if you've used a 54% to 72% chocolate instead of Mexican chocolate, you can add a few small pinches of sugar when you finish the sauce, as necessary). (The chile paste can be made ahead, cooled, covered, and refrigerated for up to 3 months or frozen for up to 6 months. Reheat before continuing.)

• To finish the sauce, add the tomato puree and stir for a few more minutes. Thin to the desired consistency with the broth, adjust the seasonings, and heat through. (The sauce can be cooled, covered, and refrigerated for up to 3 days; reheat before serving.)

• Serve over chicken, sprinkled with toasted sesame seeds.

CHOCOLATE NOTE

If you do not use Mexican chocolate, which is flavored with cinnamon and fairly sweet, start with the 1½ ounces (45 grams) of chocolate, and add a little more to taste if necessary. I most often use a 70% and find that 1½ ounces (45 grams) is the perfect amount. Whatever cinnamon and/or sugar is missing can be taken care of, if necessary, when you taste and correct the sauce at the end.

TASTING CHOCOLATE— AGAIN

I love tasting chocolate, but I'm impatient with chocolate tastings that are designed to select the "best" from a group of chocolates. It's not that I think there are no bad chocolates. But there are too many different interesting chocolates to put them on a one-dimensional scale. I feel the same way about wine.

Both wine and chocolate begin with raw materials from the soil, and both require an almost magical fusion of art and science to transform them into the products that we know and love. Details of cultivation and climate make a difference in the characteristics and quality of the result, as does each choice and step in the production process. However, unlike wine and other sophisticated foods that we love (like ripe cheeses or caviar), chocolate is not an acquired taste. Most of us grew up with it and aren't likely to need someone else to tell us what is best, regardless of whether or not our tastes have changed since childhood. When it comes to chocolate, I don't think expert opinions carry that much weight. People have to have their own experience.

I organized a blind chocolate tasting for a magazine long before the new era of small manufacturers and even before we had many imported chocolates available to us. The results said less about the chocolate than about the experience and demographics of the twelve tasters and the challenge of selecting what should be tasted in the first place. Here's what happened. The highest-ranking chocolate turned out to be the one produced locally: its familiar taste sent it right up the chart. An impressive

(and now world-famous) but unfamiliar European chocolate that was a tad fruitier and more tart than everyone was then accustomed to didn't do too well: its unfamiliar "foreign" flavor and comparative acidity cost it points. Another chocolate that was slightly sweeter than the rest also got a low rating. The tasting taught me that regional tastes and familiarity exert strong influences on our preferences, and that outliers are likely to lose points just for being different from the rest of the group. If tasters trying to rank ten oranges encounter a tangerine among them, the tangerine will probably do poorly (even if it's a delicious tangerine) because it doesn't seem to be part of the group. Blind panel tastings don't do justice to something as complex as chocolate (or anything else I care a lot about).

We nibblers, home cooks, chefs, and chocolatiers use chocolate in so many different ways. Sometimes it stands on its own—a plain bar of chocolate unwrapped and savored. Sometimes we combine it in recipes for confections and desserts and, in doing so, pair it with myriad flavors and ingredients that vary in texture, taste, and sweetness. A chocolate-covered caramel is different from a chocolate-coated nut cluster, which is in turn different from a chocolate mousse or ganache flavored with liqueurs or infused with herbs or spices—or from a chocolate chip cookie, or a slice of chocolate cake. There is no single chocolate that does all of these things best, thank heavens!

I eventually designed a new kind of tasting: we taste a small selection of chocolates with a sweet fruity ingredient (raisins), a nutty ingredient (toasted almonds), and something salty (pretzels). Instead of searching for the "best" chocolate, we explore flavor combinations that might actually occur in desserts, candies, or snacks. The exercise is fun, and it suggests a fresh approach to choosing chocolate for recipes—by taste! You can try it by making the simple seasonal chocolates called mendiants.

MENDIANTS

Soon after the *rentrée,* when Parisians return to work and school after the long summer holiday, shop windows burst with fall colors, and chocolatiers set out trays of thin satiny rounds of crisp, perfectly tempered chocolate garnished with a harvest of dried fruit and nuts. These are mendiants. The word *mendiant* literally means "beggar of alms," and it refers to the four orders of mendicant monks. Classically, chocolate mendiants are decorated with blanched almonds, raisins, hazelnuts, and dried figs to represent the white, gray, brown, and purple robes worn, respectively, by Dominican, Franciscan, Carmelite, and Augustinian friars. Of course, today's mendiants flaunt bright green pistachios and myriad jewel-toned dried and candied fruits. I even season them with pinches of spice. Mendiants may be as small as a quarter (easy to pop right in your mouth) or as big as a coaster (nice for nibblers).

A perfect mendiant is an ode to simplicity: delightful to look at and delicious to eat. Yet, once upon a time, in my youthful desire to sample every rich creamy truffle in my path, I dismissed the mendiant. It seemed too basic and I thought the garnish beggarly—rarely more than two or three bits of fruit or nut. I didn't realize I would one day find mendiants as tempting as truffles, precisely for their minimalist perfection of taste and texture.

Making mendiants is a meditation for the eye and palate. Select toppings for shape, color, and taste. There is no precise recipe; it is all up to you. Rest assured, in general, that all kinds of nuts and dried and candied fruits and peels taste good with chocolate. But "in specific," different flavors taste good, better, or best, depending upon the chocolate. If you take the time to taste your chocolate with several garnishes, first singly, then in duets and trios, you will notice how some combinations sing to you. Modern mendiants may even include a few grains of crushed flaky sea salt . . .

Mendiants keep well at room temperature, which makes them easier and more convenient than filled chocolates or truffles. Make them in advance and pack them in gift boxes with clear plastic covers to show off your artistry. / **Makes about one hundred ½-inch mendiants**

continued

INGREDIENTS

1 pound (455 grams) dark, milk, or white chocolate (see Chocolate Note)

ABOUT 2 OUNCES (55 GRAMS) *EACH* **OF THREE OR MORE OF THE FOLLOWING**

Toasted or untoasted almonds or hazelnuts, walnut or pecan halves, macadamias, or pistachios (see page 28)

Sunflower or pumpkin seeds

Dried fruits such as raisins, currants, or cherries

Candied citrus peel, crystallized ginger, or glacéed fruit

Spices, preferably freshly ground, such as dried chiles, black pepper, cardamom seeds, nutmeg, or anise seeds (optional)

Flaky sea salt (optional)

SPECIAL EQUIPMENT

Several baking sheets or other trays (they need not be heatproof)

Portable fan (optional)

DIRECTIONS

• Prepare the garnishes first. Once the chocolate is ready, you will not have time. For example, cut whole nuts in half (if desired) or chop them; dice or slice crystallized ginger or citrus peels, and so on.

• Line the baking sheets with parchment paper and tape down the edges if you plan to cool with a fan.

• Melt and temper the chocolate according to the instructions on pages 310–313. Spoon a dozen or so equal-sized pools of chocolate, at least 2 inches apart to allow for spreading, onto one of the lined baking sheets. Rap the baking sheet firmly on the counter to spread and thin the puddles of chocolate. Garnish each puddle artistically, before it sets, with 2 to 3 ingredient pieces. (If you are working with a helper, you can spoon out more puddles of chocolate at a time; do not exceed the number of puddles you can decorate before the chocolate sets.) Sprinkle some of the mendiants with pinches of spice, if desired. Let set in a cool (not cold) place, ideally in front of a portable fan, for at least 1 hour.

• Pack in a covered container with wax paper between the layers. Store in a cool dry place.

CHOCOLATE NOTE

Perhaps it is obvious that you can use any chocolate of any percentage that you desire. As long as it tastes good to you, any chocolate will make splendid mendiants.

APPENDIX

CHOCOLATE BY THE NUMBERS

A Dessert Maker's Guide to High-Percentage Chocolates

Compared even with just a few years ago, the variety of chocolate available to chocolate lovers and home cooks is astonishing. If you love dark chocolate, you are probably already nibbling more brands than you used to, with percentages that range from 55% to over 80%. If you love these chocolates, you naturally want to use them in recipes as well. Perhaps you've tried using a 70% "bittersweet" chocolate in a recipe that calls for bittersweet chocolate. If you've been lucky in your recipe choice, you've had great results. But it is more likely that you've had some dry grainy chocolate mousse, curdled sauce, gritty ganache, dry cakes, or desserts that were just too bitter to enjoy. Here's why.

Not too many years ago, bittersweet and semisweet chocolates were very similar to one another, and they were all nearly half sugar and contained less than 60% cacao. These were the chocolates called for in the recipes that you clipped over the years, jotted down on index cards, or marked in favorite books. And these are still the chocolates that many magazine test kitchens and cookbook authors mean when they call for bittersweet chocolate—but we simply don't know unless they tell us! The challenge today is that so many of the available bittersweet chocolates contain less sugar and much more cacao. A chocolate labeled "bittersweet" might contain 55%, 62%, or 70% cacao—or even more. And a 70% chocolate will affect your ganache or chocolate mousse very differently from the way a 55% chocolate does. This is why it is now so important to identify chocolate by percentage rather than by "name."

Any chocolate labeled "60%" is already stronger and less sweet than the chocolate for which most older recipes were created. You might anticipate that using a higher-percentage chocolate would simply make a dessert more chocolatey and less sweet—which might be your reason for choosing them in the first place. But it is more complicated than that. Take a look at the pie charts (opposite) showing the sugar, cocoa butter (fat), and dry solids for different chocolates and read about how each component behaves in recipes in "Chocolate Components." If you compare a 70% chocolate with a 55% chocolate, you'll see that the 70% contains one-third less sugar and almost half again as much dry solids (remember to think of dry solids as fat-free cocoa powder)—it's a whole different animal. It's now easy to imagine that using a 70% chocolate instead of 55% chocolate is like adding lots of unsweetened cocoa powder to a recipe and subtracting lots of sugar at the same time. That just begins to explain dry cake batters, dense gummy mousses, and ganache that curdles.

CHOCOLATE COMPONENTS

Let's review the three main components of chocolate shown on the pie charts, and what each contributes. Cacao is made up of nonfat dry cocoa solids and cocoa butter, which are shown separately on each chart. The third component is sugar. Some (often the most inexpensive) dark chocolates may also contain a very small amount of milk solids and butterfat—both of which I have ignored here.

The nonfat dry cocoa solids (imagine entirely fat-free unsweetened cocoa powder) contribute virtually all of the chocolate flavor. Because they are a dry ingredient and contain carbohydrates, they act a little like flour: they absorb moisture and liquid. And since nonfat dry cocoa solids are the main source of chocolate flavor, my formulas for substituting chocolates are based on comparing the average amounts of these solids in different chocolates. About 1⅔ ounces (47 grams) of 70% chocolate has about the same amount of nonfat dry cocoa solids as 1 ounce of unsweetened chocolate, so that becomes the basis of my formula—along with a sugar and butter adjustment in the recipe.

Cocoa butter is fat. It contributes smoothness, richness, and body to the chocolate. It melts at a higher temperature than dairy butter, so it is not as soft and does not melt in your mouth as quickly, but it does carry the chocolate flavor.

Sugar contributes sweetness and also keeps baked goods moist. It may also contribute chewiness, in brownies, for example, or (seemingly contradictorily) crispness in cookies—or caramelized flavor in anything.

Notice that as the cacao percentage (combined cocoa butter and nonfat dry solids) increases, the percentage of nonfat dry cocoa solids increases proportionately more than the cocoa butter. Many chefs cite the increase in fat to explain problems that arise in using high-percentage chocolates in recipes. But, in fact, the proportionately larger increase in nonfat dry cocoa solids affects the outcome far more than the increase in fat.

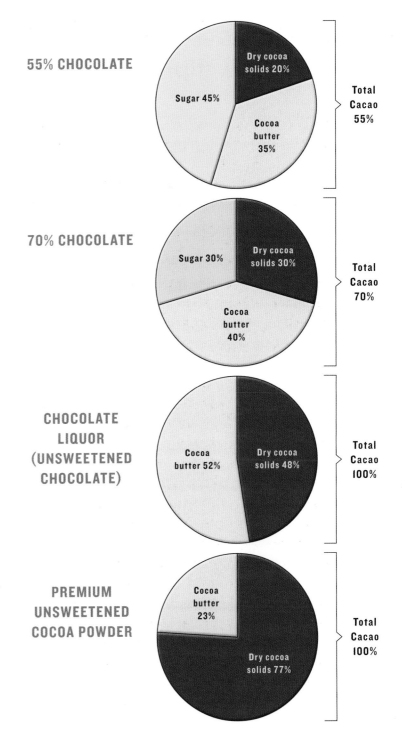

55% CHOCOLATE

Sugar 45%
Dry cocoa solids 20%
Cocoa butter 35%

Total Cacao 55%

70% CHOCOLATE

Sugar 30%
Dry cocoa solids 30%
Cocoa butter 40%

Total Cacao 70%

CHOCOLATE LIQUOR (UNSWEETENED CHOCOLATE)

Cocoa butter 52%
Dry cocoa solids 48%

Total Cacao 100%

PREMIUM UNSWEETENED COCOA POWDER

Cocoa butter 23%
Dry cocoa solids 77%

Total Cacao 100%

Formulas for Converting Recipes from One Chocolate to Another

Imagine you have a great brownie recipe that calls for 4 ounces (115 grams) of unsweetened chocolate. You love the balance of sweetness, richness, and flavor—but instead of using the same old unsweetened chocolate, you want to substitute an interesting 70% chocolate you have been snacking on lately. How much 70% chocolate should you use and what other changes, if any, should you make in the recipe? I figured that out in order to create the quartet of brownies on pages 67–69, each using a different kind of chocolate or cocoa in the same basic recipe. Meanwhile, I derived several formulas with which you can convert your own favorite recipes from one chocolate to another without risking unhappy surprises. However, just because you have a formula doesn't always mean you have to stick to it slavishly—I often use these as a point of departure only.

The formulas may seem to include finicky decimal fractions so small as to be inconsequential. However, they will make more sense after you multiply them by the number of ounces (each 28 grams) of chocolate in the original recipe and then round to the nearest ounce or tablespoon or gram. When rounding your final calculation, remember that 1 tablespoon equals 3 teaspoons, thus (for example) 1.66 tablespoons = 1 tablespoon plus 2 teaspoons. Similarly, 8 teaspoons = 2 tablespoons plus 2 teaspoons.

TO SUBSTITUTE DIFFERENT PERCENTAGE CHOCOLATES FOR UNSWEETENED CHOCOLATE

In order to substitute sweetened dark chocolate of varying percentages for unsweetened chocolate, you will need to increase the amount of chocolate to obtain the same amount of chocolate flavor. You will then need to compensate for the sugar in the chocolate by reducing the amount of sugar in the original recipe. When you add more chocolate, you are also adding more fat (cocoa butter)—so you must subtract some of the butter from the recipe as well. Recipes that do not contain enough sugar and butter in the first place cannot be converted this way. Brownies work beautifully (see pages 67–73), as do ice creams and cheesecakes. Scan the specific formula for the chocolate you want to use and check the recipe for sugar and butter before trying the conversion.

TO SUBSTITUTE 54% TO 60% CHOCOLATE FOR UNSWEETENED CHOCOLATE: For every ounce (28 grams) of unsweetened chocolate called for, substitute 2.4 ounces (68 grams) 54% to 60% chocolate; decrease the sugar in the recipe by 2.5 to 3 tablespoons (31 to 38 grams); and decrease the butter in the recipe by 0.66 tablespoon (10 grams).

EXAMPLE: If the original recipe called for 4 ounces of unsweetened chocolate, multiply 4 by 2.4 to get 9.6 ounces of 54% to 60% chocolate.

Decrease the total amount of sugar in the recipe by 4 x 2.5 to 3 tablespoons, thus 10 or 12 tablespoons (about ⅔ cup).

Decrease the total amount of butter in the recipe by 4 x .66 tablespoons, thus 2.6 tablespoons (2 tablespoons and 2 teaspoons).

Summary: If the original recipe called for 4 ounces of unsweetened chocolate, you will use 9.6 ounces of 54% to 60% chocolate, reduce the amount of sugar in the recipe by 10 to 12 tablespoons, and reduce the amount of butter in the recipe by 2.6 tablespoons (2 tablespoons and 2 teaspoons).

METRIC EXAMPLE: If the original recipe called for 4 ounces (115 grams) of unsweetened chocolate, multiply 4 by 68 grams to get 272 grams of 54% to 60% chocolate.

Decrease the total amount of sugar in the recipe by 4 x 31 to 37 grams, thus 124 to 148 grams.

Decrease the total amount of butter in the recipe by 4 x 10 grams, thus 40 grams.

Summary: If the original recipe called for 4 ounces (115 grams) of unsweetened chocolate, you will use 272 grams of 54% to 60% chocolate, reduce the amount of sugar in the recipe by 124 to 148 grams, and reduce the amount of butter in the recipe by 40 grams.

TO SUBSTITUTE 62% CHOCOLATE FOR UNSWEETENED CHOCOLATE: For every ounce (28 grams) of unsweetened chocolate called for, use 2.2 ounces (62 grams) 62% chocolate; decrease the sugar in the recipe by 2 tablespoons (25 grams); and decrease the butter in the recipe by 0.66 tablespoon (10 grams).

TO SUBSTITUTE 66% CHOCOLATE FOR UNSWEETENED CHOCOLATE: For every ounce (28 grams) of unsweetened chocolate called for, use 1.8 ounces (51 grams) 66% chocolate; decrease the sugar in the recipe by 1.33 tablespoons (17 grams); and decrease the butter in the recipe by 0.5 tablespoon (7 grams).

TO SUBSTITUTE 70% TO 72% CHOCOLATE FOR UNSWEETENED CHOCOLATE: For every ounce (28 grams) of unsweetened chocolate called for, use 1.66 ounces (47 grams) 70% to 72% chocolate; decrease the sugar in the recipe by 1 tablespoon (13 grams); and decrease the butter in the recipe by 1 teaspoon (5 grams).

TO SUBSTITUTE 82% CHOCOLATE FOR UNSWEETENED CHOCOLATE: For every ounce (28 grams) of unsweetened chocolate called for, use 1.2 ounces (34 grams) of 82% chocolate and decrease the sugar in the recipe by 0.5 tablespoon (7 grams).

TO SUBSTITUTE HIGH-PERCENTAGE CHOCOLATE FOR 54% TO 58% CHOCOLATE OR IN OLDER (OR VINTAGE) RECIPES THAT CALL FOR SEMISWEET OR BITTERSWEET CHOCOLATE

The majority of recipes that call for bittersweet or semisweet chocolates today are still created and tested with chocolate with 53% to 60% cacao (unless otherwise stated); this is still the standard in most magazine test kitchens and among many cookbook authors. And if you have vintage recipes in your files, from mothers and grandmothers, or clipped from newspapers and magazines over the last twenty to forty years, the chocolates called semisweet, and even bittersweet, were more like 50% to 55% cacao. Except for unsweetened chocolate, high-percentage chocolates were simply not available and recipes were not designed for them.

To use today's high-percentage chocolates successfully in those older recipes, or in any recipes devised for lower-percentage chocolates, you will need to use less chocolate and sometimes compensate with a little sugar and or butter. Since high-percentage chocolates can be pricier than ordinary baking chocolate, using less chocolate in a recipe will at least partially offset the extra cost! If you want a more bittersweet chocolate flavor, reduce the chocolate by a slightly smaller amount. You can also increase the intensity of bittersweet chocolate flavor by using less of the sugar adjustment.

TO SUBSTITUTE 60% CHOCOLATE FOR 54% TO 58% CHOCOLATE, OR IN OLDER RECIPES: Generally, 60% chocolate substitutes perfectly in place of these lower-percentage chocolates and in older recipes as well. If you have a truly vintage recipe that calls for semisweet chocolate, you might follow the formula for substituting 62% chocolate.

TO SUBSTITUTE 62% CHOCOLATE FOR 54% TO 58% CHOCOLATE, OR IN OLDER RECIPES: Use 10 percent less chocolate than called for.

EXAMPLE: If the original recipe calls for 10 ounces (285 grams) chocolate: Use 9 ounces (255 grams) 62% chocolate.

TO SUBSTITUTE 64% CHOCOLATE FOR 54% TO 58% CHOCOLATE, OR IN OLDER RECIPES: Use 20 to 25 percent less chocolate and add 1.25 teaspoons (5 grams) more sugar for every ounce (28 grams) of chocolate called for in the original recipe.

TO SUBSTITUTE 66% CHOCOLATE FOR 54% TO 58% CHOCOLATE, OR IN OLDER RECIPES: Use 25 percent less chocolate and add 1.5 teaspoons (6 grams) more sugar for every ounce (28 grams) of chocolate called for in the original recipe.

TO SUBSTITUTE 70% TO 72% CHOCOLATE FOR 54% TO 58% CHOCOLATE, OR IN OLDER RECIPES: Use 33 percent less chocolate and add 1.5 teaspoons (6 grams) more sugar for every ounce (28 grams) of chocolate called for in the original recipe.

TO SUBSTITUTE 82% CHOCOLATE FOR 54% TO 58% CHOCOLATE, OR IN OLDER RECIPES: Use 50% less chocolate and add up to 2.5 teaspoons (10 grams) sugar and 0.75 teaspoon (4 grams) butter for every ounce of chocolate called for in the original recipe.

TO SUBSTITUTE UNSWEETENED COCOA POWDER FOR CHOCOLATE

I have had success converting recipes for brownies, ice creams, cheesecakes, and chocolate custards from chocolate to cocoa. Although I did not explore this type of conversion in depth throughout this book, the information that follows will allow you to experiment.

The substitutions here are given two ways:

1. For the premium unsweetened cocoa powder that I used in the recipes throughout this book, which is 20% to 24% fat (1 gram of fat per 5- to 6-gram serving, if you look on the nutritional panel).

2. For ordinary cocoa powder with 10% to 12% fat (0.5 gram of fat per 5- to 6-gram serving), even though I did not use this type of cocoa in the book.

Cocoa powder is very potent, so sloppy measuring can make a bigger difference than you might think. Before you measure, stir the cocoa and press out any lumps with the back of a spoon, then spoon the cocoa loosely into the measure, heap it, and sweep it level. Do not pack or tap the cup or spoon to settle the cocoa.

Don't sift the cocoa before measuring unless a specific recipe calls for it. Use a scale rather than tablespoons for more consistent results. Small or finicky-looking measurements in the following formulas will make more sense after you multiply them by the number of ounces (28 grams) of chocolate in the original recipe and then round to the nearest ounce, tablespoon, teaspoon, or gram.

TO SUBSTITUTE UNSWEETENED COCOA POWDER FOR UNSWEETENED CHOCOLATE: For each ounce (28 grams) of unsweetened chocolate: Substitute 3 tablespoons (18 grams) premium unsweetened cocoa powder plus 2 teaspoons (9 grams) butter. *Or,* substitute 2.8 tablespoons (14 grams) ordinary unsweetened cocoa powder plus 1 tablespoon (14 grams) butter.

TO SUBSTITUTE UNSWEETENED COCOA POWDER FOR 70% CHOCOLATE: For each ounce (28 grams) of 70% chocolate: Substitute 2 tablespoons (12 grams) premium unsweetened cocoa powder plus 2 teaspoons (8 grams) sugar and 1.75 teaspoons (8 grams) butter. *Or,* substitute 1.8 tablespoons (9 grams) ordinary unsweetened cocoa powder plus 2 teaspoons (8 grams) sugar and 2.25 teaspoons (10 grams) butter.

TO SUBSTITUTE UNSWEETENED COCOA POWDER FOR 55% TO 60% CHOCOLATE: For each ounce (28 grams) of 55% to 60% chocolate: Substitute 1.33 tablespoons (8 grams) premium unsweetened cocoa powder plus 1 tablespoon (13 grams) sugar and 1.75 teaspoons (8 grams) butter. *Or,* substitute 1.2 tablespoons (6 grams) ordinary unsweetened cocoa powder plus 1 tablespoon (13 grams) sugar and 2 teaspoons (9 grams) butter.

ARE THE FORMULAS ALWAYS NECESSARY?

One of the big attractions of high-percentage chocolate is its greater flavor and relatively low proportion of sugar. Rather than using a formula to compensate for these characteristics—using less chocolate and adding sugar—you might be tempted to substitute the stronger chocolate ounce for ounce to make a dessert more chocolatey and less sweet. But only a few recipes adapt to straight substitution with only minor fine-tuning. In the baking repertoire, "nearly flourless" chocolate nut tortes like the Queen of Sheba (page 80), because of their enormous flexibility and lack of formal structure, and the lower-fat recipes sprinkled throughout this book, because they are less densely chocolate in the first place, permit this kind of substitution. They require only a little less baking time to succeed brilliantly. And in candy making, of course, you are free to use chocolate of any percentage for dipping.

However, most recipes are not so permissive. If you use a higher-percentage chocolate, you must make other adjustments to the recipe for a successful outcome.

Recipes that are essentially combinations of chocolate and liquid, or that have a chocolate and liquid component, are particularly sensitive to cacao percentage. Ganache, the combination of chocolate and cream used for truffle centers and for chocolate glazes and sauces, will break (look curdled) or separate unless there is enough liquid (from the cream) available for the nonfat dry cocoa solids in the chocolate to absorb. There also has to be enough liquid to surround the fat droplets that are formed when the ingredients are mixed or whisked together into an emulsion (see page 105).

Higher-percentage chocolates have more nonfat cocoa solids (see the charts on page 303) competing with the other ingredients in the ganache recipe to absorb the liquid needed to surround the fat droplets. These chocolates also contain less sugar, which competes with the solids to "drink" the liquid. In a ganache, eventually the sugar dissolves and increases the volume of the liquid available to coat the fat droplets; thus the sugar helps form the emulsion. But if chocolate that contains more dry cocoa solids and less sugar is substituted, ounce for ounce, for a lower-percentage chocolate, more liquid will be needed to form the emulsion and keep the ganache from breaking or separating.

Thus, for 10 ounces of 54% to 60% chocolate, you need at least 5 ounces cream (I prefer 6 ounces) to make ganache for truffles and 8 or more ounces for a glaze you can pour. But for 10 ounces of bittersweet 70% chocolate, you need at least 8 ounces cream (9 is much more dependable) and 10 ounces or more to make a good fluid glaze.

In addition to ganache, chocolate mousse or any recipe that begins by melting chocolate together with a relatively small amount of liquid (before the two are mixed with other ingredients) will also require more liquid (or less chocolate) if you use a higher-percentage chocolate. For example, 55% to 60% chocolate melts well with 1 tablespoon of liquid for every 2 ounces of chocolate; if you substitute a 70% chocolate, you must increase the water to at least 1½ tablespoons for every 2 ounces of chocolate for it to melt smoothly.

Even if there is no curdling or other outward sign of trouble as you are preparing the recipe, a 70% chocolate substituted for ordinary bittersweet or semisweet chocolate often yields a dense, dry mousse with an unpleasantly intense flavor. Rather than increasing the liquid in recipes of this kind, you can accomplish the same result by decreasing the amount of chocolate. Use the formula for substituting a 70% chocolate for a 55% chocolate (see page 306). You will use less chocolate to achieve the same amount of flavor without ruining the texture. Then, if you want a more bittersweet mousse, use less (or none) of the sugar adjustment called for in the formula.

Like Water for Chocolate: Dangerous Liaisons

One of the first lessons culinary students are taught about chocolate is that water is its enemy. Home cooks learn the same lesson when a bowl of melted chocolate transforms from a glossy molten fluid into an intractable dull, grainy paste simply because the bowl or the spatula was wet, water splashed into the chocolate, or the cook tried to flavor the chocolate with a little coffee or vanilla extract. When this happens, we say that the chocolate has "seized." Seized chocolate, because it neither melts nor flows, becomes useless for most purposes.

The problem is chocolate and a *little* water. Chocolate is composed of sugar and dry cocoa particles dispersed in fat (cocoa butter). When chocolate is melted, the dry particles float around easily in the liquid fat and the chocolate becomes beautifully fluid. If only a small amount of water is added, it is absorbed immediately into some of the dry particles. That makes those particles tacky and prone to sticking together. The more the particles stick together, the less fluid the chocolate becomes, even though it *is* melted. Unlikely as it seems, additional water can actually make the chocolate fluid again. Once there is enough water to saturate all the dry particles in the chocolate, the particles lose their stickiness and release each other to float freely once again. So, if melted chocolate and liquid seize in the course of preparing a recipe, it is probably because there is not enough liquid; you can usually fix it by adding a bit more.

CAUTION: More liquid is the fix for seized chocolate that is already intentionally mixed with liquid, but if chocolate melted alone and intended for dipping (or other uses in its pure form) seizes from a random splash of water, you must set it aside for use in a cake batter or sauce or glaze where it will be combined with more liquid or butter.

If chocolate is perfectly compatible with quantities of liquid that meet a certain "safe" ratio of liquid to fat and dry particles in the chocolate, how much is enough? Milk chocolate, white chocolate, and dark chocolate with up to about 60% cacao require at least 1 tablespoon of water for each 2 ounces of chocolate. Higher-percentage chocolates, because they contain more dry particles, require more water. A 70% chocolate needs at least 1½ tablespoons of water per 2 ounces of chocolate, and unsweetened chocolate will not melt fluidly with water unless there are at least 2 tablespoons of water for every 2 ounces of chocolate (or 1 tablespoon per ounce). These different ratios partially explain why a recipe for chocolate mousse (for example) may turn out dry and grainy when a 70% chocolate is substituted for a 60% chocolate. The 70% chocolate simply absorbs too much liquid from the mousse, unless the recipe is adjusted to compensate.

Even a "safe" amount of liquid can cause trouble: if cold liquid is added to warm or tepid chocolate, the chocolate can thicken or harden unexpectedly into little chocolate chips. One way to avoid this is to melt the chocolate with the liquid so they warm up together. If you must add liquid to already-melted chocolate, warm the liquid first to avoid the cold-to-warm shock. Another method saves a step: pour hot liquid over finely chopped chocolate, then stir until the chocolate melts.

Of course, all of these strategies are built into the recipes in this book, but understanding the relationship of water to chocolate—identifying the dangerous part of that liaison—is essential to a dessert maker's success. So many chocolate desserts and confections have a chocolate and liquid component, and problems with high-percentage chocolates show up there first.

Tempering Chocolate

A piece of tempered chocolate has a shiny reflective surface (unless it has been scuffed or jumbled with other pieces of chocolate) and an even interior color and texture. It is brittle enough to snap audibly when broken or bitten. Melted chocolate that has been tempered shrinks slightly as it cools and so it releases perfectly from molds, and it mirrors any surface with which it has been in contact. Any bar or piece of chocolate that you buy was tempered at the factory and, unless it has been damaged by heat in transit or in storage, will still be tempered when you unwrap it to eat or cook with it.

Heat-damaged chocolate or chocolate that has melted and cooled without being retempered looks dull and gray, perhaps mottled or streaky. It may be soft and cakey at first, but it will eventually become dry and gritty with a stratified interior texture. When that happens the chocolate actually tastes less flavorful and melts less smoothly in your mouth.

Whether in perfect temper or out of temper to start with, each time chocolate is melted, it can be tempered again to regain its glossy surface and crisp texture. Of course, there is no need to temper melted chocolate used as an ingredient in a batter or dessert, sauce, or glaze. However, if you want to dip cookies in chocolate that will dry hard and glossy, or if you want to make a molded chocolate rabbit, or if you want dipped chocolates to dry beautifully and keep at room temperature, you must temper the chocolate.

Melted chocolate solidifies as it cools because the fat molecules link together and form crystals that connect to form a sturdy network. Cocoa butter is a complex fat capable of taking different crystal forms, but only one of the forms is stable and will cause the chocolate to contract and harden with the desired shiny surface and brittle snap. This form is called beta.

It takes only a small percentage of beta crystals to ensure that subsequent crystals will also take the beta form as the chocolate cools. The process of tempering involves a sequence of heating, cooling, and stirring steps designed to produce enough beta crystals to set the pattern for the rest of the crystals that will form as the chocolate cools.

Under the right conditions, beta crystals form and survive at temperatures between 82° and 91°F; they melt and are destroyed at higher temperatures. Most tempering methods involve heating the chocolate well above 91°F so that all crystals (stable and unstable) are melted and destroyed, and you start with a kind of crystal-free blank slate. Then, as the chocolate cools, you create brand-new beta crystals. Once there are enough beta crystals, the chocolate is tempered. You can use a simple test to determine when this has happened.

Before you begin to practice and learn tempering, there is one important mantra to keep in mind: Tempering is not simply a matter of taking chocolate from one prescribed temperature to another, although most instruction focuses mostly on that activity. Tempering is really a function of three interrelated factors: time, temperature, and agitation (stirring). This means that your chocolate may not be in temper the moment you have completed the steps to get your chocolate to the "correct" temperature. Often, the chocolate just needs a few more minutes of stirring. Do not get so involved with temperature that you forget the necessity for time and stirring. Use the test for temper as feedback as you work, and be prepared to practice, go slow, observe, and adjust (Zen and the art of chocolate tempering).

There are several methods for tempering chocolate. The one that follows is convenient to use and easy to learn.

THE CHUNK METHOD FOR TEMPERING CHOCOLATE

This particular method requires at least 20 percent of the chocolate you start with to be solid chocolate that is already in temper—a nice shiny bar in the same condition that it was in when it left the chocolate factory. Do not be concerned about tempering more chocolate than you need for a recipe or project; leftover tempered chocolate can be reused, or eaten. Also, a large bowl of tempered chocolate is easier to keep warm and in good working condition than a small one. I like to work with at least 1¼ pounds (565 grams) of chocolate, but you can temper less.

Temper any amount of chocolate that you like, using the following guidelines.

• Choose good-tasting chocolate, not chocolate chips or coatings that are not truly chocolate.

• Do not work in a hot room.

• Before tempering, prepare whatever is to be dipped and measure out any other ingredients needed and have them at room temperature (cool or cold centers will cause the chocolate to crack when it cools).

• Do not allow moisture to come in direct contact with the chocolate: make sure that the inside of the bowl, the spatula, and the thermometer stem are all clean and dry.

• Whenever you take the temperature of the chocolate or the water, wipe the thermometer stem clean with a paper towel.

INGREDIENTS

1¼ pounds (565 grams) dark, milk, or white chocolate (of which at least ¼ pound [110 grams] is solid, in one or two big pieces, and in temper)

• Set aside one or two large pieces of the solid tempered chocolate, equal to ¼ pound (110 grams, or 20 percent of the total amount of chocolate you are starting with) to use as "seed." Chop the remaining chocolate into small pieces (½ inch or smaller) and place them in a stainless steel bowl with a 2- to 3-quart capacity. Warm the chocolate slowly, as follows, so that it registers only about 100°F (if it was in temper to start with) or 120°F (if it was not in temper) by the time it is entirely melted.

• Set the bowl in a wide skillet of barely simmering water and stir frequently at first, and then constantly, until about three-quarters of the chocolate is melted. Remove the chocolate from

SPECIAL EQUIPMENT

Instant-read thermometer

the heat and stir for 1 to 2 minutes to melt the remaining chocolate. If the chocolate is not entirely melted, replace the bowl in the skillet and continue to stir, then remove from the pan.

• If the temperature of the chocolate exceeds 100°F, let it cool to about 100°F (no need to be exact here). Drop the reserved tempered chunks of chocolate into the bowl and stir constantly until the chocolate registers 90°F for dark chocolate, or 88°F for white or milk. As you stir, you are simultaneously cooling the melted chocolate and melting the surface of the tempered chocolate chunks. As the temperature of the melted chocolate approaches 90°F, stable beta crystals from the surface of the tempered chunks start to mingle with the melted chocolate and form the "seed" to create more beta crystals. When there are enough beta crystals, the chocolate is tempered. The object is not to melt the chunks completely, but to use them to provide the beta "seed" to produce more beta crystals. In fact, if your chunks are completely melted by the time the chocolate reaches 90°F, the necessary beta crystals are likely to have been destroyed; add another chunk of chocolate and continue to stir.

• When the chocolate is at the desired temperature, it may or may not yet contain enough beta crystals to be tempered. Use the Test for Temper below to check. If the chocolate is not in temper, continue to stir for a few minutes longer, then test again. When the chocolate is in temper, remove the unmelted chunk(s) and chill them in the refrigerator for 10 minutes, then store at room temperature to be used again. Use the tempered chocolate immediately.

• If you are using the tempered chocolate for dipping, stir it from time to time and scrape down the bowl to prevent chocolate from building up around the sides. The chocolate will cool and thicken as you work. Do not allow it to get too thick: rewarm the chocolate in a pan of warm water for a few seconds at a time, or warm the sides of the bowl with a hair dryer, and stir until the chocolate regains fluidity, as long as you do not let it exceed a maximum temperature of 90° to 91°F for dark chocolate or 88° to 89°F for milk and white chocolate. If the chocolate is at its maximum temperature but still too thick, see opposite. Or you can keep the bowl in a container of warm water just 2 degrees warmer than the maximum temperature for the type of chocolate you are using. Or set the bowl on a heating pad covered with several layers of towel so that it is barely warm.

The Test for Temper Drizzle some of the chocolate onto a knife blade or a piece of wax paper. Set the test in front of a fan (preferably) or in a cool place. If the chocolate starts to set within 3 minutes and it looks shiny, it is tempered. If it looks streaky or spotted or doesn't set even after 3 minutes, it is not yet tempered.

KEEPING TEMPERED CHOCOLATE IN WORKING CONDITION

Once chocolate has been tempered, it will thicken as you work with it. Intuitively, it would seem that the thickening is due to cooling, but that is only partially true. In the course of dipping centers, for example, tempered chocolate will thicken even if maintained at its "ceiling temperature" in a water bath or on a heating pad covered with towels. Why does this happen? Remember that the formation of the necessary beta crystals in the tempering process required time and agitation, in addition to temperature. Once the chocolate is in temper, time and agitation (caused by dipping, scraping the bowl, and occasional stirring) continue to create more and more beta crystals, whether or not you want them. More beta crystals make the chocolate thicker and eventually harder to work with. The chocolate is still in temper, but there are too many beta crystals; the chocolate sets even faster than before and the gloss is a little duller. Chocolate is said to be "overseeded" or "overtempered" when it is very thick and sludgy from too many beta crystals.

The remedy? If the chocolate has cooled, rewarm it to its ceiling temperature by setting the bowl in the skillet of warm water for a few seconds at a time, and then thoroughly stirring it. If the chocolate is at the maximum temperature recommended but is still too thick, you must melt and destroy some of the excess beta crystals by allowing some of the chocolate to exceed the maximum temperature. Use the water bath as before, but let the chocolate get a little warm around the edges of the bowl. Then stir the chocolate well to mix in the warmer chocolate; otherwise your shiny tempered chocolate will show some fine streaks of gray after it cools. This should return your chocolate to a more fluid and, with luck, still tempered state. After this maneuver, always test for temper again to make sure that you haven't melted too many beta crystals and lost the temper of your whole batch.

Another way to fix overseeded chocolate is to add a little "virgin" chocolate (chocolate that has been heated to 125°F and cooled to 90° to 92°F but is not seeded or in temper) to the thick chocolate and stir it in thoroughly. This rewarms the chocolate, reduces the ratio of tempered crystals, and puts you back in business.

Glossary

ALKALIZED COCOA *See* Dutch-process cocoa.

ALKALIZING A chemical process applied to cocoa nibs or to chocolate liquor to reduce acidity. *See also* Dutch-process cocoa.

BITTERSWEET OR SEMISWEET CHOCOLATE Sweet dark chocolates that contain a minimum of 35 percent by weight of chocolate liquor. Today this 35 percent minimum is mostly an academic fact: chocolate manufacturers have been exceeding it for decades in response to consumer demand (and willingness to pay) for better chocolate. For example, a 55% chocolate is at the low end of the bittersweet/semisweet range these days, although still very mainstream. Assuming the manufacturer added 8 to 10 percent cocoa butter, the chocolate liquor content is still at least 45 percent, and thus far higher than the 35 percent minimum. Bittersweet and semisweet chocolates may also contain up to 12 percent milk solids, which may include milk fat. See page 36 for more about bittersweet and semisweet chocolate.

BLOOM Streaks, graying, or discoloration on the surface of chocolate caused by poor tempering, temperature fluctuations, and/or moisture in storage. Finely crystallized sugar on the surface of chocolate (caused by moisture) is called *sugar bloom*. A dull appearance or streaks on the surface of the chocolate caused by poor tempering or too much heat in storage is called *fat bloom*. *See* Qualities to Look For, page 39, for a fuller discussion.

CACAO The source of all chocolate and chocolate products. The term *cacao* refers to the tree and its fruit and the seeds inside the fruit (also called cacao beans or cocoa beans), which are processed to make chocolate. On a chocolate label, cacao refers to the total cocoa bean content of the bar—the combined total of chocolate liquor plus any additional cocoa butter or cocoa powder.

CACAO BEANS *See* Cocoa beans.

CHOCOLATE LIQUOR Cocoa nibs ground into a fine paste, i.e., pure unsweetened chocolate. Different types of chocolate are defined by the minimum percentage of chocolate liquor they contain. When the term *chocolate liquor* appears with a percentage on the front of a chocolate label, it refers to total cacao content including any cocoa or cocoa butter added separately to adjust the flavor or texture of the chocolate. When chocolate liquor appears in the ingredient list on the chocolate package, it may or may not be listed separately from any added cocoa butter or nonfat dry cocoa solids. For more about chocolate liquor, see pages 31–32.

COCOA (OR COCOA POWDER) Chocolate liquor that has most of the fat extracted from it, then is pulverized to a powder. Cocoa powder is unsweetened and may be natural or treated with alkali (Dutch-process). See page 34 for more about cocoa powder. The term *cocoa* is also used in a broader sense in the commodity market to mean cocoa beans. The British use the term *cocoa* to mean chocolate liquor or cacao, and, as such, it may appear on chocolate labels with a percentage.

COCOA BEANS Also called *cacao beans*. The seeds of the fruit of the cacao tree, *Theobroma cacao,* from which all forms of chocolate are made.

COCOA BUTTER The ivory-colored fat that constitutes 50 to 54 percent of the weight of hulled roasted cocoa beans; also called *cocoa fat* or *cacao butter*. Cocoa butter is extracted from chocolate liquor (ground roasted cocoa beans) in the making of cocoa powder. Extra cocoa butter is usually added to chocolate liquor to make fine chocolate. Although it has very little flavor of its own, cocoa butter melts readily in the mouth and makes chocolate taste smooth, rich, and long lasting on the palate.

COCOA MASS Another term for chocolate liquor.

COCOA MASSE The French term for chocolate liquor.

COCOA NIBS Hulled, and usually roasted, cocoa bean pieces.

COCOA SOLIDS; DRY COCOA SOLIDS Both terms are used inconsistently. They may refer to chocolate liquor, inclusive of any added cocoa butter or dry cocoa solids. But both terms are sometimes used to mean only nonfat dry cocoa solids (chocolate liquor minus all the fat).

CONCHING A prolonged, heated mixing and scraping process during the last stages of manufacture that results in chocolate's smoothness of flavor and texture. Conching grinds chocolate particles to a size undetectable by the human palate, smoothes their microscopic rough edges, and mixes and coats them intimately with fat. In the process, undesirable aromas and flavors are released through timed and controlled aeration. Fine chocolates may be conched for 24 to 36 hours, or even up to 72 hours.

COUVERTURE Chocolate that contains at least 32 percent cocoa butter. Couverture is smooth on the palate and fluid enough (due to the cocoa butter) when melted to coat candies with the relatively thin layer of chocolate considered a hallmark of fine confections. As an indicator of quality, the term *couverture* had more meaning in the past, when standard chocolate bars and cooking chocolate often contained less cocoa butter. Today, with the exception of some baking squares, most chocolate bars that home cooks buy for eating and cooking are, in fact, couverture. Chocolate chips, morsels, and chunks (with some exceptions) have less than 32 percent cocoa butter and, therefore, are not couverture.

DARK CHOCOLATE There is no official definition for dark chocolate, but the term is widely used to refer to chocolates other than milk chocolate or white chocolate and it includes (but is not limited to) semisweet and bittersweet chocolate. See page 36 for additional information.

DUTCH-PROCESS COCOA Dutch-processed, or alkalized, cocoa powder made from chocolate liquor or cocoa nibs that have been chemically treated (usually with potassium carbonate) to reduce acidity and harshness. See page 35 for a fuller discussion.

FINE CHOCOLATE Dark, milk, or white chocolate is considered fine chocolate if it meets certain simple but stringent ingredient standards set out by the Fine Chocolate Industry Association. The standards preclude chocolate from containing artificial flavorings or vanillin instead of vanilla, and fats other than cocoa butter (or butterfat where appropriate). The recipes in this book call for and were tested only with chocolates that meet the standards for fine chocolates.

GANACHE The generic term for any combination of chocolate mixed with cream (with or without flavoring or the occasional addition of butter or egg). Ganache may take the form of a flowing sauce or glaze, a firm or soft truffle center, a spreadable frosting, or a fluffy filling. The flavor and texture of ganache vary with the ratio of chocolate to cream, the method of mixing them together, the conditions of cooling, and how the mixture is ultimately handled after cooling.

LECITHIN A soy-based fat that is used in tiny quantities to emulsify the fats in chocolate.

MILK CHOCOLATE Sweet chocolate that contains a minimum of 10 percent by weight of chocolate liquor. Today, the best milk chocolates significantly exceed the minimum chocolate liquor required; many are 35% to 40% cacao! Milk chocolate must also contain a minimum of 3.39 percent milk fat and a minimum of 12 percent milk solids (inclusive of milk fat).

NATURAL COCOA Cocoa powder made from chocolate liquor or cocoa nibs that have not been chemically treated to reduce acidity. See page 34 for a fuller discussion.

NONFAT DRY COCOA SOLIDS The fat-free component of chocolate liquor, which represents 46 to 50 percent of its weight. Imagine dry cocoa solids as completely fat-free cocoa powder. Almost all the chocolate flavor resides in the dry cocoa solids.

TEMPERING Tempering is a controlled heating, cooling, and stirring process that creates stable fat crystals in chocolate. Tempered chocolate hardens uniformly, with an even color, a brittle texture, and a glossy surface.

UNSWEETENED BAKING CHOCOLATE Pure chocolate liquor to which a little vanilla and/or lecithin may have been added.

Sources

Chocolate Brands of Note

The companies listed below produce fine chocolate suitable for nibbling or dessert and confection making. Familiar American and foreign brands that you can easily find in better supermarkets are included, as well as smaller and less well-known chocolates available in specialty shops or online. Some of these brands are pricey and may seem daunting (at least at first!) to home bakers and dessert makers, but they are completely worth the price, if only for tasting.

AMADEI

www.amedei.com

This small female-owned Italian company is known for excellent chocolate.

BARRY-CALLEBAUT

www.barry-callebaut.com

This enormous Belgian company makes chocolate with broad appeal, widely used in hotel and restaurant kitchens.

BERNACHON

www.bernachon.com

World famous for truffles and confections, Bernachon also makes a small quantity of very highly regarded chocolate. The Bernachon boutique is a destination for travelers passing through Lyon, France.

CHOCOLATES EL REY

www.chocolates-elrey.com

Renowned for its earthy and complex dark chocolate made with 100% Venezuelan cacao, Chocolates El Rey also makes the best white chocolate I know.

DAGOBA

www.dagobachocolate.com

Certified organic chocolate.

DOMORI

www.domori.com

Superb Italian chocolate made from rare Venezuelan cacao.

GHIRARDELLI

www.ghirardelli.com

Known for its dark roasted cacao flavor, Ghirardelli chocolate is popular among home bakers.

GREEN AND BLACK'S

www.greenandblacks.com

Organic chocolate.

GUITTARD CHOCOLATE

www.guittard.com

Excellent chocolate from the oldest family-owned chocolate company in the United States. The E. Guittard line is particularly favored by pastry chefs and chocolatiers.

LINDT

www.lindt.com

This well-known Swiss company also owns Ghirardelli chocolate.

MADÉCASSE

www.madecasse.com

Madécasse produces chocolate in Africa (Madagascar) from African cacao. Owned by socially conscious former Peace Corps members.

MICHEL CLUIZEL

www.cluizel.com

Cluizel makes an array of excellent single-origin and single-estate chocolate bars and offers a box of tasting samples—small disks of chocolate from several different origins.

PACARI

www.pacarichocolate.com

Santiago Peralta produces award-winning organic and biodynamic chocolate in Ecuador, from Ecuadorian cacao. Pacari also makes some of the best raw chocolate available to date.

PRALUS

www.chocolats-pralus.com

Renowned for its chocolate confections, Pralus also makes chocolate, including fifteen different origin bars and four blends. Pralus has several boutiques in Paris and elsewhere in France.

SCHARFFEN BERGER CHOCOLATE MAKER

www.scharffenberger.com

Founded by John Scharffenberger and the late Robert Steinberg, and now owned by the Hershey Company, Scharffen Berger is credited with sparking the current wave of artisan and craft chocolate makers in the United States and offers excellent bittersweet, semisweet, and unsweetened chocolates, cocoa nibs, and natural cocoa powder.

SCHOKINAG

www.schokinag.com

German chocolate appreciated by pastry chefs and chocolatiers.

SLITTI

www.slitti.it

Superb Italian-made chocolate from Andrea Slitti.

TCHO

www.tcho.com

This hip new American chocolate maker supervises the roasting of its cacao in the country of origin and then produces the final product in its San Francisco facility. Visit the shop and take a tour of the factory.

VALRHONA

www.valrhona.com

Iconic French chocolate, Valrhona is beloved by pastry chefs and chocolatiers.

The Newest and Smallest American Craft Chocolate Makers

Most of the following bean-to-bar producers entered the Good Food Awards (www.goodfoodawards.org) competition in 2011, 2012, or 2013. Anyone passionate about chocolate or interested in its evaluation should taste bars from these new-wave producers.

AMANO ARTISAN CHOCOLATE

www.amanochocolate.com

ASKINOSIE CHOCOLATE

www.askinosie.com

BITTERSWEET ORIGINS

www.bittersweetorigins.com

BLUE BANDANA CHOCOLATE MAKER

www.facebook.com/BlueBandanaChocolateMaker

CACAO ATLANTA CHOCOLATE CO.

www.cacaoatlanta.com

CACAO PRIETO

cacaoprieto.com

DANDELION CHOCOLATES

www.dandelionchocolate.com

DE VRIES CHOCOLATE

www.devrieschocolate.com

DICK TAYLOR CRAFT CHOCOLATE

www.dicktaylorchocolate.com

ESCAZU ARTISAN CHOCOLATES

www.escazuchocolates.com

FEARLESS CHOCOLATE

www.fearlesschocolate.com

FRESCO CHOCOLATE

www.frescochocolate.com

FRUITION CHOCOLATE, INC.

www.tastefruition.com

JACQUES TORRES CHOCOLATE

www.mrchocolate.com

LILLIE BELLE FARMS

www.lilliebellefarms.com

MADRE CHOCOLATE

madrechocolate.com

MAST BROTHERS CHOCOLATE

mastbrothers.com

MINDO CHOCOLATE MAKERS

mindochocolate.com

NIGHT OWL CHOCOLATE

www.nightowlchocolate.com

THE OAKLAND CHOCOLATE COMPANY

theoaklandchocolateco.com

OLIVE & SINCLAIR CHOCOLATE CO.

www.oliveandsinclair.com

THE ORIGINAL HAWAIIAN CHOCOLATE FACTORY

www.originalhawaiianchocolatefactory.com

PATRIC CHOCOLATE

www.patric-chocolate.com

POTOMAC CHOCOLATE

www.potomacchocolate.com

RITUAL CHOCOLATE

www.ritualchocolate.com

ROGUE CHOCOLATIER

roguechocolatier.com

SOMA CHOCOLATE, LLC

www.somachocolate.com

TAZA CHOCOLATES

www.tazachocolate.com

THEO CHOCOLATE

www.theochocolate.com

VIDERI CHOCOLATE FACTORY

www.viderichocolatefactory.com

WOODBLOCK CHOCOLATE

www.woodblockchocolate.com

Baker's Supplies

Beryl's Cake Decorating and Pastry Supplies

800-488-2749

www.beryls.com

An awesome collection of professional tools and supplies for pastry chefs, dessert makers, cake decorators, and confectioners. Among other things: digital thermometers (including Polder, with the probe on a cable), silica gel (desiccant), custom cookie cutters, and chocolate dipping forks.

Chocosphere

877-992-4626

www.chocosphere.com

Excellent shopping site for chocolate bars from everywhere, including organic, raw, small bean-to-bar craft producers.

King Arthur Flour

800-827-6836

www.kingarthurflour.com

Ingredients for the baker and dessert maker, including Guittard, Schokinag, and Callebaut chocolates.

Parrish's Cake Decorating Supply, Inc.

225 West 146th Street

Gardena, CA 90248

800-736-8443

Equipment for the baker, including Magic Line pans with solid or removable bottoms in every conceivable size, and both 2 inches and 3 inches deep.

Market Hall Foods

888-952-4005

www.markethallfoods.com

A fabulous online resource for ingredients with two retail locations, in Oakland and Berkeley, California (www.rockridge markethall.com). The buyer and owners solicit advice from an impressive list of local cookbook authors and professional bakers (who happen to be friends): thus the store has a subspecialty in baking and decoration ingredients as well as dozens of chocolates. Madagascar and Tahitian vanilla extracts and whole and ground vanilla beans; the best candied fruits and citrus peels; honeys; chestnuts in a variety of forms, including chestnut flour; nut pastes; and more.

Penzeys Spices

800-741-7787

www.penzeys.com

All kinds of spices; Madagascar, Tahitian, and Mexican vanilla beans; and several types of cinnamon, including Ceylon cinnamon (also known as Mexican cinnamon, or *canela*). Reading the catalog is a real education about flavor ingredients and their uses.

Spun Sugar Chocolates

510-843-9192

www.spunsugar.com

"Professional" chocolates, such as Callebaut and Ghirardelli, can be ordered in less than 10-pound quantities (often the minimum elsewhere), perfect for the home cook; Valrhona, Callebaut, and Guittard, including the E. Guittard line of European-style and single-origin chocolates from Venezuela with 58%, 61%, and 72% chocolate liquor; cake-decorating supplies.

Sugar and Spice

877-902-2546

www.sugarnspicesf.com

Cake-decorating and candy-making supplies.

Sur La Table

800-243-0852

www.surlatable.com

Premium source for quality tools and equipment for home bakers; tableware including serving platters, dessert dishes, and cake stands.

Williams-Sonoma

877-812-6235

www.williams-sonoma.com

Baking tools and equipment; tableware and serving platters.

In Addition

Ceramics supply stores sell banding wheels that can be used as decorating turntables.

Restaurant supply stores sell commercial half sheet pans and cake pans, Ateco decorating turntables, and more.

Chocolate Sites of Interest

Chloe Chocolat

www.chloe-chocolat.com

Anyone passionate about chocolate should know about Chloé Doutre-Roussel, her tours and tasting classes in Paris.

The Chocolate Life

www.thechocolatelife.com

Clay Gordon presides over this forum about all things chocolate.

David Lebovitz

www.davidlebovitz.com

Chocolate and dessert lovers also love David Lebovitz. Since moving to Paris from California (where he was a pastry chef at Chez Panisse), David has become our chocolate and dessert correspondent in Paris—and wherever he travels.

Ecole Chocolat

www.ecolechocolat.com

Pam Williams started this professional school of chocolate arts in 2003. Programs are delivered online, for both beginners and professionals.

Fine Chocolate Industry Association

www.finechocolateindustry.org

Founded in 2007, the Fine Chocolate Industry Association (FCIA) is an international group of chocolate professionals dedicated to supporting the art of fine chocolate making and the preservation of heirloom cacao. Awards are given each year for best chocolate and best chocolate confections, worldwide.

Fog City News

415-543-7400

www.fogcitynews.com

Adam Smith's newsstand does have periodicals, but also hundreds of interesting and unusual chocolate bars—from the weird to the sublime—complete with staff tasting notes. FCN is a destination for chocolate lovers visiting San Francisco.

Good Food Awards

www.goodfoodawards.org/chocolate

Good Food Awards recognizes the best craft chocolate makers in the United States; check the site for the award winners.

International Chocolate Awards

www.internationalchocolateawards.com

Follow international trends in fine chocolate confections, including filled and flavored chocolate bars, truffles, and chocolate spreads.

The International Cocoa Organization

www.icco.org

ICCO is a global organization that promotes every aspect of cacao development, trade, and education worldwide.

The Well-Tempered Chocolatier

www.thewelltemperedchocolatier.com

Canadian writer, pastry chef, and chocolatier Eagranie Yuh is worth knowing and following.

Acknowledgments

A book takes more than an author. Maya Klein was my assistant through the early phases of this book, and her intelligence and creativity enriched it. The late Robert Steinberg and John Scharffenberger of Scharffen Berger Chocolate Maker allowed me to have an intimate look at the creation of a new American chocolate. Robert's friendship came with challenging questions, discussion, argument, and tasting, all of which brought clarity to my thinking. Maricel Presilla introduced me to Jorge Redmond and Rand Turner of El Rey chocolates; I thank them all for the opportunity to visit the world of cacao at the source, in Venezuela. Edith McClure was a frequent and beloved tasting partner. Jennifer Chin spent two weeks with me knee-deep in ganache. Over the years, even brief conversations with Shirley Corriher, Hal McGee, Thalia Howenthal, Jim Graham, Veronica Bowers, Elaine Gonzalez, Terry Richardson, Michael Recchiuti, Flo Braker, and Marion Cunningham added to my knowledge.

Thanks to everyone at Artisan who was involved in this revised edition, including Ann Bramson for her brilliance and loyalty to a project that turned out to be more challenging than we imagined, and Judy Pray, Trent Duffy, and Sibylle Kazeroid, for taking on this revised edition and producing an even better book. I also appreciate the efforts of Michelle Ishay-Cohen, Kara Strubel, Nancy Murray, and Barbara Peragine. As always I thank my agent and friend, Jane Dystel, for her support and good counsel.

Thanks again to Deborah Jones for her always-inspired photography, Sara Slavin for the prop styling and art direction of our fifth book together, Sandra Cook for styling the ice cream and savory photos, and Jeri Jones and Brook Buchanan for being part of the team.

Thanks to everyone who was involved on the first edition, including Deborah Weiss Geline and Judith Sutton. I remain grateful to Nancy Nicholas for her help with writing and organizing the first edition as well.

Writing a book takes place in the real life of the author. I can't close the last chapter of this book without thanking the people who made a difference to me with their love and encouragement, wisdom and insight. Thus, to my family, friends, and teachers of every kind—in particular Joan and Jon Nackerud, Edith McClure, Beryl Radin, Christine Blaine, Amelia Saltsman, Barbara and Bob Blackburn, Suzanne Samson, Steve Keneipp, Kelly Dobbins, Sarah Leverett, Christina Lapides, Bev Frances, Albert Abrams, and of course my daughter, Lucy Medrich—thank you.

OPPOSITE: Warm buttered corn tortillas filled with butter, cinnamon sugar, and cocoa nibs (see page 254).

Index

Note: Page numbers in *italics* refer to illustrations.

Praline (cont.)
  topping, 203
  in Walnut Praline and Blackberry
    Sundae, 64
Preheating the oven, 22
Premelted chocolate, 38
Preserves. See Jam
Prosciutto:
  Nibby Asparagus with, 282–83
  in Nibby Pesto Crostini, 279
Prunes, White Chocolate Ice Cream
    with Armagnac and, 60
Pudding:
  Italian (Budini), 91–92
  Nibby, 256
Pumpkin seeds, in Mendiants, 297–99

Quark cheese, in Marble Cheesecake,
    210–13
Queen of Sheba, The (torte), 75, 80–81,
    144
  about, 78–79
  variations on, 82–92

Rabbit, in Lapin au Vin, 291–93
Racks, cooling, 23
Ragout, Wild Mushroom, 284–86
Raisin(s):
  and Nut Cookies, Nibby, 261, 267
  Rum, White Chocolate Ice Cream
    with, 60
Raspberry(ies):
  -blackberry sauce, for Walnut
    Praline and Blackberry Sundae,
    64
  -Chocolate Cakes, Molten, 178–79
  jam, in Cocoa Bean Almond Roulade,
    268–69, 270
  in Julia's Cake, 176–77
  -Laced Chocolate Cake, 218–19

-Laced Chocolate Cupcakes, with
    marbled glaze, 147, 219
  in Strawberry Celebration Cake, 147,
    167–70
  in Tribute Cake, 175
Real Chocolate Wafers, 233, 267
Reduced-fat recipes, about, 44, 152–53
Red wine, in Coq (or Lapin) au Vin,
    291–93
Reine de Saba, La, 75, 78; see also Queen
    of Sheba, The (torte)
Ribbons, chocolate, 38
Rich Hot Chocolate, 162–63
Richardson, Terry, 99
Roasted Squash Soup with Cocoa Bean
    Cream, 281, 290
Roden, Claudia, 79
Rolling pins, 24
Rose Cream, Bittersweet Semifreddo
    with Sesame Crunch and, 132–33
Roulade:
  Bittersweet, 159–60
  Cocoa Bean Almond, 268–69, 270
Ruffles, Chocolate, 198
  in Strawberry Celebration Cake, 147,
    167–70
Rugelach, Currant and Nib, 265–66, 267
Rum:
  in Strawberry Celebration Cake, 147,
    167–70
  use of, 28
Rum Raisin–White Chocolate Ice Cream,
    60

St. George Spirits, 28, 111, 148
Salad, in Crunchy Baby Greens, 275, 290
Salmonella, raw eggs and, 122–23
Sarah Bernhardt Chocolate Glaze, 194
Sauce(s):
  Alice's Chocolate, 240, 241

Alice's Cocoa Fudge, 243
Bittersweet Hot Fudge, 242
blackberry-raspberry, in Walnut
    Praline and Blackberry Sundae,
    64
Chocolate, 240
Giuliano's Sweet and Savory Meat,
    with Chocolate, 287–88
Little, for Pasta, A, 289–90
Mole Coloradito, 294–95
Sherry-Cocoa Pan, Chopped Chicken
    Livers with, 280
Strawberry, Peanut Butter–Chocolate
    Torte with, 84–85
Saucepan Fudge Drops, 234
Scales, 24
Scharffenberger, John, 10
Scharffen Berger Chocolate Maker, 10,
    11, 15, 36, 39, 100, 156, 243, 275,
    278, 318
Schmidt, Steven, 221
Schulze, Joan, 116
Scones, Cream, with Chocolate Chunks,
    238–39
See's, 12
Seeds, sunflower or pumpkin, in
    Mendiants, 297–99
Semifreddo, Bittersweet, with Rose
    Cream and Sesame Crunch,
    132–33
Semisweet chocolate, 13–14, 32, 36–37,
    302, 314
  in Classic 60% Brownies, 68
  Giuliano's Sweet and Savory Meat
    Sauce with, 287–88
  in Mole Coloradito, 294–95
  substitutions for, 305–6
  see also Bittersweet chocolate; High-
    percentage chocolate
Serrated knives, 25

United States:
    chocolate consumption in, 12-13, 14-15
    chocolate industry standards in, 36
Unsweetened chocolate, 34, 66, 316
    in Coq (or Lapin) au Vin, 291-93
    in New Classic Chocolate Brownies, 68
    substitutions for, 306-7
    in Wild Mushroom Ragout, 284-86

Valrhona, 33, 39, 100, 318
Van Houten, Conrad, 35
Vanilla, use of, 29-30
Varietal chocolates, 32-33

Wafers, Real Chocolate, 233, *267*
Walnut(s):
    Espresso Tart, 228
    Praline and Blackberry Sundae, 64
    toasting, 28
Warm Bittersweet Mousse, 126-27
Warm Mocha Tart, 226-28
Water:
    in chocolate mousse, 123
    and seizing of chocolate, 309
Water bath, 40-41, 42

Waters, Alice, 116
Wax paper, 24
Whipped:
    cream:
        in Bittersweet Semifreddo with Rose Cream and Sesame Crunch, 132-33
        Chocolate Meringues with Berries and, 143
    Ganache Filling:
        Chocolate, 189-91
        Gianduja, 190
        Mexican Cinnamon, 190
        Mint-Infused, 190
        Mint-Infused White Chocolate, 191
        Mocha, 190
Whisks, 26
White chocolate, 12, 37-38, 42, 309
    in Cold Creamy Truffles, 102-3
    Ganache Filling, Whipped, Mint-Infused, 191
    Ice Cream, 59-60
        with Dates, 60
        with Prunes and Armagnac, 60
    -Lemon Truffles, 119
    in Mendiants, 297-99

Mousse, 134-36
    -Citrus, 136
    with Fresh Mint, 135
    -orange, in Triple Mousses, 137-39
    -Rum Raisin Ice Cream, 60
    -Toasted Coconut Ice Cream, 61-62
    Truffles, 118-19
White confectionery coating, 38
White Meringue, 142
    in Carmen Meringay, 183-85
Whitman's, 12
Wild Mushroom Ragout, 284-86
Williams, Chuck, 95, 171
Williams-Sonoma, 95, 171
Wine, red, in Coq (or Lapin) au Vin, 291-93
Winters, Lance, 111
Wire whisks, 26
Women of Taste Truffles, 116-17

Yves, Thuries, 122

Zabar's, 13
Zaslavsky, Nancy, 294
Zest, citrus, in White Chocolate-Citrus Mousse, 136
Zester, 26